The Ride, the Rose, and the Resurrection

THE RIDE, THE ROSE, AND THE RESURRECTION

A True Story about Crisis, Faith, and Survival

DAVID CHARLES STIELER

iUniverse, Inc.
Bloomington

The Ride, the Rose, and the Resurrection
A True Story about Crisis, Faith, and Survival

iUniverse books may be ordered through booksellers or by contacting:

iUniverse
1663 Liberty Drive
Bloomington, IN 47403
www.iuniverse.com
1-800-Authors (1-800-288-4677)

ISBN: 978-1-4759-7307-5 (sc)
ISBN: 978-1-4759-7308-2 (hc)
ISBN: 978-1-4759-7309-9 (ebk)

Library of Congress Control Number: 2013901853

Printed in the United States of America

iUniverse rev. date: 02/18/2013

CONTENTS

For
Carole

FOREWORD

—ༀ—

Dave and Carole are personal friends of mine from teenage years. This account of a tragedy that neither of them had asked for nor could have ever anticipated is all too common and will strike a chord with all readers. Even if you have never been associated in any way with a situation like this, you will be drawn into the extremely personal account that rocked every part of Dave and Carole's world—including, but not limited to, the survival of their marriage. As their pastor and friend, I was included in many parts of this incident, but until reading the details, I didn't realize the full impact this traumatic event had on every fiber of their lives.

In this gripping account of their intensive journey through a personal tragedy, Dave walks us through the psychological, spiritual, and real battle for survival from a near-death experience. The battle consumed them on every level. The insurance companies seemed intent on paying the least amount possible, all the while dragging their feet on any settlement and subjecting the insured to rigorous scrutiny and redundant paperwork as they struggled to recover from their injuries.

Dave's vivid descriptions, combined with his attention to detail, will draw the reader into the personal battle as though he is in a cloud hovering above the events as they unfold. The spiritual implications are stunning—of God working through tremendous strains in our lives when circumstances stop one dead on the highway. Trite phrases and well-intended scripture verses cannot ever cut short the ongoing battle that God fights for us within our deeply human struggles. His intent is to bring us to a point of growth where, in many instances like this, closure will never happen this side of heaven.

I highly recommend this read, and I have a deep respect for Dave as he lays out in print his personal and into-the-heart honest struggle with life after near death.

Pastor Michael Hollenbeck

ACKNOWLEDGMENTS

—◊—

Making the quantum leap from repairing farm equipment while occasionally writing speeches and editorials as a sideline hobby to organizing and creating a full-length book required more than a few adjustments. Shortly after this project was launched, it became obvious that my comparative writing skills were the equivalent of a second-grade elementary school student's. Figuratively speaking, I was suddenly the college guy who had enrolled in an English literature class while still learning how to read.

I am forever in debt to Harry Dickenson and his logical outline. The literary organizational skills that teacher force-fed me through three years of high school speech and English classes carried me from beginning to end yet again.

My wife, Carole, provided the inspiration to put our story into print. Although I have never been able to get her to admit it, I believe she was the one who anonymously contacted the publisher and forced this project out of the file cabinet and onto the desktop.

Nicole, my little girl and my guardian angel, never flinched. She stayed by my side, counseled me, and inspired me to be a better person. Her encouraging support carried me through desperate discouragement and horrendous storms.

Jeremy, my best friend and my oldest son, never failed me. He was there at the touch of the telephone to hold my hand and walk me through some of the toughest times ever.

Jason, my elusive child, forced me to learn through his absence how to pick up the pieces and move on in the face of total heartbreak.

My brother in music, Kevin Cribbage-Coffee Cook, a.k.a. Uncle Weird Beard, was and always will be with me through thick and thin. Thank you, Z!

Roger Jones, my most treasured cousin, shared my grief as well as my triumphs over insurmountable odds. He has always been the one whose respect I have most cherished.

My friend Pastor Michael Hollenbeck and the small congregation he leads quietly provided the strength I needed to persevere when all seemed lost. Dan and Tanya, Paulette and Elwin, Mary, Don, Michelle, Val, Joyce, and the occasional visitors who joined our small group on Monday nights helped me maintain sanity when nothing else in my life seemed to make sense.

The Christian Motorcyclists Association and select members of ABATE of Michigan Region 7 sent prayer requests that generated responses from fellow Christians as far away as Australia. Fellow Christian motorcyclists Kenny Gainsforth, Eddie Cash, and Jim "Fingers" Crenshaw were the first three faces I remember seeing when I awoke in the hospital.

Bill, Floyd, Brian Bennett, Lenny and Terri, Tom and Debbie, Roger and Leslie, Mike "The Musician" Sheets, Joey and Barb, Billy Lee Cox, and all of my other friends who held our hands and encouraged us after tragedy struck helped remind me that the life we live is about the people who are in it.

And, of course, the gift to write and the strength to see this project through to its completion was only possible through the grace of God.

INTRODUCTION

—∭—

Nobody wants to be unhappy. I would go so far as to say that everything we humans do translates to the pursuit of pleasure in one exciting form or another. We don't flinch when facing the roiling rapids, because calamity is always expected to be someone else's problem. We simply hedge against the improbabilities, paying for insurance that promises to guarantee our safety in the aftermath of any unforeseen brush with disaster. Then, with safety straps and a false sense of security firmly in place, we launch another death-defying adventure in our quest for happiness.

The thrill of victory, that euphoric high that has become a fundamental component of the American dream, has caused the human race to not only work its knuckles to the bone in search of the illusion but also to conquer and squash anyone who stands in the way. The afflicted become so completely obsessed with the image of comfort and joy that they literally abandon pleasure to achieve it. In simple terms, it's called getting ahead. It is a lesson we have all been taught since childhood.

So it's *Forward ho!* as we arise every morning, taking one more step into adulthood, replacing tractors and bicycles and other toys of our youth with fast cars, motorcycles, and airplanes. Each quest for happiness becomes jam-packed with stuff designed to enhance the experience. We seek bigger and better, trading our compass for a GPS and overflowing the storage unit with playthings that at one time or another represented the potential for an exciting encounter. And that is how we have learned to define adventure.

The promise of adventure is what lures people out onto the highway. Nobody really knows what lies ahead. The best anyone can do is chart a course based on hindsight and hearsay, and then plunge recklessly straight into the future, full stride, with all the confidence of a blind man unaware of the stairwell he is about to encounter.

When tragedy strikes and we wake the next morning all bruised, bandaged, and bewildered, the world around us takes on an entirely different color. Like Humpty Dumpty, none of the king's men will ever succeed at reassembling what has been shattered. After life has been hung in the balance, the very definition of living becomes obscured to the point of identifying with the calamity instead of the cure. From that moment forward, the stuff we own just doesn't matter anymore.

The real gifts of life are often so taken for granted that their true value is only discovered after they are gone. And the loss can be devastating. An empty nest, a missing loved one, or the breakup of a close friendship will defeat even the strongest of men. Whether we want to admit it or not, only God's grace will put us back on our feet after a life-altering event hangs us by the ankles and shakes the spare change out of our pockets.

I had never been able to figure out whether the definition of my happiness would be found in the journey or the destination. Looking back, I would have to say the smiles on my face have been put there by a little bit of both. But staring death in the face solved that riddle with answers that surprised even me. My life turned on a dime. Without warning, everything I was able to recognize was scattered into the wind. A prison that had no bars replaced peace, harmony, and my sense of security.

This is my story of life, death, and resurrection.

CHAPTER 1

SQUARE PEG—ROUND HOLE

—⁄⁄⁄—

Whoever said that happiness is watching a workplace disappear in the rearview mirror has never been forced to sit idle. Trading a livelihood for leisurely living may sound appealing when the hounds are howling, but after all of the stressful issues have finally been resolved and the dust has settled on that last decisive challenge, the overwhelming sense of uselessness that comes with inactivity is crippling. The longer a guy is out of the game, the more he is inclined to crave being a player.

Sometime during the winter of 2006, thoughts of retirement began seriously crowding my scenery. Visions of laying down the wrenches and kicking back into a life of leisure had always been in the back of my mind, but other than putting money into an IRA and paying off the mortgage, I had not formulated much of a plan for crossing that career-ending finish line. It occurred to me that making the transition from dream to reality was no longer all that far into the future, but gazing over the hill at the backside of fifty also presented an interesting dilemma. Do people actually put away their careers and still have purpose? More to the point, could I ever realistically afford to stop working?

For years I had been quietly observing the lifestyles of the retired and anonymous. At one end of the spectrum, the golden years seemed to be characterized as winters spent in Florida playing shuffleboard, Tuesday morning tee times, and a wardrobe consisting of plaid polyester slacks and polo shirts. On the flip side there was Bubba in his backyard next to the outdoor refrigerator,

1

charring burgers on the grill, a spatula in one hand and a beer in the other, sporting a sleeveless football jersey and a ball cap with his favorite NASCAR driver's number on the back.

Both images screamed *"Run for your life!"* Although certain aspects of nearly every lifestyle held a measure of appeal, the thought of a pigeonholed existence to any extreme scared me to death.

Understandably, my idea of front-yard, hands-on hobbies would likely be considered intolerable inside one of those sterile gated communities full of perfectly manicured lawns and painted driveways. Likewise, I would find no comfort living in a neighborhood full of cars on blocks, staring at the engine parts spread across the guy next door's front porch.

In other words, if I decided to spend my retirement years on a golf course, it would probably have to be as the cart mechanic. Fun is relevant, but there needs to be something more tangible than bragging rights to show for the time I invest in leisure activity. A score card just doesn't do it for me.

And there lay the problem: What exactly was retirement supposed to look like, anyway?

Dad was a World War II veteran who had lost his leg to a German mortar. If anything, the challenges he faced as a leg amputee inspired him to rise above the obstacles and show the world that he did not need crutches. He pursued happiness through independence and self-discipline.

Like most folks of his generation, war and strife had hardened Dad. Growing up without a mother during the Great Depression of the 1930s forced him and his eight siblings into survival through the school of hard knocks. Nobody had held their hands when they were faced with adversity, so they weren't about to hold anyone else's. When it came time to introduce their own children to the ways of the world, all they had to fall back on was their pitiless self-confidence.

When I was somewhere around the age of nine, Dad tagged me with the nickname Daze, probably because I always struggled when handed chores that didn't come with instructions. It never occurred to me that his approach to getting things done might actually have been a vote of confidence in my ability to handle them on my own.

It was disappointing after each project had been finished to watch Dad review my bent-nail-and-split-board quality of workmanship with head-shaking frustration while grumbling under his breath. My nickname was eventually changed from Daze to Dunce. I pictured myself in the front corner of the classroom, wearing one of those cone-shaped hats while classmates pointed and snickered.

In spite of feeling as though I would never be able to please him, I still loved my dad. Adolescence wasn't all that bad by comparison. Our guidance had certainly been laced with impressive doses of fear, rejection, disappointment, and uncertainty, but at the time, there seemed to be nothing unusual about the way my brothers, my sister, and I were being raised.

By the time I was a teenager, life for the most part had become void of any recreational interaction with my parents. I always had a job at the family business to earn spending money, so there was never any lack of opportunity to learn the value of a buck. But once the time card went through the clock at the end of the workday, the Dunce was usually nowhere to be found.

Dad frequently tracked me down to lend a hand with his backyard projects, but even on a good day our working relationship was halfhearted at best. We had little patience for each other.

About halfway through one of those father-and-son weekend encounters, progress at the work site came to a screeching halt when I finally threw down my tools out of frustration and staged my own protest. I was tired of trying to read his mind only to be scolded for having misinterpreted some elusive gesture. I got into Dad's face and took a full swing at his chin with a closed fist, but I pulled the punch inches before making contact when something in my eighteen-year-old brain suddenly brought me to my senses.

Firing a warning shot across his bow certainly seemed to get his attention. After that showdown, Dad dropped the nicknames and began making a noticeable effort to include me during the planning stages of every project we launched together. Owing to what appeared to be a total change of heart, my father found ways to explain what he was trying to accomplish while we worked. My little mutiny had somehow earned his respect.

The episode also established in me a significant sense of sovereignty. It goes without saying that someone must lead and others should follow, but following felt a lot like being pushed around to me, and that was unacceptable. One successful rebellion against authority and I was ready to make it through life on my own. Unfortunately, because of that bullheaded independence, I never learned the art of losing.

Looking back, I have to admit that Dad's tough love seemed an appropriate way to teach self-discipline. Personal responsibility was deeply ingrained. Aside from his one-legged swagger, he was very much like many of the other dads I knew. The world today might be a better place for everyone if misbehaving juveniles with their droopy drawers and flat-brimmed attitudes were forced to face Dad's brand of discipline.

Through my teenage years in the 1960s, our small rural community experienced its share of economic euphoria. Following the terror brought on by World War II and the Korean War, Americans were industrious and profitable, but their bullish behavior spawned a generation of overfed, rebellious children later known as the Baby Boomers. Public optimism began to wane only after the first shots had been fired in Southeast Asia. That's when the all-knowing, all-seeing politicians in Washington, DC, started shipping young men into the jungles of Vietnam to fight an enemy nobody knew how to identify.

Vietnam was an unpopular war to say the least. Nobody wanted to go there, but once the US Army's draft lottery numbers had been drawn, those who were chosen faced very few options. Many Boomers rose up and rebelled against the war. Some left the country, while others burned their draft cards and joined the growing number of protesters. I stood on the sidelines and watched, trying to avoid a trip to Vietnam by attending college.

There was a very real fear of what the future had in store for my generation. In spite of President John F. Kennedy's inaugural address and Dr. Martin Luther King's "I Have a Dream" oration, civil unrest and cultural disharmony seemed to prevail. But Dad's method of raising children had not only taught us to ignore the color of another man's skin; he had also inadvertently prepared me to face the jaws of death without flinching.

After two miserable years trying to maintain a grade point average high enough to avoid flunking out of school, I finally gave up. At the age of twenty, with no particular interest in anything beyond finding a paying job and getting on with life in 1969, I became the family's first college dropout.

Factory jobs weren't hard to find in those days, so the transition from student to laborer went smoothly. In no time my pockets were full of spending money and I hadn't a care in the world. That was obviously an extremely shortsighted point of view. It didn't take long for the US Army to receive word that I was no longer a student. In August 1969, friends and hippies exploring their communal peace of mind headed for the little town of Bethel, New York, for an event called Woodstock. I, on the other hand, landed a round-trip bus ride to the Armed Forces Induction Center at Fort Wayne, Detroit, to undergo the army's preinduction physical examination.

While being herded from room to room in our underwear during the physical examination process that day, a group of us who had been crammed together in a corner discovered the military's lottery within the lottery. We watched a marine liaison emerge from his cubicle, walk over to a line of draftees, and tag every third guy as an inductee into the Corps.

"Can they do that?" I whispered to the guy standing next to me. "They can't draft guys into the marines, can they?"

"Apparently they can," he whispered back. "I know my number's comin' up, so when I get out of here, I'm gonna go see the navy recruiter. There's no way I'm gonna be a marine!"

Everyone knew that both the US Army and the Marine Corps guaranteed its soldiers an all-expense paid trip straight into the jaws of combat. Contemplating that bone-chilling prospect sent a wave of fear shivering through my body.

A week later I paid a visit to the US Air Force recruiter in Port Huron, Michigan. He put my name on the list for the next scheduled session of air force entrance exams and stuck my application into his files. Thank God for that bit of foresight. On behalf of the war department, Uncle Sam sent me a Christmas card that year with a personal invitation to join the party. One frantic phone call to the air force recruiter's office, and the army's paperwork was intercepted. Two days later I signed on the dotted line and became a brand-new US Air Force recruit through the delayed enlistment program, although the delay wasn't nearly as long as I would have preferred. Three more months of civilian life and I was wheels-up aboard a military charter flight, wondering what had happened to that freedom everyone always talked about.

For entirely different reasons, both Woodstock and the military were interesting and eye-opening experiences. Country Joe sang protest songs to the throngs of young adults crowding the stage set up in the Catskills while GI Joe waded through the jungles, trying to avoid contact with the Vietcong.

My twenty-first birthday came and went while in basic training at Lackland Air Force Base in San Antonio, Texas. My next stop was twelve weeks of aircraft maintenance training. On August 1, 1970, I married my girlfriend, Carole, and then climbed aboard a flight bound for Southeast Asia.

So much for avoiding the war in Vietnam.

Although I never experienced a real fear of dying while overseas, I honestly did not expect to come home alive. One night in October 1970, two months into my tour, that fatalistic premonition rubbed shoulders with reality when a C-130 I should have been aboard went missing. My friend Tom Bosnick was on that flight. We were both very upset by the fact that our squadron commander would not authorize me to join him as his maintenance assistant. Tom took off for Taipei, and I returned to the barracks. The wreckage and remains were finally found two weeks later, plastered to the side of a mountain seventy-five miles off course. Everyone aboard had perished.

Shortly after that airplane went down, I was taken off the flight line and assigned a desk job. So ended the threat of having to fly into a firefight at treetop level over the jungles of Vietnam.

I wasn't one of those who were spit on when they came back stateside, but I sure didn't receive a hero's welcome either. "Ignored" would be a more fitting description of the reception received when I was feet-dry on American soil. Regardless, I was proud to have served my country honorably, and nobody was going to take that away from me.

The public's lack of respect didn't really faze me. I was just happy to be back in the arms of the girl that I had married only two weeks prior to shipping out for Taiwan.

I came home to Michigan and rejoined the family business after being discharged from the air force in September 1973. There were a lot of other career opportunities to explore, but I had been programmed to take the safe, conservative route. Buying into and owning the family business seemed to be the socially accepted and responsible thing to do at the time, so into the cauldron I dove.

I was haunted by my decision to walk away from college, and this caused me to seriously contemplate the future. The key to happiness would be independence, but independence required an education. Thanks to the GI Bill, college tuition funding was available. I spent my nights and weekends pursuing a degree, one course at a time.

The wheels hauling my young family unit toward financial security were in motion, but it wasn't long before that train derailed. I finally abandoned my plans to take over the business in 1979, when Dad had an emotional meltdown and leveled his sights on me after verbally firing defensive rounds into every corner of his executives' offices. Once again, the plunder of disappointment had carried the day.

Slipping back into survival mode, I walked away from the family operation for the last time and spent the next few years traveling as a working musician until leaving the road to finish college and start a home-based bookkeeping business. Carole supported the kids and me while I struggled to develop a future.

Near the end of the recession that had lain to waste so much of America's industry in the 1970s, men in black suits from the IRS audited my parents' livelihood and retirement plans into oblivion. Witnessing the way our government had allowed one of its agencies to turn so venomously on my father, a disabled veteran, was breathtaking. The IRS agents sent to conduct an audit were the equivalent of Nazi storm troopers dispatched by the SS. Those guys weren't there to help preserve the operation; their assignment was to gut what few assets remained and leave the carcass for local buzzards to pick apart.

Our parents' encounter with that bureaucratic death squad taught me to be wary of the potential for destruction at the hands of strangers whose sinister authority granted sufficient power to crush lives. Looking back I can see how the experience ignited in me a bitter fear of failure, which might explain my cynical attitude and relentless effort to keep my own little world from unraveling.

Generally speaking, however, there was not much remorse among my siblings and me over the unfortunate demise of the family business. Compassion during our formative years had never been a prime directive. Besides, we had all moved on to other things in our own lives, so the end of a would-be legacy presented no personal sacrifice. We just stood with hands in pockets on the sidelines watching Mom and Dad's ship go down, dragging their little nest egg with it.

Growing up in a family business while living in a rural farming community offered very little opportunity for becoming streetwise. A couple of pyramid scams handed me some hard lessons, but there were still a few enticing shell games to trip over until my necessary education in survival had been polished.

While I was still struggling to get my little bookkeeping business up and running, an old high school friend approached with a plan for saving his floundering manufacturing operation. I needed an income, and he needed someone with experience to manage his business operation, so we joined forces. His offer included ownership in the operation in lieu of a decent salary. The arrangement seemed legitimate and provided all the incentive needed to sign on with reckless abandon. The deal was done on a handshake. He dangled the bait, and I swallowed it hook, line, and sinker.

After investing a year in what I thought was going to be a solid future for both of our families, the guy finally let his true intentions leak out. Hiring me to run the business for him was nothing more than a way of buying time against foreclosure at the hands of the bank that had financed his operation. My friend regarded me, his business manager, as little more than a disposable human tool. Once the operation had been financially stabilized, the doors were closed and the assets liquidated, and I was back on the street, looking for work.

Sheer desperation and a couple of months on the bricks landed me a middle-level management position inside a two-hundred-million-dollar Forbes 500 manufacturing operation. It didn't take long for me to realize that I had jumped out of the frying pan and into the fire. Being a survivor in that high-dollar, fast-moving, world-class manufacturing operation meant learning how to pass the buck and suck it up. Independence and entrepreneurial skill is seriously frowned upon in such an environment.

Through a combination of hard work and attrition, I stepped off the top rung on that middle-management corporate ladder and into an unforgiving executive-level management position. The challenges for advancement were not as much about climbing the ladder as they were about maintaining a grip as the rungs were randomly being chopped out from under the climbers.

The experience would best be described as a form of sanctioned brutality. Rarely did a day go by without me being threatened by someone from the ranks above and below. I received very little support from peers, and being a team player usually meant allowing others to take credit for the work being accomplished. "Dog eat dog" would have been a very appropriate title for the communal cannibalism that occurred daily.

The Dunce was clearly in over his head.

Four years later, on December 12, 1989, at eight thirty in the morning, an otherwise promising corporate career came to an abrupt halt. I was forty years old without a dime invested in a retirement plan and once again out of a job. No matter how hard I swung the bat, I just couldn't seem to make it to first base.

Is everyone struggling like me? I kept asking myself. *What is the secret to success?*

Weddings and weekend bar gigs with the boys in the band provided some income, but unless another road gig opened up, I would have little chance of earning enough money playing music to feed a family, much less fund a retirement plan. The situation for this college-educated scrapper was becoming desperate.

Several months of scouring the bushes for a livelihood worth pursuing finally uncovered the deal of a lifetime in the spring of 1990. I used $8,500 from my savings account to buy an estimated $150,000 worth of tools and inventory from a guy who wanted out of the automotive starter rebuilding business. Driving home with a brand-new career in the back of a twenty-six-foot rental truck made me feel that the future was filled with fresh hope, totally unrestricted, and more promising than ever.

Visions of the first American pioneers danced in my head. Without a clue what the future had in store, men had struck out into the wilderness with their families and everything they owned piled into the backs of ox-drawn covered wagons. Facing the unknown held more appeal for them than trying to fit the mold society had formed. Just like those pioneers, I was headed in a whole new direction. There were no guarantees, but the adventure came with a clean slate.

Life for my wife and me during the summer and fall of 1990 evolved around the construction of a new building on the property next to our house. On January 1, 1991, my little starter repair shop opened for business. I spent the next two months organizing benches and equipment while listening to news reports covering American troop involvement during the opening phases of Desert Storm. By the end of March, America had become committed to spending its resources in the deserts in the Middle East, while my little establishment had begun to turn a profit sufficient to cover the overhead.

My ship had finally been turned around. Self-confidence improved. Submission became a thing of the past. Getting ahead meant taking control and never looking back. Fueled by a deep desire for independence and a desperate fear of losing, I immersed myself in the operation far beyond any previous commitment. This one was mine. Regardless of the level of soul sacrifice required, I was determined that little repair business was going to succeed.

Launching a business and surviving was all the proof needed to show the world what success and invincibility looked like. Symbolically thumbing my nose at past employers and counterparts sent the perfect message: my gain was their loss.

Nevertheless, there was no shortage of people willing to share their advice. Among the more popular opinions I received was that a sound business plan included strategies to conquer and eliminate the competition. Being competitive made sense to me, but it seemed a waste of time to focus on beating up the other guy to get ahead. Zeroing in on what it took to be a reliable, trustworthy repairman for those who sought after my services made a lot more sense.

Executive decision number one: The competition could do it their way. I was going to do it my way.

Occasionally that freshly reinforced sense of self-confidence came across a little harshly. Along with everything else Dad taught us, he had provided the incentive to be independent simply by teaching us how to hate being told what to do, especially by someone seeking help. I had no problem handing a part back over the counter to anyone arrogant enough to claim he or she knew more than I did about fixing it. That whole thing about the customer always being right went straight out the window the first time someone tried to tell me how to do my job.

"My reputation is the only thing I have to offer," I would explain. "You might find it cheaper somewhere else, but you won't find a better product. If I can't do the job the way I believe it needs to be done, I would just as soon you take the work somewhere else."

11

Such a willful mind-set!

Fortunately most of the people bringing work into the shop appreciated that straightforward approach. Self-confidence seemed to enhance the customer's confidence in the work being performed. Some folks were a tad offended by such an abrasive attitude, but when I refused to blink, they clearly understood their choices were to either trust me or take the work to someone else. Many who opted for the latter eventually returned, hat in hand, apologizing for having doubted my integrity.

In reality, that inflexible style was backed by a solid track record for delivering quality. Too bad that reputation for doing good work didn't come with a large dose of humility. The little starter repair business grew successfully almost in spite of the attitude coming from the Dunce behind the counter.

Part of me missed being on someone's team, but experience had already demonstrated that being a team player usually meant becoming someone else's doormat. It didn't matter. I had built a successful business from the ground up using my God-given talent.

Instinctively I thanked God daily for having given me an open mind and numerous opportunities to learn exactly what I did not want to do for a living. Otherwise, the way to self-employment would likely have slipped by me and my wife unnoticed. His grace was the real reason for our independence.

Blazing our own trail wasn't easy for my wife and me. We had never earned enormous amounts of income. Stubborn pride kept us from taking advantage of the numerous entitlements or welfare handouts available during many of our early years together. We chose instead to make it on our own, which required determination and a level of self-discipline not encouraged by a spoiled, lazy society. None of what we owned had been handed to us, so we were driven never to let any of it be taken away.

We also shared a wide range of interests, and our way of pursuing those fantasies usually added a third dimension to the adventure. Never wanting to settle for second best, we spared no effort or expense in our pursuit of happiness.

Friends and family would probably agree that my wife and I had been flirting with disaster since we first met in high school. In many ways they were probably right. We felt safe when we were together, so we sort of approached life with reckless abandon, living as though nothing we wanted to do came with any tangible risk. We were never satisfied with the mundane. Figuratively bungee jumping our way from one day to the next, our restlessness carried us to the rim of the canyon on more than one occasion. We did not consider ourselves thrill-seekers, but we certainly did not fit the description of the average sideline spectator.

Success came through hard work and dedication, satisfying our independent spirits. But for several years I had been wondering if the drive to survive had, in fact, transformed me into a materialistic workaholic.

Owning a lucrative alternator and starter repair business combined with Carole's income from her job as circuit-court administrator ultimately afforded us a level of financial flexibility we probably abused. Over the years, we bought and paid for more things than many people ever dream of owning, and we rarely got rid of anything. Our kids jokingly told us numerous times that when we finally left this world they would probably just set fire to the house and everything in it rather than try to sort through the mess.

We were both hands-on people who reused a lot of things other folks would have simply sent to the landfill, but between the two of us, Carole, without a doubt, ranked higher in creativity. Her hands were never idle. She would knit or crochet while we sat in front of the TV. She also demonstrated some artistically attractive decorating techniques throughout the house using photos, flowers, weeds, rocks, vines, baskets, buckets, lights, and other odds and ends.

Clearly not afraid of work, she never flinched at digging her fingernails into flowerbeds or picking up a paintbrush to retouch the window trim. When it was time to mow the lawn, she usually took it upon herself to grab the push mower and trim around the trees and planters spread over our two acres.

We had also developed a keen interest in traveling. We dreamed about visiting places all over the United States. In fact, there never seemed to be boundaries to the exciting activity we imagined in our future together. Our minds were filled with ideas and plans. We wanted to see it all, do it all, own it all, and tell all about it. The trouble was that we had failed to allow breathing room to mobilize the adventures. Dream-building sort of took center stage.

It wasn't as though we had lost the ability to have fun. We just never seemed to get around to it. The dilemma was that I could never figure out exactly how we were going to afford the fun we had always dreamed of having. It was looking as though I would be chained to the workbench forever, just trying to earn enough money to maintain all of that stuff we had accumulated. There was a distinct possibility that I would grow too old and feeble before the opportunity to play with any of it would ever present itself. In reality, our toys owned us.

In spite of everything we owned, Carole, during the summer of 2005, had started dropping subtle hints about wanting to buy a motorcycle. Having not had the opportunity to ride a motorcycle since prior to joining the air force, the thought of climbing back into the saddle appealed to me on several levels. The notion of buying a bike, however, seemed more like adding one more expensive toy to the inventory that would only wind up being stored and ignored. We lived in a beautiful home on three wooded acres in the country with a backyard magnificently landscaped and sufficiently elegant to have hosted two wedding ceremonies and a number of family reunions. Because our life had already been filled with other distractions, we rarely found time to appreciate any of it. When would we ever make room in our life for a trip on a motorcycle!

In contrast to my conservative, stifling, no-nonsense approach to life, living, and recreation, Carole was ready to hit the road on a moment's notice and head for any part of the world her heart desired. She had an amazing spirit for adventure. Her only concern appeared to be the time and money we needed to get to where we were going. From my perspective, it never seemed to occur to her that planning for the return trip might be of equal importance. She seemed content to just let nature take its course and deal with life's challenges as they came along; it seemed she felt that any problems encountered along the way would work themselves out. "Let the rough end drag" was her motto.

In all fairness, Carole deserved a lot of credit for her ability to redefine the meaning of that old expression "You only live once." I should have taken lessons from her.

While picnicking at a roadside park on the shores of Lake Huron one sunny afternoon in June 2006, a young couple rode in on their full-dress road bike and stopped to stretch their legs. Within a few minutes they were back in the saddle and headed out onto the highway. Carole and I sat quietly observing. As they were pulling away, Carole made a remark that really struck a nerve.

"That could be us," she said.

"What do you mean?" I asked her.

"That could be us riding around on a motorcycle. I think it would be a lot of fun."

"You're probably right," I said, "but do you think we would use a motorcycle enough to justify the cost of owning one?"

"Tom and Kay own one," she replied. "So do Nicole and Rodney. Roger and Leslie are always going somewhere on their motorcycle. I just think it would be fun to go riding around with them and do stuff together."

She had a point. There was really nothing preventing us from owning a motorcycle, and it sounded like a fun way to launch a whole new adventure. It also seemed like a good way to do some traveling without breaking the bank at the gas pumps, as our airplane and Corvette were inclined to do.

That was all it took to get me into the buying mode. A few days later, just to be safe, I decided it would be a good idea to recheck her thinking.

"Last week at the lake," I said, "when that couple rode in on their motorcycle, you made the comment, 'That could be us.'"

"Yeah," she said. "So are you thinking about buying one?"

"That all depends."

"On what?" she asked.

"On whether or not you were serious," I said. "Don't toy with me here. 'Cause if you want us to own a motorcycle, I'm ready to go find a deal on one."

"I wasn't kidding," she said. "I think it would be fun tooling around on a motorcycle. Like I said, Nicole and Rodney own one, and so do several of our other friends."

Wow, I thought to myself. *Just about every guy I know would love to have this woman for a wife!*

Two weeks later, I landed a deal on a 1990 Harley-Davidson that had been tastefully customized. The day that motorcycle showed up in our front yard was, ironically, one of Carole's happier moments in life.

Neither of us had a clue that that day would also mark the beginning of the final countdown toward the end of a life we shared.

CHAPTER 2

LIVING IN LIMBO

—◊◊◊—

We spent the rest of that summer and part of the autumn of 2006 exploring the countryside from the seat of our motorcycle. We were both still working full-time, but that did not matter. Having a new toy to play with had become an energizing experience for both of us. Any plans we had for trading our jobs for retirement simply got pushed to the back burner as we headed down the highway in blissful economic ignorance, enjoying the American dream.

For a long time, I had lightheartedly referred to retirement as showing up for work because I wanted to, not because I had to. Hidden in that statement was my surreptitious fear of having built a little empire that could not be maintained on a retiree's income. That is probably why, in spite of visions of grandeur, our life in general remained unsettled. Plans to get away from the machinery needed to start rolling, but shutting down the business to make it happen would never be a comfortable or viable option. I knew there had to be someone willing to come in and run that little repair business without finding it necessary to throw me, the old guy, into the street.

Everything boiled down to the fact that successfully retiring without compromising our lifestyle hinged on a steady source of revenue. Retirement investments, savings, and Social Security combined would barely maintain the estate. Doing things and going places required additional cash. Working part-time three or four days a week would be enough to generate the necessary supplemental income, but someone would have to take the helm every day to keep the ship from sinking. That full-time position would be best suited for a partner—someone with a personal stake in the operation's success. As bad as the job market had become, there was nobody willing to invest his or her time building sweat equity. Qualified people searching for work seemed to be looking for a high-paying free ride with benefits.

The hope of turning a family business over to the next generation has been part of an American dream shared by independent, hardworking entrepreneurs since the idea of profit-driven capitalism had been hatched. That had always been my dad's dream. Generally speaking, it's a sound concept, but personal experience had proven to me that turning the reins over to the kids is also an extremely fragile process that is difficult to execute without resulting in shattered relationships. Having been raised in and around a family-owned business, I had learned valuable lessons about how not to bring relatives onto the payroll and why certain protocols needed to be followed when family members joined the team.

The first rule in my personal guidebook for future success was to never assume my children would want anything to do with the family business should I be fortunate enough to someday own one. The second rule was to never violate the first rule.

Shortly after opening the doors for business at that little repair shop, someone asked my wife and me if we were planning to work at it together. "No," I replied without hesitation. "Carole and I talked about it briefly and decided to stay happily married." In retrospect, that may have been one of the most intelligent decisions either of us had ever made.

All three of our children, on the other hand, had been given the opportunity to learn my trade. Two were already well into their careers elsewhere, and the third had not yet tested the world on his own. Even if the business were to be handed down to the next generation in our family, it didn't look like it would be happening anytime soon.

Our older son, Jeremy, showed no interest. In June 2006, after three overseas tours during his eleven years in the US Army, he decided to abandon his plans to be a career soldier. Had he chosen to reenlist, there was a better-than-average chance he would have immediately been redeployed indefinitely to the Vietnam-style war that continued raging in Iraq and Afghanistan. I suggested that he could return to Michigan and take over the business, but he had bigger fish to fry in the Washington, DC, area pursuing high-paying opportunities he would never have had either from the ranks of the enlisted men or as a partner in my business. So his name went to the bottom of my list of possible business partners.

Our daughter, Nicole, had put herself through college while working with me in the shop part-time. She caught on quickly and could have easily taken over the entire operation, but after graduating from college with a paralegal degree, she landed a job at the Tuscola county courthouse in Caro, Michigan. It came as no surprise that Nicole was happily on her way to pursuing something other than motor vehicle repair. I was still the company's sole owner.

Our younger son, Jason, had finished college and still lived at home, helping in the shop as a part-time employee. The business was his if he decided that he wanted it.

Early one morning just before Thanksgiving in the autumn of 2006, I sat by the kitchen window, sipping from a fresh cup of coffee while gazing out over the frost-covered lawn in our backyard. Immersed in a soul-searching melancholy, restlessly contemplating the future, my mood was tepid. A little voice inside kept telling me to find another road map on my quest for self-preservation.

Then, from out of nowhere, in one stunning epiphany it became clear that I had been trying to become my son's employee. Shamefully recognizing my self-absorbed strategy for semiretirement, the plan vaporized like frost disappearing under the rising morning sun.

Jason was my last hope for a successor, but he had never held a paying job anywhere else. Although he seemed to show a genuine interest in learning the operation, I knew from experience that if he ever hoped to settle successfully as a permanent partner, he first needed to explore his other career options. Dragging Jason into the business before he had a chance to see what the rest of the world might have to offer would be a fool's choice. Clearly the only fair and reasonable course of action was to cut the strings and send him into the cold world that was sure to pummel his senses the way it had so brutally bruised mine. Sometime during the next few days or weeks—I cannot recall because time had become so agonizingly irrelevant—I encouraged my son to find another job.

—ᴍ—

It was another one of those gray Michigan Sunday mornings in February 2007. The Christmas season was behind us. My books had been closed and turned over to the accountants to have the annual tax returns prepared and filed. The world outside was in hibernation somewhere under the frozen, snow-covered scenery.

Life in general just didn't seem to be panning out quite the way I had always imagined. Losing my last chance at handing control over to a sidekick, struggling to survive in a crummy economic climate, and facing a sense of loneliness that promised to define the rest of my life had seriously sobered the mood.

Carole had already left home to attend morning worship services at Grace Bible, a church we had occasionally talked about visiting together. I opted to stay home and hide inside the peace and quiet of my private sanctuary.

I found church attendance as an adult to be of little comfort, most likely because the whole religious experience had been tainted from childhood. As a kid during the 1950s, being dragged out of bed on a Sunday morning was usually an unpleasant experience. It involved getting all dressed up, piling into the back of the family sedan, and driving down dusty roads to a little country church in the middle of nowhere. The church sanctuary was a place where wiggling wasn't allowed. Sitting through another long, boring episode of blah, blah, blah made the hands of time turn painfully slow for a young boy wishing he could be anywhere else.

Mom was the church organist, and Dad seemed bent on demonstrating to the congregation that his family represented the holiest of worshippers. Our parents were Christians, but as is the case with most other folks claiming to have found salvation, the church had become their god. Meanwhile the children in the congregation were expected to serve as examples of their parents' faithfulness. It was a suffocating affiliation, and my fidgety restlessness usually earned at least one scowling glare from my father every Sunday morning.

As I got older, those childhood experiences were amplified by endless exposure to twisted translations of scripture. Politically corrected versions of salvation through tolerance in one church directly conflicted with sermons spewing warnings of hellfire and brimstone at another. None of it felt the way Christianity should feel. Corrupted religion laced with legalism had permeated most, if not all, of the mainstream denominations.

Self-proclaimed messiahs like Jim Jones were cropping up everywhere. On November 18, 1978, more than nine hundred people followed that man to their graves in the name of religion during what has become known as the Guyana massacre. Like rats following the Pied Piper out of Hamelin, people seemed willing to validate every crackpot who claimed to know when the world was going to end. How rational people could be drawn in so completely escaped logic. Avoiding the scene altogether seemed the safest route to me.

By the time the year 2000 rolled around, contemplating church attendance conjured up in me serious fears of being sucked back into yet another series of guilt-laden obligations serving no other purpose than to manipulate my conscience, absorb my already limited free time, and leave me wishing I had simply remained anonymously disconnected. Exploring yet another new congregation seemed to be tempting fate. Just showing up for Sunday morning services was akin to asking for work assignments.

The final straw was drawn for us around February 2001, when the secretary at the church where we had been attending sent a calendar of events in the mail that included our names on the list of volunteers. Carole and I had been assigned to host the postservice coffee hour for several of the upcoming Sundays. Neither of us had been asked if we were willing, let alone available, to fulfill those assigned time slots. In spite of previous requests to be contacted before being involuntarily volunteered, we were once again tied by surprise to a schedule that had little, if anything, to do with the worship services. Preparing the coffee hour, in fact, usually kept us from participating in the very thing we had gone to church for in the first place.

Our quietly disappearing without explanation or apology finally put an end to the obligations. From then on, we usually spent our Sunday mornings in silent splendor on the couch in the den with a cup of coffee and a good book.

Michael Hollenbeck, the pastor at Grace Bible, was a high school pal of both Carole and me who had come back to his hometown to occupy the pulpit at the church where he attended with his mother and father all through high school. Mike spent a lot of his free mornings during the week visiting with me, drinking coffee, and sharing ideas about life, living, and religion. He knew that I had all but given up on Sunday morning worship services as a source of peace and promise, but his persistence never faltered.

My pastor friend was often sitting behind the counter in my little repair shop when customers came through the door turning the air blue with language that would have made a sailor blush. I usually had to turn away so nobody could see me grinning from the reaction Mike got from the potty mouths when introductions were finally made. Mike never flinched. He just went right on with the conversation as though those four-letter words were a normal part of everyone else's vocabulary—which, sadly, in many instances they were.

It was no secret that Mike wanted us to join his congregation. Our responses to his tactfully subtle invitations usually involved changing the subject. One morning, sensing his urgency, I addressed the matter head-on.

"Michael," I said, "I'm not coming to your church. I don't want to risk wrecking our friendship."

He just laughed, and we continued our conversation.

Staring outside at snowdrifts covering the frozen landscape while Carole was at church that Sunday morning in February brought haunting memories of the smart-aleck remark I had made to Mike in response to his invitations. Nothing had changed in our relationship; I just didn't see the point in going to church. Deep resentment lingered from the guilt that had been laid on my soul for having failed to worship properly in the eyes of those doubting the believers and doing the preaching. At some point, curiously, it had occurred to me that most of the guilt-producing sermons had not come from the pulpit.

I sat as motionless as a mannequin by the window that morning as thoughts racing through my subconscious began to surface in the form of lyrics and a melody. In a spooky sort of way, the theme seemed to contain a gentle spiritual warning of things to come based upon what life had already turned out to be. Without a doubt, hundreds, maybe thousands, of songs had been written and recorded with the same idea, but this particular inspiration was a new one in my repertoire:

> *There were times I didn't want to bother*
> *Too busy with a world I couldn't see*
> *And a life full with everything that's empty*
> *Lord, what's happened to me?*

Because of my background in music, there was nothing unusual about the way the song had materialized; that sort of thing happened frequently. But past experience had proven that unless the idea was recorded as it came to me, the entire piece would vaporize into thin air. For once the songwriting program on the computer opened without any glitches, and within minutes my fingers were flying while a flood of ideas appeared on the screen. An hour later the first draft was finished. My review of the freshly completed work crystallized my unsettling thoughts of a future filled with uncertainty for both my son and me. Jason was facing the front end of his career search while I was staring out the back door into an empty nest.

Although Jason's search for work had so far come up empty, I remained quietly in the shadows, wringing my hands, anxiously observing while he diligently combed the job market for employment opportunities in an economically depressed area. He managed to uncover a few entry-level positions that paid well, but the competition was fierce. My hope was that he would land a well-paying job close enough to home for us to continue growing our father-and-son friendship as adults.

The warmer weather of spring was just around the corner. With it would come the seasonal rush of repair work on farm equipment being dragged out of storage and readied for spring planting. More than once I picked up the phone to invite Jason back into the shop to earn a living but hung up the receiver before dialing the last digit. It was a struggle biting my tongue, but unless he asked for help, he was on his own. I was determined to stay out of his way.

Near the end of February, reaching a point of desperation in his job search, Jason stopped by his sister's office at the county Friend of the Court building in Caro. Frustrated, discouraged, and rapidly running out of options, he asked Nicole if she knew of any employment opportunities.

"Why not put your application in at the Lighthouse?" one of Nicole's coworkers suggested. "I heard they were hiring."

"What is the Lighthouse?" he asked.

"It's a neurological rehabilitation center," she said. "Their main office is less than a mile east of Caro."

"I've never heard of the place before," Nicole said.

"Neither have I," said Jason. "What do they do? Wouldn't you have to have some sort of special training to work there?"

"It can't be that tough to get a job there," she said. "A friend of mine works there, and he hasn't had any special training. I'm told they have a pretty strict screening process but they're good people to work for."

Prior to that day none of us had ever heard of the Lighthouse Neurological Rehabilitation Center even though it had already been in operation for nearly twenty years. Their primary function, we learned, involved care and rehabilitation for individuals who had experienced traumatic brain injury (TBI).

Following his sister's advice, Jason submitted his job application to the Lighthouse. Early in March 2007, he was called in for an interview, which led to orientation, on-the-job training, and then a full-time job as one of the staff members.

The news brought a sigh of relief. My son had found a job within commutable distance from our house, enabling him to continue living with us until he could establish a place of his own. His pursuit of job opportunities in a nearby town meant there was still a remote possibility that he would return someday to take over the little business I had built, but the most important part was that our youngest child had finally opened a door that promised an identifiable, independent future.

There was no way that anyone could have known how forcing my son to leave the business and go out on his own would ultimately translate to a key component of my recovery from a near-death experience. Nor did we have any idea just how important a part Jason's new employer would play in our family's personal lives.

CHAPTER 3

THE RIDE

—◊—

Carole and I spent the rest of that winter and early spring of 2007 mostly talking about strategies to avoid spending another summer missing out on the things we wanted to do. We also spent a considerable amount of time discussing ideas for launching an affordable retirement.

We were both still working full-time, Carole at the courthouse and I in my little repair shop. After thirty-six years of marriage, our financial plan still amounted to little more than paying off the mortgage. Our only goal had been to achieve debt-free living. After that—well, we just never thought that far ahead. Doubling and tripling monthly loan payments kept us tied pretty tight to the harness. Retirement age was creeping up on us, but it was hard to pin down the means and method of making the leap. I knew almost to the penny what it cost to turn the lights on in the shop every morning but had only developed a vague idea of how much money it took to own and operate our home. We had never bothered to prepare a household budget. We just kept putting in our time, hoping to someday magically reach economic independence.

It didn't take a mathematician to recognize the impact inflation was having on the net worth of our investments and retirement accounts. The decreasing value of the dollar meant that our little nest egg would never be enough to support the standard of living we had grown accustomed to. Even if we cashed everything out and seriously scaled back our spending habits, I calculated there would barely be enough to get us through five or six years before we would be flat broke. We weren't alone. Most of our friends faced the same dilemma; many had not yet come to realize it.

We weren't just spinning our wheels financially. We had budgeted very little free time into our daily routines. Every year, it seemed, as warmer weather approached, our calendar would fill up with five days' worth of events scribbled into each weekend; many of those activities were linked to obligations we had not willingly chosen. Volunteer work with one organization or another seemed to soak up every spare minute of our lives, and the pace was taking its toll. We had reached a point in time when protecting our plans for the upcoming summer became our primary concern.

Dragging myself from the shop and into the house at the end of another exhausting day, I kicked off my shoes, cut through the kitchen, and folded into the most comfortable chair in the living room. Carole was around the corner in the kitchen, rattling pans and pulling cooking utensils out of the drawers.

"How was your day?" I asked over the noise she was making.

"It was a zoo at the office today," she replied. "I guess people just think I have nothing better to do than sip coffee and listen to them babble on about their silly little problems. How 'bout you? How'd your day go?"

"Man, I'm beat," I said, "and I've got a meeting to go to tonight."

Carole stopped what she was doing and stood up, turning her undivided attention in my direction as though she had just caught a severe weather bulletin and was listening closely for further details.

"With who?" she asked. "I didn't know you weren't going to be home tonight!"

"There's a board meeting at the airport," I said as my head flopped back against the chair. "I thought you knew."

"No, I didn't know," she said as she returned to her work in the kitchen. "I don't remember you telling me anything about it. You look pretty tired. Are you still going?"

"I'd stay home and skip the meeting, but I'm the one who called it," I said. "I need to talk to the rest of the board about this volunteer treasurer's job I've had for the past eleven years. Either someone is going to start sharing the load or I'm going to start writing myself a paycheck from the airport's treasury. So yeah, I'll be going to the meeting tonight." I gave a sigh of resignation. "Tomorrow night I have a VFW meeting," I added.

Both of us were overcommitted. There never seemed to be a tactful way to decline invitations to social activities or say no to requests when volunteers were needed for some civic duty. Our time always seemed to belong to someone else.

"I get so tired of constantly being on the run," I said, "and it seems like I'm always running around doing things for someone else. When are we ever going to have time for ourselves?"

Carole closed the oven door and came into the living room to put her feet up while supper warmed. "Yeah," she said, letting out a big sigh as she collapsed onto the couch. "It's like we never have time to sit and relax, much less do things we would rather be doing."

"It's the same old thing," I continued. "We make all these plans to go places and do things, but when the snow finally melts in the spring, all these other commitments start cropping up. Every fall when the snow starts flying again, I look back on the summer that's just passed and realize that once again the things we wanted to do never seemed to make it off the back burner."

We talked about it, pondered the dilemma, examined our personal desires, and wondered aloud why we tolerated such circumstances. It wasn't the first time we had had that discussion. We had already arrived at the obvious conclusion that it was time to become a little more selfish with our time.

"Something's got to change," Carole said. "We need to take our summer back. I'm not spending one more weekend catering to everyone else."

"I think the first thing we need to do," I said, "is learn to say no to people. We need to change our priorities."

"I can't argue with that," she said.

"Maybe it's just a philosophical thing," I said. "Maybe it's a matter of learning why we need to say no. I remember a guy telling me once, 'Dave, there are only twelve weekends in a summer, and it's going to rain on at least four of them.'"

Judging from the expression on Carole's face, I could tell the wheels were turning.

"Rule number one," I said, "should be that we never commit to anything without talking it over between us first."

"You're right," she said. "We both need to work on that. Got any suggestions?"

"Let's look at the calendar," I said as I walked over to pull it off the hook in the stairwell where it was hanging. "Let's start circling some dates we do not want to give away."

The first thing we did was resurrect date night—one night a week set aside to spend time exclusively with each other. Declaring a date night had proven effective for carving out a piece of privacy when the kids were all still young and living at home. There was no reason for us to believe that our date night arrangement couldn't work just as well twenty years later, when it was only the two of us against the outside world.

Pursuing date night was fun. We took turns lining up things to do. Sometimes we went to one of our favorite restaurants, and other times we would sit at the dining room table and play card games. Occasionally we used our date nights to do our grocery shopping. If the weather was nice, we would hop on the motorcycle and ride to Lake Huron to enjoy a picnic at our favorite roadside park next to the shoreline. Regardless of the activity, the date night objective was to tune out the rest of the world and reconnect with each other. And it worked. It wasn't long before we craved the luxury of expanding our private time.

"This date night thing works pretty good," I said, "but it's only one night a week. I think we need to block off more time for ourselves."

"Okay," she said, "so what's your plan?"

"Do you ever daydream about things you would like to do, like take a trip or go somewhere for a weekend?" I asked.

"Sure," she said, "all the time."

"Then let's write those things on the calendar," I said. "If we can't pick specific dates for things we want to do, let's at least hang notes by the calendar as a sort of wish list."

We started plugging the calendar full of personal-choice ideas. No matter how far-fetched, we wrote any activity or event remotely appealing to either of us on the calendar, and those items became cause for pause when we were asked if we were available. That little trick derailed a lot of decision-making agony.

Not long after starting back up with our date nights, our son Jeremy landed two prime seats to see Bob Seger in concert at the Verizon Center in Washington, DC, and he wanted me to join him. As a performing entertainer, my bookings usually conflicted with those sorts of events, so attending a concert as part of the audience promised to be a new experience. It was a bonus that my son wanted to spend some time with his dad and the time away sounded rather appealing.

It was a whirlwind trip, flying into Reagan International on a Thursday, attending the concert with Jeremy on Friday, and flying back home on Saturday. We had a blast!

That was the sort of adventure I wanted to share with Carole, so I landed two tickets to see the groups *Chicago* and *America* together at a concert coming up in June. We were not in the habit of doing such things for ourselves, so buying those tickets felt just a little bit extravagant.

So this is what it feels like to stretch out on our own, I thought to myself.

Expanding date night and filling slots on the calendar made us feel as though we were scoring major victories. Early in May our conversations began focusing on the upcoming Memorial Day weekend.

"I heard some guys talking about Rolling Thunder," I said to Carole over supper one night. "They said it's the largest single demonstration in Washington, DC. Hundreds of thousands of motorcycles from all over the United States meet up at the Pentagon, ride through the National Mall, and wind up at the Lincoln Memorial."

I looked up Rolling Thunder on the Internet. Rolling Thunder is the name of the organization that keeps pressure on our government officials to negotiate for the return of POWs and MIAs from various wars around the world. While doing the research, I came across an article that told of their recent success in having a Korean War veteran's remains finally returned home.

"All we have to do is show up with our motorcycle and we're part of the ride. You wanna go?"

"Yeah, that sounds like fun!" she said. "I'll put in for that Friday off work if you want to go a day earlier. Maybe we can spend a day with Jeremy while we're there."

"Okay," I said, "I'll set up the trailer so we can haul the motorcycle. We can drive to Jeremy's house in Dumfries on Friday, and then on Sunday morning we can ride the bike into DC."

We skipped the local VFW's annual ritual that year and hauled our motorcycle to Washington, DC, to ride with the brotherhood. Participating in that once-in-a-lifetime adventure was amazing. Over 750,000 motorcycles showed up, filling the north, east, and south parking lots at the Pentagon. Judging by the colors worn, more than half of those riders were veterans like me.

Because I am a Vietnam veteran, that political demonstration struck close to the heart. It was the homecoming I never received, so I felt justified trading up from the local level to the national scene. The boys at the VFW post weren't any too pleased with my decision to deploy and leave them to tend the 2007 ceremonies in my absence, but I was determined to shed the shackles.

After that appetizer we started searching for other affordable, entertaining overnight activities and places of interest to visit. Some of our best entertainment tips came from our kids, now grown and sharing their own travel experiences.

As hard as we tried to plot activities that we could share, every so often we missed the mark. Because of a breakdown in communication, we had accidentally made conflicting plans for the upcoming July 4 celebrations. Talk about being independent!

Carole had made arrangements to go camping in Michigan's North Country with Nicole. I was preparing my gear for a weekend hiking trip into the Adirondacks. We each knew of the other's plans; we just never paid attention to the date until we both realized we had made our plans for the same weekend. I had hoped my wife would join me in the mountains, and she was expecting me to join the two of them with their tents in the woods.

We were both a little dismayed when it finally occurred to us that we would be going in opposite directions during, of all times, a holiday weekend. Our method of planning ahead apparently still had some wrinkles that needed ironing out. Nevertheless, we were extending the trend of doing things we wanted to do instead of draining our time filling someone else's well. We vowed to be more careful when making future plans and moved on.

Michigan weather conditions in June were usually perfect for flying. Our airplane had not been out of the hangar in nearly a year, so I opened the logbooks to review pilot currency and aircraft maintenance records. Moving the Cessna and myself back onto the flight line in airworthy condition presumed that we might be more inclined to find spontaneous excuses to take to the skies in search of adventure.

The sunrise on Sunday morning, June 17, gave way to another beautiful cloudless day, so off to the airport I went. At the top of a stack of fliers tacked on the bulletin board in the pilot lounge was an announcement for an upcoming pancake breakfast sponsored by the flying club at the Sandusky, Michigan, airport eighteen miles away. Their doings usually attracted many of our friends and fellow pilots, so I penciled the event into my pocket calendar.

I towed the airplane out of the hangar and onto the ramp and spent the rest of that morning brushing the dust off the aircraft and my piloting skills. Two hours and four practice landings later, the airplane was back in the hangar and I was on my way home to tell Carole about the following weekend's event at the Sandusky airport.

Monday, June 18, rolled around, and we returned to our parallel worlds that were filled with chores and responsibilities. On Wednesday of that week, Carole packed her bags and left town with a coworker to attend a two-day state court seminar in Gaylord, Michigan. While she was away, I spent my evenings alone, packing hiking equipment and preparing the motorcycle for the July 4 trip into the Adirondacks. We were both looking forward to time away from work in spite of the fact that we wouldn't be spending the time together. Saturday, June 23, started out with us on the patio, catching up on the previous week's activity and enjoying each other's company.

"I talked to Diane last night," Carole said.

Diane was an old high school friend who had moved to California with her husband, Ernie, a few years earlier.

"Yeah? What did Diane have to say?" I asked.

"Ernie isn't doing too well," she said. "I think he's losing his battle with cancer."

"I thought he was on the mend," I said, sadly reflecting on the fact that we might never see him again.

"So did I," she said. "Diane said it was horrible reliving the nightmare, watching her husband slip away the same painful way she had lost her mother and sister. She covers it up pretty well, but I know she's having a really hard time."

Once again I felt the Grim Reaper peeling away another part of my life. Death prepared to visit Ernie the way it had claimed my friend Tom Bosnick when that airplane crashed in Taiwan. Because I had never learned how to deal with the loss of someone close, the thoughts just rolled through my mind and wound up tucked somewhere deep in the shadows.

Shoving any further depressing thoughts aside, I hooked up the flatbed and drove off to the lumberyard to pick up landscaping and building supplies. Carole returned to whatever it was she had been doing in her craft room and spent the rest of that Saturday afternoon routinely sorting through our individual lists of chores. Around eleven o'clock that evening, Carole went to bed. I retired to the backyard to spend the night trying out my new camping stuff.

June 2007 has to be a record month for sunshine in Michigan's Saginaw Valley. Sunday the twenty-fourth turned into another comfortably warm cloudless day. We were anxious to pull the Cessna out of the hangar and take advantage of the weather. I was a little stiff from having slept on the ground the night before, but the body only limbers with exercise, so I began the day by forcing rebellious muscles and joints to bend. Aside from our plans to attend the fly-in at the Sandusky airport, there was nothing in particular going on that day. The excitement of diving into another day filled with spur-of-the-moment choices and no obligations added a spring to our step.

Carole had heard the telephone ring during the night, so when it was time to crawl out of bed, she checked the answering machine and discovered a message from our friend Diane. Ernie's cancer had finally taken him from this world and into the next great adventure during the night. It was a sobering way to start the day, but we resolved to celebrate the life we had shared with him by continuing to renew our own.

Our flight to Sandusky that morning was as smooth as glass. Radio traffic was moderate to heavy as airplanes arrived from all over southern Michigan. We squinted into the distance, trying to spot the mosquito-sized aircraft descending from various altitudes and coming in from every direction. I joined the traffic pattern, lined the airplane up with the designated runway, and made respectable tire-to-pavement contact just past the crowd of spectators standing alongside the approach end of the airport's east-west landing strip. The only remaining available aircraft parking space was out in the middle of a freshly mowed hayfield behind the rows of hangars, so we bounced over the rough terrain and parked wingtip-to-wingtip next to the Piper that had touched down just ahead of us.

We climbed out of the cockpit and headed across the field to join the long line of hungry pilots, passengers, and local airplane enthusiasts that had formed in front of the breakfast hangar. A large group of motorcyclists on an organized cross-country run had assembled on the street side of the building. We finished breakfast, spent some time visiting with fellow pilots and biker friends, and then hiked back across the hayfield where our airplane sat waiting to take us home.

After spending a deliciously beautiful morning flying low and slow across the flatlands of Michigan's Thumb, closing the hangar door felt wrong. The day was still young, and it was very tempting to pull the airplane back out and pick another destination to fly away to.

"What a gorgeous day." I said. "We really need to do this more often. What do you want to do with the rest of the day?"

"We could go home and build a campfire back in the woods," Carole suggested. "Maybe roast some hotdogs and just hang out."

"That sounds nice, but I don't think I could relax in our own backyard within sight of the unfinished projects that are everywhere," I said. "It would be too tempting to pick up a shovel or a rake."

As we piled our flying gear into the back of the car, we talked about taking in a matinee at a nearby theater, but the weather was too perfect to be cooped up inside. Taking a picnic to the lakeshore didn't sound all that bad even though it involved another forty-five minute road trip to get there. It is sad to say, but whatever we decided to do for entertainment, we needed to do it somewhere away from home.

On the drive back from the airport, Carole turned to me and said, "Hey, I know what we can do. Let's take a ride on the motorcycle!"

"Okay," I said. "Where do you want to go?"

"Nowhere in particular," she said. "It just feels like a good day to ride."

"All right," I said, "as soon as we're home, I'll get the bike out while you get into your riding gear. When we get to the end of the driveway, you pick the destination."

The temperature was rising into the eighties, and the thought of cooling off with the wind in our face was irresistible. Carole wasted no time getting ready to ride. Before I could get the bike out of the garage, she had unloaded her things from the car, put on her boots and helmet, and was back outside. She stood there patiently, camera tucked neatly into the front pocket of her leather vest, waiting for the okay signal to climb on.

"So which way to you want to go?" I asked.

"Let's ride over to Caro and see if there's anything going on," she said.

In no time we were out of the driveway and headed north, shifting through the gears and regaining that feeling of freedom on the open road. Beautiful groves of trees lined both sides of the highway, providing patches of shade on the hot asphalt under our tires. Beyond the canopy of leaves in the blue skies where we had been less than an hour before, we spotted several airplanes flying home from their visit to the airport in Sandusky. Coming at us in the other lane of traffic was a long line of custom hot rods and classic cars out for a Sunday cruise. The world was alive with people taking advantage of a perfect day.

The fragrant smell of freshly mowed hay occasionally interrupted by the sickening sweet odor of decaying roadkill filled our senses as the scenery changed with each passing mile. Cedar swamps alongside the country roads provided shade as we rode through low-lying areas and penetrated pockets of cooler air. The blast of heat rising from the blacktop at the edge of the darkness was always a little breathtaking.

Forty minutes later, we rolled into Caro and parked the bike to while away some time pawing through discounted merchandise at the sidewalk sales. After a couple more stops my pockets, Carole's backpack, the luggage rack, and both saddlebags on the bike were crammed full of stuff we had impulsively picked from the shelves. Tying all of our things to the motorcycle brought back visions of the mopeds in Southeast Asia threading their way through traffic with a dad, a mom, three kids, and a stack of chicken crates strapped on board.

Our favorite method of traveling could probably be best described as aimlessly wandering. We still weren't ready to go home, so we turned into the first handy place for some ice cream and took our time with a couple of cones before getting back on the bike for the return trip. It was truly amazing what sort of adventure could be discovered when there were no particular routes to follow and no restrictions on how much time it took to get to where we were going. We rode out of Caro and took the long way home.

Arriving in Kingston from the north, I opted to continue the scenic ride to the south through the hills and curves, taking in the smells and sights all the way to Clifford, and then back to the east into Marlette. The road between Kingston and Clifford made for a great ride when the weather was cooperating. Cresting the hills, smoothly downshifting into the turns, gradually accelerating as we proceeded through each curve, and then opening the throttle as the bike came onto the straightaway was exhilarating.

Experiencing life from the seat of a motorcycle offers a perspective that no other form of transportation can provide. We were enjoying the ride. There was nothing more urgent than the moment at hand. As we rolled into Marlette from the west, it felt like we were enjoying the first day of the rest of our lives. I pulled the bike into the left turn lane at the main intersection in downtown Marlette and stopped to wait for the light to turn green. With the motorcycle engine hot and idling, I turned to Carole over my left shoulder.

"This was worth the time spent," I said. "What a beautiful day!"

37

Carole wrapped her arms around my waist and hugged me from behind. "Thanks for a fun day," she said.

"I think I can go back and work in the yard now," I said. "This was exactly what I needed to recharge my batteries."

The traffic light changed to green and we pulled away from the intersection, slowly shifting through the gears while heading north out of town for the last three and a half miles of our trip. Up ahead, just past the outskirts of town, a car came tearing out of a trailer park and onto the highway.

What an idiot! I thought to myself. *If we had been at that spot ten seconds sooner, he would have run over us.*

The driver recklessly sped away ahead of us, his car weaving erratically between the lines. I just shook my head and kept my distance. I wasn't going to allow a stupid motorist to ruin my mood, so I turned my attention back to the scenery.

The fields on both sides of the highway were lush with fresh soybean and corn plants sprouting out of the ground. Groves of tall maple trees lined the fence rows in the distance. Elusive deer herds were undoubtedly decimating the farmer's crops at that very moment as they wandered through the rows planted in those fields. Fleeting thoughts of the upcoming deer season triggered visions of corn-fed venison cooking on the grill at Thanksgiving.

As we approached the intersection of M-53 and French Line Road, we caught up with the car that had careened onto the highway from the entrance to that trailer park. The car was stopped and sitting on the right-hand shoulder of the road.

What is this guy doing? I thought. *Talking on a cell phone? Making a turn? Maybe his car broke down.*

Who knew! At least he would be behind us once we made it past him through the intersection and safely home in another—

CHAPTER 4

HIT-AND-RUN

—⟋⟍—

Sleeping … I must be dreaming … feels like I'm lying on the ground.
That looks like a Schwann's truck rolling past me. I wonder why the taillights are white and not red.

—⟋⟍—

Dennis, a volunteer firefighter from the Caro department, was southbound on M-53 a quarter of a mile north of the intersection where Frenchline Road crosses the highway. As he crested the hill, Dennis saw our limp bodies still sliding across the middle of the intersection ahead. He had to have caught sight of us a split second after the impact.

Like most firefighters in the area, his vehicle was equipped with various lights and flashers, along with a light bar bolted to the top of his pickup cab. Dennis pulled up to the scene and parked his truck across the middle of the highway to block oncoming traffic, turning on all of his emergency lighting before getting out of the vehicle.

His initial assessment was that we had simply lost control of the motorcycle and dumped it in the middle of the road. One quick survey of the scene and Dennis knew we were in serious trouble. He grabbed his cell phone and quickly dialed 911 while simultaneously evaluating our condition. When the emergency operator answered his call, Dennis provided the vital information. Then, stressing that we both were critically injured, he advised the operator that medical airlift evacuation should be dispatched to the scene immediately.

While tending to our injuries, Dennis glanced up and noticed a vehicle sitting on the shoulder of the road next to the southbound lane just south of the intersection. A young man was standing next to the vehicle, staring back at us as we lay unconscious in the highway. Thinking he was just a passerby, Dennis instinctively made a mental note of the car and its driver; he then turned his attention back to Carole and me.

One by one, passing motorists pulled off the road and jumped out of their vehicles to help in whatever way they could. Dan, the second or third person on the scene, was a friend of ours. He was no medical technician, but he could tell we were in desperate condition. A lady who had stopped ran up to Dan and asked what she could do to help. Dan told her to hold me down.

"Sit on him if you have to," Dan said. "Do not let him get up!"

Dan later told me that I took off my helmet. My foot was mangled, and he said that I was struggling to breathe, but I kept trying to get up to look for my wife, who was lying unconscious on the highway twenty feet away. He said Carole's loss of blood and labored breathing terrified and sickened him. He knew her life was slipping away right before his eyes.

Medical first responders, firefighters, EMTs, and police officers soon arrived at the scene, and everyone scrambled into action. Crews were deployed to the nearest intersections in all four directions, and traffic was diverted while a two-mile section of M-53 was temporarily closed to through traffic.

—◊◊◊—

While Carole and I spent that Sunday, the twenty-fourth of June, enjoying life playing with the airplane and the motorcycle, our daughter, Nicole, and her husband, Rodney, spent the morning with the Burlington Fire Department at the annual Michigan State Fireman's Association conference in Imlay City, Michigan.

Sharing her husband's passion for helping people in distress, Nicole had joined the fire and rescue squad shortly after they were married. Both Rodney and Nicole found the emergency volunteer work gratifying, so they hooked up with Burlington's medical first responders (MFR) rescue unit. Nicole so enjoyed the medical side of her activity that she took the required training and became an emergency medical technician (EMT) working part-time with the Marlette Ambulance crew.

Rescuing crash victims, coordinating emergency medical evacuations, and handling critical injuries during that first "golden hour" following an incident is something the human spirit needs to be called to do. The gruesome scenery is not for the weak. I have thanked God over and over that both Rodney and Nicole thrived in that environment. Through their combined emergency and medical training, they had unsuspectingly prepared themselves for an accident scene and emergency room trauma the likes of which none of us could have imagined.

On their way home from the conference that afternoon, Nicole, Rodney, and the other first responders in their group diverted to answer a medical emergency call from Central

Dispatch. They treated the patient, turned the care over to Greg, one of Nicole's EMT partners who had arrived with an ambulance, and then climbed back into their vehicles and headed for home. No sooner were they out on the road than another call came in requesting response to the scene of an accident at the corner of M-53 and Frenchline Road.

With more than a full day's activity already under their belt, the team turned straight for the fire hall to grab their turnout gear. On the way to pick up their equipment, Rodney remarked that they were probably going to be asked to set up the medical evacuation landing zone for the helicopter that had also been dispatched to the scene.

He was right.

Back at the fire hall, Nicole ran to the rack, grabbed her equipment, jumped into the rescue truck with two other MFR volunteers, and rushed to the scene ahead of the others to clear and secure an area for the aircraft to land safely. Rodney stayed behind and waited for the rest of their personnel to arrive, and he then made his way to the scene with his crew packed into the squad truck.

—ᴍ—

Mark was a close friend of Nicole and Rodney who, through their relationship, had also become a friend of ours. Mark had signed on as a volunteer with both Burlington and Marlette fire departments, but he had not gone to the conference with the rest of the crew from Burlington that day, so when the call went out, he responded as a part of the Marlette crew. He grabbed his gear from the Marlette fire hall and beat it straight to the scene of the accident. When he arrived, he found both Carole and me in desperate condition. One ambulance had arrived, and a crowd had already gathered. Some were assisting in whatever way they thought would be helpful; others were looking on, wondering what they could do to help.

From out of the confusion someone suggested that it might be a good idea to get Carole into the Sanilac ambulance and rush her to the Marlette Regional Hospital a mile and a half back toward town. The group lifted Carole into the back of the rig, and then Mark jumped in behind the wheel and headed south, away from the accident scene. He continued talking anxiously to Carole over his shoulder as he sped down the highway, urging her to hang on while the medics worked to keep her alive.

At that same moment, Nicole hurried through town behind the wheel of the rescue truck and headed north out of Marlette, toward the crash site. She knew a motorcycle had been involved and had an eerie feeling about what lay ahead for her and the team.

Nicole and Mark's emergency vehicles passed each other on the road in front of the entrance to the mobile home park where that car had come tearing out and onto the highway just seconds before we had crossed that stretch of pavement on the motorcycle. Our daughter told me later that in that split second as their vehicles zipped by each other going in opposite directions, her eyes met with Mark's. She said the look of fear on Mark's face sent a chill down her spine. She knew that something was wrong—that she was heading toward a scene unlike anything else she had experienced.

"This isn't going to be good," Nicole mumbled to herself.

As she arrived on the scene, Nicole rolled the rescue rig to a stop alongside the Lapeer EMS unit, jumped out, and grabbed her gear. Moving as quickly as possible, she pulled the bunkers (firefighter's pants) over her tender, sunburned legs. Dressed and ready, she rounded the back of the Lapeer EMS unit and stopped dead in her tracks, her worst fears unfolding before her eyes. There, lying in the middle of the highway, was our motorcycle. Our helmets were scuffed and lying in the road as though they had been randomly tossed from the ditch. Blood stained the pavement where our bodies had skidded to a stop. Panic began to well up from within her as she quickly absorbed the scene. Turning around, she recognized my boots on the ground, and then she saw me lying on my back inside the ambulance.

Nicole leaped into the back of the ambulance, pushed Leslie (the EMT who was working on me) aside, and looked into my eyes.

"Hi, Dad," she said softly.

"Hi, Nic," I replied, stunned and groggy.

In startled disbelief, Leslie spun her head around and looked up at Nicole. "Is this your father?" she asked.

"Yes," Nicole replied.

"You need to get to the hospital," Leslie told her with wide-eyed insistence.

Nicole jumped out of the ambulance, looked around, and realized she had no transportation to go anywhere. Not knowing what else to do, she jumped back into the ambulance to be with me. Leslie looked up and saw Nicole back at my side.

"What are you still doing here?" Leslie asked. "I told you that you needed to get to the hospital."

"How am I supposed to get there? I don't have a ride!"

"Go find a ride from someone," Leslie said. "I said you need to get to the hospital so get going. *Now!*"

Nicole jumped back out onto the pavement and caught sight of Rodney, who had just arrived in the squad truck with his crew. She ran straight to her husband and looked him in the eyes.

"It's Mom and Dad."

"Yeah, I know," Rodney said. "I can see his bike."

Rod looked around and spotted one of the police officers standing nearby.

"We need to get to the hospital, and you need to take us. Now!" Rodney said to the officer.

The officer, realizing who they were, turned to one of the deputies and told him to load Rodney and Nicole into the squad car and take them both to the hospital.

When Rodney and Nicole arrived at the Marlette hospital, they were escorted to the EMS room adjacent to the ER, where the staff was working feverishly to keep Carole alive. She was not breathing on her own, and the team could not get the breathing tube into Carole's lungs. They were pumping oxygen into her lungs using a hand-operated bag valve mask (a CPR-type oxygen mask with a hand pump bag attached to a supply of oxygen).

Neither Nicole nor Rodney was allowed into the area where Carole was being treated, so after a short while, Rod went outside to call Jeremy and Jason. Nicole went out to the lobby to wait with her team.

Jason was on his way to his job at the Lighthouse when he answered the call from Rodney on his cell phone. Reeling in disbelief from the brain-stunning news, Jason turned his Chevy S-10 around and phoned his girlfriend, Rhonda, as he sped straight for the Marlette hospital.

Rhonda was driving home from our house and had been detoured two miles out of her way because of the roadblocks the police had set up to divert traffic around the scene of the crash.

She had no idea her short trip home had been extended because of what had happened to us.

As soon as Jason hung up his cell phone, Rhonda called her mother and father to give them the shocking news, and then she made a beeline for the hospital emergency room. Shortly after she and her parents pulled into the hospital parking lot, Jason arrived and joined the rapidly expanding crowd of friends, family, and emergency responders gathering inside and around the entrance to the waiting room outside the hospital's ER.

—◊◊◊—

Jeremy had just returned home to Dumfries with his wife and daughter after a weeklong vacation at Virginia Beach. It was about two o'clock in the afternoon. Their belongings had all been hauled from the car and piled on the floor in the middle of the living room. They were contentedly worn out after several days of fun in the sun, sand, and surf, but they still had a few chores to finish before kicking back to bask in the afterglow of their latest family adventure. Jer's next job was to start unpacking the dirty clothes so he could fire up the washing machine with a load of laundry. He was standing in the kitchen, taking a short break, when the phone rang. It was his brother-in-law, Rodney.

"You need to come home, Jer," Rodney said. "There's been an accident."

Jeremy went numb as Rodney shared the gloomy details regarding our condition. Ten minutes passed before the initial shock finally began to dissipate. Jeremy started calling airlines to book the next available flight to Michigan, finally landing a seat on a plane leaving Reagan International the next morning. Then he called Rodney to forward his flight information so someone could meet him at Bishop Airport in Flint when he arrived on Monday.

"Jer, you need to come home tonight," Rodney insisted.

A frantic sense of panic began to replace the stillness that followed the initial blow. Jeremy called the airline back and finally connected with an assistant who, recognizing the urgency of the call, changed the flight reservation to a first-class booking for a coach price and then advised him that his flight would be boarding at 4:30 that afternoon.

Jeremy plucked his duffel bag, still full of dirty clothes, from the pile of belongings in the middle of the living room and dashed out the front door, headed for the airport. Uncertainty and fear swirled through his brain as he hustled his way through traffic and into the terminal building at Reagan International in Washington, DC, sprinting headlong into the opening chapter of his grim pilgrimage.

—ᴡᴠ—

Meanwhile, as the airwaves were being filled with the shocking news of our accident, Mark was in the lobby outside the ER, kneeling on the floor in front of Nicole. She asked Mark what was going on, and all he would say was, "I can't tell you, Nicole." She pressed him for details, but he refused to tell her anything.

Nicole's EMS partner, Greg, was in the emergency room. He had arrived during the melee with a transfer—the patient Nicole and her team had treated and turned over to him earlier in the day. The crew in the ER was still struggling to get a breathing tube down Carole's throat and into her lungs. In desperation, they called Greg over and asked him for some assistance.

Greg immediately took control, skillfully inserting a laryngoscope (a round, curved silver tube with an end that looks like a duckbill) into Carole's esophagus. Greg carefully inched the device into the back of her throat and then rotated the cylinder, pulling the tongue forward and opening the airway so a breathing tube could be inserted. He turned on the oxygen supply and transferred the breathing apparatus from the hand pump to a machine, buying Carole a little more time.

—ᴡᴠ—

I'm lying on my back. I can't sleep this way.

By the time the St. Mary's helicopter landed in the middle of M-53 at the scene, the EMTs had me prepped for the ride. Before anyone else could lay a hand on me, Jim Rye and the other Burlington medical first responders elbowed their way through the team of medics.

"Stand aside," they said to the EMTs. "He's one of ours. We'll load him."

They lined up on both sides, lifted me onto the gurney, and wheeled me to the helicopter. The medics from St. Mary's obediently stepped back and followed as my extended family of MFRs and firefighters carefully and prayerfully rolled me toward the chopper and slid me into the emergency airlift vehicle.

This bed feels like it has wheels and it's rolling. Why can't I get up?

What a strange feeling! I think I'm being slid headfirst into a big silver tube. What's going on? Now the floor is shaking.

Whump!

That sounded like an aircraft door closing, and this bed is shaking faster. Am I in a helicopter? Why am I going for a helicopter ride?

I was the combat soldier being hauled off the battlefield, and my brothers were determined to see that I made it out safely.

—⁓—

After clearing the accident scene, all of the firefighters and medical responders who had been called to the rescue hurried back into their vehicles and reassembled on the highway in front of the hospital. Ambulances, fire trucks, rescue rigs, and other various emergency vehicles lined the streets outside the hospital's emergency entrance with their emergency flashers glowing and lights twirling, warning passing motorists to keep their distance. Every piece of equipment remained in place, diverting traffic, doubly insuring that nothing would impede Carole's FlightCare evacuation. It was an extremely tearful moment for all of the people who witnessed that demonstration of compassion, but their sentiment was not surprising; those diverting traffic were, after all, our close friends and family who had come to our rescue. For years Carole and I had actively supported the local firefighters and emergency responders, and every one of them loved us as a part of their own personal kin.

Carole was the collateral damage—the innocent bystander whose life her brothers and sisters were determined to save.

CHAPTER 5
THE MARATHON

—⁂—

The airborne ambulance crew loaded Carole onto a stretcher, transferred her to the helicopter waiting outside the ER, and lifted off for Flint's Hurley Medical Center. One by one, emergency personnel climbed into their vehicles, turned off the flashing emergency lights, and quietly slipped away. After the aircraft had finally disappeared beyond the treetops, family and close friends gathered to take a deep breath and figure out their next move.

There was a bit of confusion over which direction everyone was to head in. Nicole and Jason knew they would have to split up because Carole had been transferred to Flint and I had been flown to St. Mary's in Saginaw. Why separate hospitals? Nobody knew, but that's the way it was, and no one was going to waste time arguing about it. They just knew there needed to be a family member at both places to make critical decisions regarding procedures or proposed treatments.

Someone needed to coordinate the deployment, so Brian, one of the Burlington firefighters, took over.

"Okay, who's going with who?" Brian asked.

Nicole and Rhonda piled into Brian's vehicle and set out for Flint, Michigan. Rodney and Jason jumped into Jason's pickup and headed in the other direction, toward St. Mary's in Saginaw.

"Oh my gosh, Brian, wait!" Nicole said as they started to pull away from the hospital in Marlette. "Mom didn't have her purse with her. That means she's on her way to Hurley without any ID or medical information. We need to swing by my mom and dad's house before we go to Flint. I hope I can find her purse without having to tear the house apart."

The reality of each scene replaying in Nicole's mind must have been sending numbing shock waves into nerve endings already tingling with the fear of losing her mother and father. Thoughts were probably spinning and bouncing through her brain like pinballs as they raced from "now" to "when," passing through "what if," searching for answers. This was no practice drill, and the victims were not strangers whose lives had only briefly brushed elbows with the rescuers. This was her mom and dad who had suffered deadly critical injuries.

Fortunately, as soon as Nicole walked into the house, she went straight into the kitchen and spied her mother's purse where it had been left lying on the dining room table. They were back in Brian's car and on their way to Hurley in less than a minute.

As the story was later told, everyone involved was holding his breath waiting for the next bit of news about the end that may or may not have already come. Had the tables been turned with me running to save my daughter's life in a race with life-and-death consequences, I doubt I would have dealt with the situation nearly as well as she handled ours.

Amy had graduated from high school with Jeremy and had also been maid of honor in Nicole's wedding. She had been so much a part of our family while the kids were growing up that she had been identified in Nicole's wedding program as the sister of the bride. Some people actually thought Amy was our daughter.

Carole and I had proudly followed Amy's progress through college as she earned a bachelor's degree with emphasis in graphic design and drawing. The Disney images she hand-painted on Nicole's bedroom wall while still in school became the room's centerpiece. Amy eventually earned her master's in education, K–12, and landed a teaching position in the art department at the Lapeer schools.

Amy had recently finished the school year and had nicely settled into summer break where she lived—near Flint, Michigan. Nicole figured it would be best to have familiar boots on the ground at the hospital in Flint before Carole arrived in the airborne ambulance, and Amy was the only person she could think of who might beat the helicopter to its destination. So as soon as Brian pulled out of the hospital parking lot, Nicole turned on her cell phone and called Amy to deliver the news and to ask Amy to go to the hospital in Flint so someone who knew Carole would be there when she arrived.

Amy was shocked and momentarily paralyzed by what she had just been told, but she quickly collected her thoughts and wasted no time seamlessly moving into action. She arrived at the hospital ahead of the helicopter and went straight to the ER and provided as much information about Carole as she was able; she then found a chair by the nurse's station and waited. Shortly after the helicopter arrived, as the medics wheeled Carole into the emergency room, Amy caught a glimpse of her unconscious body, which was covered with blankets and bandages.

On her way to Flint, Nicole called our parents, all of whom lived in Florida at the time. My parents took the news in stride, as though they had been expecting this sort of incident report since the day they heard the news that we had bought that motorcycle. Carole's mother and father, on the other hand, were seriously stressed and had already begun to panic before Nicole could hang up the telephone.

After delivering the news to her grandparents, Nicole dialed Kevin Cook, a.k.a. Uncle Weird Beard, a fellow musician I had toured with and who had become like a brother to both Carole and me. Kevin immediately dropped everything, called his son with the news, and headed for the hospitals to be at our side.

Nicole had just enough time to contact Carole's friend Bonnie before Brian pulled up to Hurley's emergency entrance. As soon as the car came to a stop, Brian, Nicole, and Rhonda jumped out and headed straight for the ER. Amy and Brooke—Nicole's EMS supervisor, who had already arrived at the hospital—greeted them in the waiting room.

Nicole and Rhonda went directly to the nurse's station and identified themselves. The attendant at the nurse's station who had been waiting for their arrival dropped what she had been doing and immediately went into action.

"Wait right here," she said as she swiftly disappeared into the next room.

Within a few seconds, the nurse returned with the doctor who had been assessing the extent of Carole's injuries.

"This is the patient's daughter," the nurse explained as brief introductions were made.

"Your mother experienced a serious brain trauma," the doctor said to Nicole.

"How serious is it?" Nicole asked the doctor.

"I have to be honest with you," the doctor said with a grave expression. "Her chances of making it through this are slim."

Nicole let out a deep breath, relieved to discover that her mother was still alive. Her EMT training had provided her with a better-than-average understanding of medical terms and conditions, so she pried the doctor for more specific details.

"You realize, of course, that brain injury is extremely difficult to diagnose and treat," the doctor said. "At this point all we can do is wait and watch."

"Yes, I understand," Nicole said, focusing on the chance that her mother could still pull through. "I know there is no guarantee, but she's strong. Is there anything else you can do?"

"Are you her legal guardian?" the doctor asked.

"No," she said, "but we both know that, as her daughter, I can authorize whatever treatment you recommend."

"We would like to attach a pressure monitor to her skull so the staff will be able to track changes in brain pressure, but we need someone's permission to proceed."

Without hesitating, Nicole signed the necessary forms authorizing the doctors to screw a brain pressure monitor onto Carole's head.

"Do whatever you have to do to keep her alive," Nicole said to the doctor before returning to the waiting room.

As the doctor said, Carole was not expected to survive her injuries. Her left clavicle and scapula were broken, her left elbow had been shattered, her left hand was seriously injured, and she had suffered two herniated discs in her lower spine. All of the ribs on her left side were broken, and her punctured lung had collapsed and had been slowly filling with blood. Burns and abrasions covered her right arm. Blood had been coming from her ears, mouth, and nose.

But those injuries were Band-Aid wounds compared to the blunt force trauma she had suffered to her head. Carole had collided with enough force to crack the motorcycle helmet she had been wearing, and the resulting whiplash effect on her brain was the haymaker.

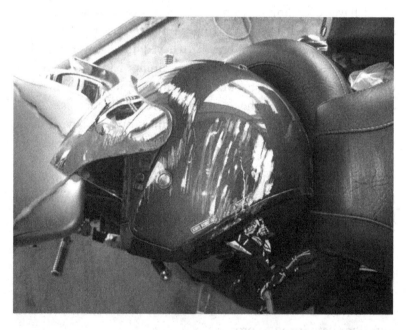

The human skull is as hard and inflexible on the inside as it is on the outside, so the brain has no room for expansion. Bruising or bleeding caused by severe trauma usually results in some degree of swelling. Since there is no room for the traumatized brain matter to grow in size, swelling tissue begins to compress itself. Increasing pressure typically results in permanent damage to the brain tissue, causing disability or death, depending upon the severity of the injury and the amount of pressure that builds.

Even if Carole's wounds could be miraculously healed and her other biological functions somehow amazingly continued, not many of her medical attendants believed she would ever be able to walk or talk again after having suffered such a traumatic blow to the head.

When Nicole and Rhonda were finally allowed into the trauma unit to see Carole, her situation looked dreadfully hopeless. Carole had been placed on a ventilator, and the pressure monitor was attached to her forehead. Doctors stayed with them for a moment to explain the extent and the severity of the injuries she had suffered, and then they left the room so the girls could be alone with Carole. A few minutes later, Nicole and Rhonda were forced to vacate the unit to make way for another incoming patient.

Although Carole's life expectancy was no longer being measured in terms of minutes, all the doctors could say was that they wouldn't know anything for the next twenty-four to forty-eight hours. Assuming she survived, their plan was to keep Carole in a drug-induced coma the entire week following the accident to minimize brain activity and avoid any further swelling caused by unnecessary stimulation. During that time, the staff would be monitoring her brain for increases in pressure. They would simply attempt to deal with any changes as they occurred.

Frontal lobe damage was detected; further trauma was anticipated. The prognosis was grim.

My wounds, although not nearly as critical as my wife's, were nevertheless crippling and potentially life-threatening. The ER doctor approached Rodney and Jason as soon as they arrived at St. Mary's.

"He has stopped breathing twice because both of his lungs collapsed while we were stabilizing his condition and assessing the extent of his injuries," the doctor said. "We need to insert a tube through the ribs on his left side to reinflate his left lung, but there are serious risks involved."

Rodney understood the implications but decided to allow the doctor to continue for Jason's benefit.

"When the tube is installed into his left lung," the doctor said, "there is a better-than-average chance his right lung will collapse again. We may have to put him on a ventilator to keep him alive." He paused, took a deep breath, and said to the decision-maker, "I need to know if there are any DNR [do not resuscitate] orders on your father-in-law."

Rodney told the doctor to do what he had to do as long as it wasn't simply for the sake of keeping my body functioning.

"I know there are serious risks," Rodney said, "but if he's going to just wind up a vegetable, pull the plug. He would not want to live the rest of his life that way."

An hour later the doctor reappeared and, with a sigh of relief, reported the procedure had been completed successfully. The doctor told Jason and Rodney that I was resting comfortably and everyone was confident I would survive.

They were relieved at the news but still anxious about Carole's condition. Rodney and Jason had been out of communication with everyone else since they had left the hospital in Marlette. Fear of the unknown began to creep into their heads. Knowing that Carole's injuries were far more critical than mine were, Rodney sent Jason to Hurley to be with his mother and to call back with an update on her condition as soon as he got there. Rodney realized too late that he had left his cell phone and identification in the vehicle Jason was driving. As soon as Jason was out the door, Rodney was completely isolated from the rest of the group.

Rodney stood leaning against the wall in the hallway outside the St. Mary's emergency room, head down and angry, asking God why he had been left there so all alone. He was completely isolated from friends and family with no transportation, no cash, no means of communicating, and no way of proving who he was. He half expected at any moment to be identified as a vagrant and escorted off the premises.

When he looked up, Pastor Mike Hollenbeck had just stepped out of the elevator down the hall with Dan Krueger, another friend of ours, at his side. The two of them were rounding the corner and walking toward him.

Rodney looked toward the ceiling and said, "Sorry, just kidding!"

A nurse passed by just as Rodney spoke.

"Pardon me?" she asked.

"Oh, nothing," Rodney responded. "Just having a private conversation."

———

During the short time Nicole and Rhonda were at Carole's side in the trauma unit, Rhonda's parents and three of Nicole's friends had arrived to join the vigil. Nicole and Rhonda retreated to a private waiting room that Amy had located and joined the group. While they waited for an update from the medical team, Nicole went outside with her cell phone to call Rodney but could not get him to answer his cell phone, further adding to her anxiety.

A short while later the doctors emerged to inform Nicole they had a room prepared for Carole in the ICU on the fifth floor of the hospital.

"Give us a few minutes and we'll meet you up there," they said.

Meanwhile Jason arrived and met up with Rhonda and Nicole at his mother's side in the ICU. Knowing there was nothing more she could do, Nicole left them alone with Carole. She knew a family member needed to be present, and Jason could cover that responsibility for his mother at Hurley, so Nicole headed for St. Mary's to find her husband and check in with the doctors tending my wounds.

Jason and Rhonda had decided they were not leaving his mother and settled into a couple of chairs they had dragged into Carole's ICU. Sometime during the night, a nurse escorted the two of them to a private family room down the hall, gave them a key, and left them there to rest more comfortably. That tiny efficiency unit would be the family's temporary living quarters for the next nine days.

—◆◆◆—

Fleeting thoughts of death, dismemberment, and permanent disability flashed through Jeremy's mind as he drifted in and out of the tasks at hand that Sunday afternoon. Airport security checkpoints and preboarding formalities at Reagan International passed in a blur of uneasiness. The distressing phone call from his brother-in-law just two hours earlier had brought back painful memories and ugly scenes from his tours as a soldier in the Middle East. He didn't know what he was coming home to, but he sensed the experiences that lay ahead were not going to be pleasant. After endless, emotion-filled hours of anxiously wondering what lay waiting for him at the end of his journey, Jeremy's flight finally landed in Flint. Amy met him at the arrival gate, and they left the airport headed for Hurley Medical Center just after midnight.

Stunning silence and disbelief enveloped him as he spent half an hour at his mother's bedside inside Hurley's ICU. They piled back into Amy's vehicle and headed to St. Mary's in Saginaw, where they sat for another hour at my bedside. The scenery at both hospitals had been dismally depressing and emotionally traumatizing. Carole's life hung in the balance. My condition was critical but stable. Barring any further complications, I was out of the woods.

It was nearing four o'clock in the morning, and both Jeremy and Amy were thoroughly drained. They dragged their tired bodies back to the car, headed out onto the highway, and stared through the windshield for the remaining hour-long leg of their trip. Amy finally pulled into Nicole's driveway sometime around 5:30 a.m. Shortly after seven o'clock that morning Alf, a biker friend, called to check on our condition. Jeremy answered the phone and filled our friend in on the few details he had.

"Have they caught the SOB who hit your folks yet?" Alf asked. "Because we're lookin' for him!"

—m—

The gates opened that first Monday morning to an around-the-clock marathon that split everyone's time between Flint, Saginaw, and Marlette. Rodney and Nicole headed straight for St. Mary's, and Jeremy went to join Jason and Rhonda at Hurley.

Amy was already busy providing a taxi service for anyone needing transportation to or from the hospital, regardless of the distance. She was prepared to cook and run errands whenever and wherever she was needed, and she opened her house to anyone who wanted a place to rest between hospital visits. She helped handle communications, put herself at the disposal of anyone needing anything, and provided everything she had available that might translate to support for the family. Our surrogate daughter became the family's liaison and served as an indispensable resource for everything from food and shelter to a shoulder to cry on.

Carole's father had grabbed the first flight he could book out of Tampa that morning. By the time his flight arrived in Flint, Nicole was at Hurley, so she and Amy drove to Flint's Bishop Airport and met him at the arrival gate. The man was inquisitive and visibly upset. There were a few tearful moments before they headed for the hospital, but he seemed to be handling their gloomy reports without any serious trouble. As they walked into the ICU where Carole was lying in a coma, he became visibly grief stricken and paralyzed from the shock of seeing his daughter lying in a hospital bed, unconscious and dying. He struggled emotionally and showed signs of serious instability, causing concern among those who were with him during his short visit to Michigan. He accepted Amy's hospitality and stayed at her house along with Jeremy Monday night. The next morning he went back to the hospital to spend Tuesday silently surveying his daughter's condition, and he returned to Amy's that night to get some sleep.

When Wednesday came, Carole's father asked for a ride to the airport and caught a flight home to Florida. Before boarding the plane, he said he would be coming back. It seemed obvious to the kids that their grandfather was emotionally out of sorts and not handling his daughter's perilous condition well at all. A brief telephone conversation between Nicole and Carole's sister in Tampa made the rest of Carole's family aware of the need for a chaperone to accompany Grandpa on any future visits.

—⁓—

By midday Monday, my condition had been sufficiently stabilized to address the non-life-threatening wounds. My brother Geoff had arrived during the night from a business trip in Toronto and had joined Nicole and Rodney in the waiting room at St. Mary's. The attending physician approached Geoff and began going over the procedures he was about to undergo in the operating room.

The doctor needed authorization to proceed. Geoff deferred the doctor's request to my daughter, but Nicole had been traumatized. It was at that point that Rodney's triage training from Burlington's MFR team guided him through a series of critical decisions. Rodney knew that Nicole was approaching an emotional meltdown, so he grabbed control of the situation.

"What do you need, Doc?" Rodney asked him.

"I need a signature authorizing the removal of your father-in-law's foot," the surgeon explained to Rodney.

Most people would have simply signed the paper, but not my son-in-law.

"Is it life threatening?" Rodney asked.

"What do you mean by 'life threatening'?"

"What I want to know," Rodney replied, "is whether or not his life is going to be in danger if the foot is not removed. Is there any life-threatening risk if you leave his foot the way it is?"

"I can't say he will ever use it again," the surgeon replied. "His foot is crushed, and there is no way he will ever be able to walk on it. Life threatening? No."

"Then leave it on. As long as that mangled foot is no threat to his survival, leave it where it is. Amputation is going to be his decision, not ours."

"All right. We'll bandage it the best way we can, and we'll leave the decision regarding amputation for him to make," the surgeon said with a sigh.

The doctor returned to the operating room, pulled on his mask, and went to work trying to save my foot. Given the way the ankle had been shattered, there had to be fragments of bone like shards of glass everywhere under the skin. That doctor had his hands full. He reset the bones in my foot three times before finally turning off the lights and sending me to recovery. Further surgery would be required if I was ever going to walk again, but the man went the extra mile for me instead of simply pulling out a hacksaw and filling the trash can with mangled body parts.

Someone told me that I drifted in and out of consciousness during the entire ordeal, talking to the attendants all the while they worked on me. I recall none of it.

—∿—

Okay I'm awake now. Wow, what a dream! That was too real.

I thought I was being loaded into a helicopter. I wonder if I had that dream because we went for a ride in the airplane yesterday.

I don't remember going to bed last night. I must have been really tired.

What did I do yesterday? I wonder what time it is. I sure hope this isn't how the rest of my day is going to go. I'd better get out of bed and get this day started.

Wait a minute; it's not morning, and this isn't my bedroom. I don't recognize this room. Where am I? Am I still dreaming?

I couldn't move. It felt like one of those dreams where I was being chased by a pack of wild dogs but no matter how hard I tried, my legs just wouldn't let me take another step.

I must still be asleep. Why can't I wake up? This dream gets weirder by the minute.

Tilting my head forward, I caught a glimpse of my right leg.

No wonder I can't move. That leg looks like it's all tangled up in a blanket.

Whoa! That's not a blanket; that's a huge bandage!

I vaguely remember waking up to a dull throbbing sensation and seeing a huge bundle of bandages and splints where my right foot was supposed to be. I knew something bad had happened, but I did not yet fully understand what. I don't think it ever occurred to me that my foot might have been missing altogether.

Something is strapped to my head ... little plastic hoses stuck in my nose. It feels like there is air coming through them. What is all of this stuff for?

Holy Cow! There are needles sticking out of the back of my hand with rubber tubes attached to them. Why don't I feel any pain? How did those needles get there without me knowing about it?

This looks like a hospital room, and it's full of people. What happened? Why is everyone standing around the foot of my bed?

I wish I could wake up. This dream has turned into a nightmare.

Wait a minute ... I don't think ... I'm ... dreaming ...

"Hi, Dave."

It was as though I had been gently awakened by someone's voice telling me it was time to get up.

"Hey, how ya' doin'? What are you doing here all the way from Tennessee? I didn't even know you were coming to visit. Sorry I'm still in bed. I'm really tired."

It seemed odd that Jeremy's in-laws were in my bedroom. But this wasn't my bedroom. And this was no dream!

Gradually I became aware that my daughter, Nicole, was sitting on the edge of the bed beside me, holding on to my right hand.

"Where am I?" I asked her.

"You're in the hospital, Dad."

"Why? What happened?"

"You and Mom were in a motorcycle accident."

Accident.

An *Accident?*

An ACCIDENT!

Shock waves coursed through my body. *Accidents happen to other people,* I thought to myself. *Careless people; not people like us.*

Everything around me felt surreal. My daughter's words struck me one by one, each syllable adding weight to the dizziness spooling up in my head.

"We're not sure exactly what happened," Nicole said, "but we know it was a hit-and-run. The police have found the car that you ran into."

The car that I ran into! I am not a reckless driver! How could I possibly have run into someone!

"The police are trying to track down the driver."

"An accident on the motorcycle?" I asked skeptically.

No wonder I didn't remember going to bed yesterday. Or was that today?

Images raced through my brain in search of an explanation, but nothing was making any sense. Automatically blaming myself, I figured I had to have unconsciously done something wrong to cause the wreck, but I could not comprehend the idea of having rammed into the back of another vehicle sitting innocently in the middle of the road. How could I have possibly missed *that?*

Then suspicion crept in as the phrase "hit-and-run" began to register. I had heard about people who, for whatever reason, hated motorcyclists so much that they would simply run the rider, any rider, off the road. I had actually witnessed a dramatic cat-and-mouse duel between a motorcycle and an automobile on the expressway near Fort Myers, Florida, during one of our vacations. The cyclist escaped, but the exchange left a dramatic visual image. Had we become victims of just such a biased mentality?

My God! Carole was with me on the back of the motorcycle. If I'm banged up, she must be hurt too. Suddenly a shot of adrenaline surged through my body. Panic wrenched the muscles around my stomach.

"Where's Mom? *Is she all right?*" I asked, forcefully.

Why is my son-in-law standing there with tears in his eyes? What does he mean that he "had to make some tough decisions but I'm going to be all right"?

"Where is your mother!" I demanded before Nicole could answer the first time that I asked.

"She's at a different hospital, Dad," Nicole patiently replied.

That's all anyone would tell me, and I was apparently too stunned and full of painkillers to fully comprehend anyone's vague responses to questions about my wife.

Other than a dull throbbing coming from my right foot, accompanied by a lot of sensitivity in my shoulders, ribs, and left hand, I felt no serious pain. That I was still alive began to register as a miracle in itself. The fact that nobody could, or would, tell me anything about my wife cultivated a dimension of anxiety I had never before experienced. My thoughts shifted from curiosity to terror, and then disbelief. Moments later those temporary spikes in my emotions would dissolve like sugar in a glass of tea, and my mind would return to neutral, void of any particular emotion or concern.

My sense of time was gone, and things relevant to my life in general were confined to the space in my hospital room. Lying on my back in a medically induced haze, I tried to interact with the growing crowd of visitors who were creating a constant invasion of activity at the foot of my bed. Our youngest son, Jason, emerged from the group and leaned over to whisper something in my ear.

"I bought Rhonda a diamond, Dad," he said in a hushed voice.

"Really? That's cool, Jay!" I said, apparently with a little more enthusiasm than he had expected.

Appearing startled by my response, Jason quickly glanced around the room to see if anyone had heard me. I had no idea he had not yet shared the news with anyone else.

"Yeah," he said as he got closer and quieter, "but don't say anything to anyone about it. I haven't even told Rhonda yet."

"Okay," I whispered. "Your secret's safe with me! I won't tell a soul. Have you told Mom yet?"

"Yeah, but she probably won't remember. She's pretty out of it right now."

Well, of course she was "out of it." Jason knew that his mom was still in a coma, but he couldn't tell me that. He, like everyone else, was still wondering if she would even survive.

Out of the confusion, someone interrupted our private conversation and handed me a telephone. Paul, one of the deputies from the Sanilac County Sheriff's Department who had been dispatched to the scene of the accident was on the other end of the line.

Paul was a personal friend I had met through Carole's job as circuit-court administrator, so my initial thought was that he had called to see how I was doing. As it turned out, he was actually handling the investigation surrounding our accident. He was contacting me on police business to see if I could possibly share any details that might help solve the mystery over how the accident was caused.

I shared the few bits and pieces that I could remember from the time we rolled around the corner at the stoplight until waking up in the hospital. I knew my testimony was not very helpful, but Paul did say they had already confiscated the car we ran into and had the guy in custody that had been driving it. All he would tell me was that the stories the guy told the police did not seem to match the evidence they were uncovering.

"Don't worry," he said. "We'll get this thing sorted out."

Paul also told me that when he had arrived at the scene, he'd had no idea that it involved my wife and me. When he ran the license number of our motorcycle through the DMV and my name came back, he nearly dropped his phone onto the pavement. A bulletin was immediately sent out for any information regarding a vehicle appearing to have recently been involved in a collision. Other than skid marks on the pavement, the only piece of evidence found at the scene indicating that another vehicle may have been involved was a piece of a broken taillight lens found lying in the road near the point of impact.

That driver who left us lying in the highway may as well have shot a cop for the attention he drew. Neither Paul nor any of the other deputies will admit to having prioritized their response to our accident, but judging from the attention we were given, I am guessing everything else involving the Sanilac County Sheriff's Department was set aside until our situation had been brought under control.

As each day passed, I became more consciously aware of just how serious our crash had been. I sensed a heightened concern over Carole's condition, but answers to my questions remained vague. Visitors at my bedside were cautious about sharing details. Surges of adrenaline shot through my system as my brain progressed through the various levels of comprehension, struggling to grasp the full scope of our situation. *Where was my wife? Was she all right? How badly had she been hurt?*

I realized I had been stripped bare and rendered defenseless against a merciless world. Was this some sort of a test? Was there a message in all of this that I had not yet figured out?

Gradually a sense of quiet peace fell over me like a soft veil covering a delicate piece of art. I sat propped up in bed, alone in my room, staring at the wall, quietly talking to an invisible force that enveloped me. Although it had not yet registered just how close both of us had come to meeting Him face-to-face, God seemed to fill the room with His comforting presence, and time momentarily stood still. While absorbing the magnitude of this life-changing event, I quietly thanked Him for watching over us.

"Okay, God, you have my attention," I said aloud. "Now, what was it you wanted me to do?"

During the days and weeks following the accident, people shared details that helped me piece together what had happened. Each tidbit of information depicted a new dimension to a personal calamity that was sure to galvanize an abrupt change in the direction our lives were heading in. Regardless, I was still in denial. I fully expected to be discharged in time to attend the *Chicago* and *America* concert at DTE that Friday. Nicole indicated that the doctors were probably going to keep me in the hospital for a few more days.

"Even if you were released in time to make the concert, Dad," Nicole explained, "there's no way Mom is going to be able to go with you."

"Well, then, what do I do with the tickets?" I asked, frustrated.

"Why don't you give them to someone?"

"Do you want them?" I asked her.

"No," Nicole replied hesitantly, "I don't think Rodney and I will be able to go. Is there someone else who might want them?"

"Why don't you see if Roger and Leslie want them?" I replied.

I was disappointed that we were missing out on the concert event Carole and I had so looked forward to.

Oh well, I thought to myself. *At least we still have our July 4 weekend camping trips to enjoy. I hope being off work this past week doesn't wreck those plans too.*

Little did I know!

CHAPTER 6
A STUNNED COMMUNITY

—◦◦◦—

Shocking, horrible reports greet us daily, but those are always stories of unfortunate tragedies in other people's lives. We tend to see ourselves as immune to disease, bulletproof against society's wickedness. The truth is that we merely allow ourselves to be lulled into a false sense of security, convinced that bad things only happen to other people. Our safe, peaceful environment is a cocoon that is easily unraveled when a crisis strikes close to home.

Word of our accident exploded through the streets like a windblown forest fire. As usual, most of the rumors circulating were inaccurate and seriously exaggerated by the time they had reached the coffee shops and social hangouts around town. The fact that two separate FlightCare helicopters had been called to the scene of the same accident made the incident appear all the more spectacular. Those sightings only added fuel to gossip spread by the misinformed, needlessly increasing the dimension of the drama. The reality is that the collision of metal and flesh was already perilously spectacular without colorful exaggeration.

Friends we had not been in touch with for more than twenty years heard about the crash on the evening news. Radio broadcasts were interrupted with a bulletin requesting information regarding the whereabouts of any vehicle that may have been recently involved in a collision. Fellow motorcycle enthusiasts, including some whose reputations may be questionable, put word on the street that a biker was down and the person who had laid us in the highway was still on the loose.

On a tip from the manager of that trailer park we had passed half a mile down the road from where the accident occurred, the police tracked down the vehicle. They matched the piece of taillight lens found at the scene to the broken taillight on the car and took the car into custody. That tied their investigation to the car's owner, but the driver was nowhere to be found.

Amazingly, when the police finally caught up with the guy several days later, he told the arresting officers that he didn't even realize anyone had hit him. Incredible! The side of the car was caved in, and the rim on the flat tire in the trunk was bent like a bottle cap where the brake pedal on our motorcycle had made first contact. After hooking the wheel rim, the heavy steel pedal on the motorcycle had twisted 180 degrees backward and wrapped itself around my ankle. The inertia from the impact had to have flung the motorcycle violently sideways, tossing Carole and me onto the pavement like rag dolls riding a toy bike.

The police report contained a statement made by a homeowner three houses from the intersection where the collision had occurred. The man approached one of the officers at the scene and reported that he had just witnessed a guy changing the left rear wheel on his car on the side of the gravel road in front of his house. The driver looked like he needed help, so the homeowner walked out to offer his assistance, but the driver seemed to be in a hurry. He refused any help, didn't want to talk, and, when the spare was on, threw the bent rim and flat tire along with the car jack into the trunk and sped away in a cloud of dust as though someone were chasing him.

A close friend of ours, also a highly respected attorney in our community, was seated at a table in one of the local restaurants when someone came through the door and announced that Carole had been killed in a motorcycle accident just an hour earlier. She rose from her table, left the restaurant, and walked to her office two blocks down the street, crying the entire way. She later told me that she locked herself inside and spent the rest of the day sobbing after receiving the horrible news.

The term "shock and awe" might describe the impact our accident had on the surrounding community. That doesn't necessarily mean that my wife and I, as individuals, were all that important or that our accident was any more or less tragic than the widely reported deaths of American soldiers who had lost their lives during gun battles in the streets of Baghdad. We just knew lots of people, so our crash struck a nerve in a lot of lives.

Carole and I were lifelong residents of Marlette and had been actively involved over the years with many clubs and organizations around the area. Even those who didn't know us on a personal level knew who we were. We considered ourselves average, private parents who were stressed, like everyone else who was trying to get through everyday challenges.

In essence, word of our accident seemed to carry with it a sense of vulnerability. Folks throughout the community deliberated over how something so critical could ever happen to two upstanding citizens who appeared to have built such an organized, safe, controlled, got-it-together lifestyle. That was, of course, an extremely inflated image of who we really were, much like the colorful reports of our accident that creatively gained momentum as they circulated. Those who knew us would agree that we were far from saints, but there were those who saw us as Samaritans, which prompted the speculative question, "Why does God let bad things happen to good people?"

Admittedly, I too spent many lonely hours wondering why we had been violated, but asking why God lets bad things happen is, in my estimation, the same as blaming God for our behavior, and that seems a bit arrogant. The truth is that good and bad things happen to all people. I do not believe that God lets anything happen—at least not in the context in which we use the word. Sometimes we cause things to happen, and other times we are victims of someone else's carelessness, greed or outright negligence. The fact that some idiot left us for dead in the middle of a busy highway had nothing to do with God's will, and it had nothing to do with us having been good or bad. The guy who turned into our path wasn't paying attention. Somewhere along the way, I might have missed a cue. The bottom line is that watching out for each other was our responsibility, not God's.

I do believe, however, that God's hand cushioned the fall and kept us alive. The experience may have been painful and traumatic, but we survived against astronomical odds. God's answers to prayer are the reason we were spared. "And we know that all things work together for good to them that love God, to them who are the called according to his purpose."[1]

There is no logical explanation for the chain of events that left my wife and me lying in the highway. The cause may have been a random act, but the outcome was straightforward as a center-field homerun. Simply put, our tragedy had the effect of a mortar round nobody heard coming. And when it hit, the explosion touched a lot of lives.

Thankfully, friends and neighbors who believe in the power of prayer launched our first wave of defense. Christians throughout our community gathered, spread the news, and added our names to prayer lists in every congregation. Prayer vigils everywhere were being held on our behalf, and prayer requests were spreading across the land as fast as the news of our accident. It wasn't long before intercessory petitions of prayer for our souls and safety were being conducted all over the country as out-of-state friends and family received the grim news of our condition. Before the day was out, our brothers and sisters in the CMA (Christian Motorcyclists Association) had set up a prayer chain that literally extended around the world. I have no doubt the reason we survived that initial deadly encounter was a result of groups who hit their knees, petitioning God for our safety.

I was humbled by the fact that people I would probably never meet had accepted the request to petition God for our deliverance. The impact was dramatic. My wife and I had never been on the receiving end of that sort of consideration, and I found myself totally disoriented from all of the attention—an amazing reaction given my extensive exposure to churches and Christian congregations since childhood.

Fellow members of ABATE, a nationwide motorcycle rights organization, and the CMA later told us they were horrified by the news of our accident. There was a steady stream of bikers visiting me at St. Mary's in Saginaw and, later, at our home. A handful of them were able to see Carole at Hurley Medical Center in Flint before visitation was restricted to family members.

I was later told about a plan that had begun simmering and circulating through the various groups of motorcyclists craving revenge. There was talk of ferreting out and stringing up the guy who had left us for dead on the highway. Vengeful gossip conjured up images of scenes from old Western movies. Colorful details were undoubtedly embellished, but I have learned not to completely ignore such talk. Stranger things have happened. The outcome is unpredictable when vigilante fever gets its grip on a group of people who won't hesitate to go outside the law to settle a score.

That idiot who drove off and left us for dead will probably never have a clue just how close he came to spending eternity looking up at the ore boats from the bottom of Lake Huron.

Through the ordeal, I discovered that next to God's grace, respect is probably the most significant gift anyone can claim.

Over the years, I had been on the opposite side of the political, economic, and religious table, engaged in debate of one form or another with many of the leaders in and around our community. I was that person in their lives who had never been afraid to challenge an issue, even if only to defend a principle. That rebellious side of me would never let code be compromised even in the face of public ridicule or damning scrutiny.

Ironically, many of those with whom I had engaged in public disagreements showed up at our front door asking how they could help. I believe those people offered their support out of respect, and I was modestly flattered to know that I had earned theirs.

Much the same way our nation reacted to the terrorist attacks on September 11, 2001, individual reactions to the news of our accident on June 24, 2007, varied. Most folks were angry. Undoubtedly there were those who had heard about it, shrugged, and gone about their day without skipping a beat. But anybody witnessing reports of our misfortune was shocked and in disbelief that one human could drive off and leave another lying in the middle of the highway.

One thing was for certain: literally everyone in our small rural community heard, in one way or another, about what had happened to us that day; and whether they knew us or not, most were affected.

CHAPTER 7
WEEK ONE

—◊◊—

St. Mary's

Being torn apart on the highway, rescued from the jaws of death, and then sewn back together in a hospital provided me with a whole new level of appreciation for the quality of medical care available in America. The experience also reinforced a healthy respect for nurses and their assistants. Those are the people keeping the machine oiled and the wheels of recovery rolling.

My description of a nurse's job would definitely not include words like "glorious" or "glamorous." Rooms littered with bedpans, bandages, and grotesquely filthy unbathed bodies do not make for pleasant working conditions. Not only would that be a difficult daily work environment to endure, but the job also appears to be a thankless one. Nursing is a profession not everyone is called to do. Spending every day caring for patients in a hospital's trauma unit would be next to impossible for me; I would find nothing fulfilling, encouraging, or entertaining about watching people suffer.

Nevertheless, there they were, those nurses, and there was plenty of evidence of their presence. Tubes, wires, and medical apparatuses were stuck into, stuck on to, or coming from what seemed to be every part of my body, and those attendants kept a faithful watch on each piece of equipment.

Wednesday, three days after the accident, after everyone had finally gone home for the evening, I sat alone in my bed, trying to digest the magnitude of my dilemma. Details of our accident that had been shared with me earlier in the day, while I was slowly regaining consciousness, whirled through my brain. Realizing that my wife and I had been left for dead in the middle of M-53 made me swoon. I was amazed by my surroundings, marveling at the gadgets and apparatus all within my reach. The hospital room resembled a US Army MASH unit. Bags hanging from racks next to the hospital bed were filled with clear liquid slowly dripping into hoses connected to IV needles sticking out of veins in my arm and the back of my hand. The oxygen being pumped through clear plastic lines jammed up my nose made my throat so dry it was nearly impossible for me to swallow. When it occurred to me that I had not used the toilet for a noticeably long period of time, I lifted the hospital gown and found the catheter that had been installed. That discovery generated a slight hot flash as an itty-bitty amount of modesty momentarily surfaced. Silly, I was in a hospital. No nurse was going to see anything on me they had not already seen!

Was I hurt that badly? I thought to myself, *or is all of this equipment here just to make it look like I was?*

It was a frightening thought because every piece of that equipment was, in fact, very necessary.

How could anyone be hurt this badly and not feel it?

Drugs.

In addition to the body's natural ability to block out traumatic mental images and extreme physical pain, the pharmaceutical industry has developed ways to deaden nerves and ease discomfort through the use of chemicals like morphine and Vicodin. We've come a long way from the days of Florence Nightingale, when a soldier was given two shots of whiskey and a piece of rawhide to bite on while the surgeons sawed his leg off.

As the days passed, the dosage of painkillers was reduced and my level of discomfort increased. With the pain came an acute awareness of just how serious things were.

By the end of the fourth day, taking a deep breath or trying to move in any direction resulted in an excruciating, stabbing pain in my left side. Four of the ribs on my left side had been broken.

A slight stinging sensation persisted on top of the joint at the tip of my left shoulder. Tubes and needles prevented me from taking a good look under the hospital gown to see what was causing such persistent discomfort, but eventually the wound was exposed while the dressing was changed. There was a road rash abrasion about the size of a slice of bread. The skin was gone, and all that remained was raw flesh. I was amazed that it did not hurt worse than it did. The less-than-expected pain was probably a result of the small amount of morphine still dripping into one of the tubes attached to an IV.

By the fifth day, blankets and sheets under my left hand were saturated with fluid coming from somewhere.

"I think I sprung a leak," I said to the nurse as she came in with a hypodermic to give me another shot of something in my abdomen.

"Really? Where?" she asked coyly, as if she were responding to a weak attempt at humor.

"Right there by my left hand," I said, pointing to the spot with my eyes.

"Oh, so you have!" she said, suddenly taking me seriously. "It looks like the IV has failed. I'll be right back."

Fluid coming through the drip tube was seeping out of the hole in my skin, running off my hand, and soaking the bedsheet.

A few minutes later, the nurse returned with a fresh needle.

"Let's get that needle out of there and see if we can't fix that leak," she said as she disconnected the tube and tore open a fresh IV kit.

That doesn't feel as tight as it should, I thought to myself as she wrapped a tourniquet above my elbow. *I wonder if that's because it's too loose or because of the painkillers still in my body.*

A distinctly painful pinprick grabbed my attention as the nurse stabbed the back of my hand with the new needle.

Nope, I thought to myself. *I felt that real good. I don't think the tourniquet is tight enough.*

After several painful failed attempts at finding a vein with the new needle, she called for help.

Should I tell her that I think the tourniquet should be tighter? I wondered to myself.

"I'm sorry to be so difficult," I said.

"Oh no!" she replied with a reassuring smile. "You haven't done anything. Sometimes dehydration makes it hard to find a vein."

"Still," I said, "I'm sure you've got more important things to do than fiddle around with this."

"Don't worry about it," she said softly. "I'm going to go find someone to help me with this."

The attendant and her new assistant switched to my right hand and started drilling for a new blood vessel. Two unsuccessful tries later, the two nurses left the room in search of reinforcements. A third nurse showed up and wrapped the rubber tourniquet around my right arm, squeezing it so tightly it felt as though the skin would tear. Veins started popping up all over the back of my hand. She zeroed in on a fat, healthy vein and drilled one more hole with a fresh needle.

"There," she said. "Finally found one."

A short time after the nurses packed up and returned to their other chores, fresh bruises started showing up on the backs of my hands at the various points of injection. Including the new IV, there were six new puncture wounds. It was hard to tell where the damage from the accident left off and the wounds from the needle tracks started up. To their credit, the nurses were professional, comforting, and apologetic, and as far as I could tell, they had done everything according to procedure. For some reason I found myself apologizing to them for having been such a difficult patient.

I wasn't bashful about asking for explanations any time someone showed up with another needle tray. In turn, the attending nurses were happy to explain the various chemicals that were being pumped, dripped, or injected through my system. Every few hours a nurse would come by with a couple more pills and an occasional hypodermic filled with an antibiotic or something.

During one session the nurse explained that she was giving me an insulin injection. Panic set in. There is a history of diabetes in my family, but aside from borderline hypoglycemia, I had shown no sign of having inherited the disorder.

"Am I diabetic?" I asked the nurse.

Sensing anxiety, she gently explained.

"No," she said, "severe trauma can cause sugar imbalances in the human body. We're giving you insulin to stabilize your sugar level."

Whew!

While I was in the ER, surgeons had slid a rubber drain tube into my chest cavity between two ribs on the left side of my chest. Only when that tube was extracted five days after the collision did I appreciate just how securely it had been held in place.

Not only had the tube been stitched to the skin, but layers of surgical tape had also been applied from chin to navel to prevent the point of insertion from being disturbed by my thrashing around in bed. By the time the tube was removed, every square inch of skin under that massive, solid layer of tape had begun to grow as one with the adhesive.

Not a single medical procedure, puncture, break, abrasion, or therapy produced pain that compared to the torment of having tape peeled from my hairy torso. One guy held me down while the other proceeded to skin me alive, leaving little spots of blood seeping out of the tears in my raw pelt. It was impossible to suppress the guttural screams of agony. Any man with a hairy chest can attest to the painful experience of having someone grab a handful and give it a yank. Multiply that times the number of plucks it would take to weed the hair from an entire torso and you might come close to the waxing I received.

While still trying to catch my breath after the unexpected hair and skin removal, the doctors proceeded to clip stitches and remove the drain tube. I swear that vinyl hose jammed through the hole between my ribs was forty feet long, and every inch of the tube came reluctantly, stretching and tearing tender flesh that had grown attached to it.

I was happy to learn that the broken ribs would simply be left to heal on their own.

Before the physical therapists at St. Mary's would sign a release, I had to pass their gauntlet of tests. The obstacle course included such things as using the toilet unassisted, moving around with a walker without putting any weight on my damaged foot, and navigating up and down steps without winding up in a heap at the bottom of the staircase.

Four broken ribs made the use of crutches simply out of the question. Using a walker to support my weight was extremely painful because of the still undiscovered tendon damage in my shoulders, but after the tape-and-tube-removal episode, just about any other kind of pain was bearable.

Having failed the climbing test in the hospital's stairwell, I simply explained that I would be staying at my daughter's home until able to get around without assistance. Since our daughter's house had no stairs, there would be no need for me to learn how to climb up or down them. Truthfully, I had no intention of going anywhere but home. The goal was to get myself out of that hospital the quickest way possible. Hiding the pain and choosing the correct responses finessed a discharge that probably should not have taken place for at least another week.

The first hint that I may have manipulated the system to my own detriment came with the realization of just how exhausting it was to do the simplest things. Engaging in casual conversation had become physically demanding. Five days lying in a hospital bed had melted away nearly twenty pounds of body weight and had thoroughly depleted my stamina. I had become as weak as a baby. For the first time since I had returned home from Southeast Asia, the scales topped out at 150 pounds.

By the time Saturday came around, six days after the crash, news of our accident had spread to friends from all over the area. From midmorning until the last visitor went home that evening, the flow of traffic in and out of my room had been practically nonstop. At first it was comforting to see all of those familiar, friendly faces, but it soon became tenuous trying to carry on conversations with anyone amid all of the confusion.

Visitation throughout the following day, Sunday, became excessive. The crowd was eventually moved to a visitors' waiting area near the nurse's station to avoid any further disturbance to other patients on the floor. I was speechless. Not in my wildest imagination would I have ever expected that much love and attention from so many people.

All of that caring and compassion, though, had taken a toll. By late Sunday afternoon, Nicole began recognizing signs of serious fatigue and asked if I wanted to go back to the room. Mercifully she didn't need an answer. She thanked everyone for coming to visit and wheeled my dog-tired body back down the hallway to the private sanctuary of the hospital bed.

Just after visiting hours were over Sunday night, the staff brought me a roommate. That Korean War veteran was truly a gentleman. We shared some war stories before lights-out, but as soon as he dozed off it became obvious to me that he would be the only one getting any sleep. Bless his heart, that soldier's snoring would have kept the birds from landing in the backyard.

To make matters even more insoluble, the night shift attendants sounded as though they were playing a game of street hockey in the hallway outside our room. I later discovered the door to the emergency room was on the other side of the wall facing my bed. The constant banging that continued through the night turned out to be the ER door slamming open and closed.

Shortly after midnight, I felt a pressing urge to use the bathroom. I hit the call button for help but could not get anyone on the staff to respond. Fortunately all of my IV needles had been removed and the only apparatus remaining was the oxygen hose strapped to my face. Desperate to find relief, I gingerly sat up, pulled the tubes out of my nose, swung my legs over the side of the bed, and slid to the floor, balancing on one leg. Using a walker that was leaning against the wall next to my bed, I managed to drag myself all the way to the bathroom and back without incident. It took me nearly half an hour to take care of business.

Exhausted and struggling to catch my breath, I crawled back onto the bed. An increasingly intense level of pain coming from broken ribs and a smashed ankle took center stage. Raw nerve endings responded violently to every heartbeat. Once again I pressed the call button, but nobody came to my rescue.

On the other side of the curtain, each breath my fellow veteran took produced a remarkable variation of noises that resembled a malfunctioning foghorn. Jittery anxiety saturated my body, keeping my eyes open and my senses tingling. Sleep deprivation fueled an absurd level of fatigue, hypersensitizing my raw nerves and generating in me an indescribable level of irrational anger.

At four o'clock that Monday morning, I crawled back out of bed, seriously agitated, and sat in the visitor's chair, propping my leg on the mattress. The hospital table on wheels was just about the right height to comfortably lay my head in the crook of my arm and try to sleep. After dozing for what seemed like hours, I raised my head and looked at the clock on the wall to discover that only five minutes had passed.

Around 6:30 a.m. a nurse came in for her morning rounds and found me sitting there sleepless, angry, and writhing in pain.

"What are you doing out of bed?" she asked in disbelief.

"I've been out of bed all night," I said angrily. "I couldn't sleep."

"Why didn't you call for help?"

"I did," I tersely replied. "I pressed that button until my thumb went numb, and nobody came to see what I wanted."

Within five minutes a hospital maintenance man came into the room and discovered that the call-release button on the wall was stuck.

A couple of hours and an aggressive dose of pain medication later, I was back in bed, feeling somewhat relieved but extremely agitated and anxious to go home. By noon on that day, Nicole had returned and was seated at my bedside, listening patiently to my nonstop complaining. Every few minutes I would doze, and then I would wake up, startled by my surroundings, and start complaining again.

"Has the doctor been here yet?" I asked her after several brief episodes of semiconsciousness.

"No, the nurse says nobody has seen him yet this morning," she said.

"Have any of the nurses said anything about when I'll be able to leave?" I asked.

"They're not even sure you'll be leaving today, Dad," Nicole patiently replied.

"Oh, I'll be leaving today. You can count on it! I can't spend another night here with nonstop snoring going on over there on the other side of the curtain."

Nicole didn't say a word. She just patiently sat by my side, absorbing the verbal abuse as though she had sworn an oath to avoid conflict at all cost. It had to be extremely difficult for her to stay at my side, let alone remain calmly civilized after being on the receiving end of such abusive and irrational behavior. It would have come as no surprise to me to see the staff lined up and applauding my departure, happy to see me leave.

By then I didn't care. I needed to be with my wife.

—∽—

Hurley

Nicole handled the discharge from St. Mary's that Monday afternoon and then drove me straight to Flint to see Carole, who was still in the ICU on the fifth floor at Hurley. Although everyone had done his best to keep me cautiously informed regarding my wife's condition, there was no way for me to properly prepare for the setting I was about to behold as Nicole rolled me through the door and into Carole's glass-enclosed unit.

The scene took my breath away. My beloved soul mate was lying there, eyes closed, with tubes in her nose, down her throat, in her side, and out from under the white hospital blankets that mostly covered her limp, lifeless body.

A respirator was doing Carole's breathing for her. IV needles were stuck in the backside of her right hand. Her right arm was covered in bandages. Her left arm was completely wrapped in a cloth splint from shoulder to wrist, with nothing but the tip of her swollen, purple, scraped and bruised left hand exposed. Wires attached to monitors hanging all around Carole's bed had been taped to various places on her chest and body. Beeping and clicking noises came from a horde of electronic life-support equipment.

The manner with which all of the gadgets and lifelines had been arranged gave the curious illusion that she seemed to be plugged into her room the way an engine is installed under the hood of a car. It appeared to me as though if any single part of the apparatus in that room had been unplugged, everything, including my wife, would have ceased to function. The surreal setting made me wonder if she was alive or simply operating as an integral part of the equipment she was attached to.

Carole's legs were limp, and her feet dangled lifelessly at odd angles. Thoughts of spinal injury flickered through my already overwhelmed imagination.

"Is she paralyzed?" I asked the nurse who had been standing next to the bed making notes on a slip of paper attached to a clipboard.

"I'm afraid there's really no way of knowing yet," she said.

Turning to my daughter, I repeated the question.

"Have you seen her feet move?" I asked Nicole.

"No," she said. "I've been wondering the same thing, but I keep avoiding it."

Carole's pulse was displayed on one of the monitors hanging over the bed. Every few moments her body would convulse as she coughed and gagged on tubes sucking fluids from her lungs. As soon as she went into one of those convulsions, an alarm would sound, the graph showing her pulse would display spikes, and her face would turn purple. Those spasms made it appear as though she were in the process of choking the rest of the way to death.

Mercifully the brain pressure monitor that had been attached to her forehead just above the hairline had been removed a couple of days earlier, so a bald spot and wound where the monitor had been located were all that remained. I was relieved at not having to see the appliance installed.

The entire scene hit me like a tidal wave. Dumbstruck and speechless, a mild shock coursed through my body. Carole did not seem to be suffering any particular pain, but she was obviously uncomfortable.

Rising out of the wheelchair using what little strength that remained, I managed to balance myself on one foot and stand next to her bed, leaning over the rail, searching her face for some sign of life. What happened next unleashed an unexpected groundswell of emotion.

Carole's eyes opened and met mine. In that split second her entire expression changed. Her face relaxed, and her lips parted slightly as though she were trying to tell me something. My body folded itself over the railing, collapsing forward onto the bed beside her, weeping uncontrollably; at that moment I was helpless, hurt, and so desperately sorry for the shape she was in.

Without a doubt, the brutally shocking scene had triggered a radical realignment from the depths of my soul. My partner and soul mate was slowly slipping away, and there was nothing that I could do to stop it. Such a helpless, lonely feeling!

Scenes from a lifetime of self-centered neglect flashed before my eyes as yet another episode of the reality show I was living through hit home. Curiously, we never seem to fully appreciate those around us until after they are gone. Memories of things I had failed to take the time to do flooded my brain. Lying there with my face buried in blankets, overwhelmed by deep regrets for wasted years, I felt exposed and incredibly vulnerable. Overpowering guilt surfaced as a result of my having shamelessly taken her love, devotion, and companionship so much for granted.

A few hours later, after the initial shock had somewhat numbed my sensitivity, I sat alone beside Carole's hospital bed, softly reading psalms aloud to her from the pocket Bible a friend from the Christian Motorcyclists Association had given me. Again that soft cloak of peace shrouded the room, with only the muted sounds of monitors and medical machinery beeping in the background.

With considerable effort I rose back out of the chair and leaned over the side of Carole's bed, balancing on one leg. While holding her hand and gazing into her eyes, the phrase "for better or for worse" came to mind. Through tears, I quietly spoke my vows to my wife as she lay there.

"I know you're in God's hands, Carole," I whispered. "I don't know whether you will come through this or not, but I promise that I will see to your care and well-being, even if I have to spend the rest of my life feeding and bathing you.

"I will never leave your side." I said with tears streaming down my cheeks.

She never responded.

When visiting hours were finally over, Nicole wheeled me back to the parking lot, piled me into her car, and headed for home on the final leg of that trip back from eternity. The afternoon at Hurley had been a solemn, emotionally and physically draining experience.

Riding in the backseat, watching the landscape outside the window fly by, created a surreal sensation. Fleeting scenery brought back childhood memories of staring for hours through the rear window of the family sedan while Dad drove to faraway destinations on a family vacation. On this adventure, though, the child was hauling the dad. In an odd sort of way, the past and the future blended together and defined the current state of affairs. Clearly there was no way to avoid the difficult choices that lay ahead, and the responsibility for making those decisions had fallen squarely on my shoulders. Memories blended with intensely anxious moments of grief and compromised rationale. Praying was a given; but for what, I had not a clue.

My repair business had been in a solid growth mode for several months straight, but that didn't matter. If the little enterprise had a chance of surviving temporary closure, it could not be shut down for more than a month. Economic survival became my prime directive.

I shouldn't have any trouble paying the bills, I thought to myself, *as long as I can open the doors back up before the end of July.*

I have never been so badly beaten up that I wasn't back on my feet in a few weeks, I reasoned. *Even if I have to hobble around on crutches, I should still be able to turn wrenches and earn a living.*

Comprehending the extent of our injuries was simply beyond my ability. Just how thoroughly both of us had been physically torn apart would not sink in.

Eight days after Carole and I had pulled out of the driveway on the motorcycle I finally made it home, wrecked and disabled. Nicole pushed the wheelchair with me in it through the front door and into the house, where family waited to welcome me back. Homecoming was an eerie experience. Nothing had changed, yet nothing had remained the same. There was a distinct feeling of destruction and death in the air. I sensed evil demons circling overhead, waiting for the opportunity to bring the remaining darkness down around us.

Still seated in the wheelchair, I hugged my son Jeremy, his kids, and everyone else standing around me, and I then started looking for a way to escape the confusion. I so longed to be back in my own room! Executing as tactful an exit as possible, I climbed out of the wheelchair, crawled on my hands and knees up the stairs to our bedroom, and closed the door behind me. Finally, a good night's sleep was only moments away.

The next challenge was to pull myself up and onto the bed.

Carole's fragrance was everywhere. Tears filled my eyes as I looked over at her side and stared at the emptiness filling our personal, private space. Reaching over to touch her invisible body, my hand smoothed the blanket as though my imagination could make her appear out of thin air. There, neatly folded under her pillow, was the soft, silky nightgown she had slept in the night before the accident a week earlier. The latest romance novel she had been reading lay next to the lamp on her nightstand with a little slip of paper marking the page where she had left off before going to sleep.

Is this real? I thought to myself. *Could we have really been laid at death's door, or am I just waking from another horrific nightmare?*

The reflection did not last long. Soon after my head hit the pillow, it became painfully obvious to me that lying down had been a huge mistake. This was not an elevated hospital bed; this was a flat, hard mattress.

While I lay there glaring at the ceiling, a mild panic set in. Not only was the unbearable tenderness from broken ribs making it difficult to breathe, but my physical strength had been zapped as well. Trying to sit up was futile. The only maneuver I could manage was to roll over onto my side, and that hurt like the dickens. Both shoulders were throbbing from overexertion and internal damage. Any way I cut it, getting back off that bed promised to be a challenge. No matter how delicate the maneuver, there was simply no gentle, painless way for me to move in any direction, so I braced for the inevitable. Inhaling a deep breath through clenched teeth while squeezing my eyes shut, I half flung myself back onto the floor alongside the bed with one bone-grinding effort, trying at all cost to avoid landing on my damaged ankle. After crawling back down the two flights of stairs past the group of surprised onlookers, I finally settled into one of our cheap recliners in the family room.

I spent the next four weeks trying to sleep in one of those chairs with my splinted leg propped up on the other chair. Hobbling back and forth to the bathroom, crawling up the stairs to the kitchen, and piling myself into the backseat of Nicole's car to head for another day at Carole's hospital bedside was the extent of my physical activity.

Jeremy scrambled to piece together as much as he was able in order to salvage our future. He dug through our files, sorted through our mail, got a handle on our household bills, and made sure as many loose ends as possible were tied up before returning home to Virginia.

Jason withdrew. He seemed determined to drop out of sight.

Nicole's job reassignment earlier that year in January had provided enormous flexibility in her schedule, so carrying her work with her to the hospital to care for her parents presented no problem. Her days were arranged to accommodate our personal needs. Our daughter became a primary source of transportation, a liaison between family and friends, and a personal guardian angel.

CHAPTER 8

THE STORY OF THE ROSE

—⚍—

Weather conditions in southeastern Michigan had been oppressively hot and dry. It was already July 2007, and we hadn't seen a drop of rain for weeks. Lawns resembled patches of shredded wheat. Leaves on stunted cornstalks had rolled into tubes, and the rows of soy and navy bean plants covering gently rolling hills all across the countryside were turning prematurely yellow from lack of moisture.

From the rear seat of Nicole's car, I sat staring off into the distance along I-69, my mind wandering from one disconnected thought to another.

There were many similarities between our harrowing encounter and the dehydrated and dying vegetation along the highway outside. Although death had nearly separated us just a week and a half earlier, I was in a relatively neutral mood, resigned to the reality that our daily routine would never be the same. Carole's condition had stabilized. Our time on earth may have been shortened, but like those dried-out bean plants, with a little water and nutrition, life would return, and it could be better than ever.

I thought about Kevin (Uncle Weird Beard) and Dan (another musician Kevin and I had toured with while playing music for a living). Kevin lived in Westland, Michigan, and Dan had moved to Spring, Texas, several years earlier.

Kevin, a privately faithful man, was one of those who truly had a gift for teaching. He never preached his beliefs as much as he demonstrated them. Kevin was comical with his unkempt beard and thin, scraggly hair; hence the name Uncle Weird Beard. He was usually the center of attention at any social gathering, and as an entertainer, he knew how to mesmerize a crowd with or without a piano at his fingertips.

Dan's calling was to support the mission. Any mission. He had his own unique approach to every situation. There was usually a bit of drama adding color to his tales, but he always knew what he was talking about whether anyone agreed with him or not.

Whenever Kevin and Dan got together, their philosophical theatrics were usually quite interesting. I spent most of our time together just listening to the two of them banter theories back and forth.

Although Kevin's first encounter with Carole shortly after I joined the group had been slightly confrontational, the two of them had developed a close relationship. Kevin jokingly pronounced her name "kah-Role," with the emphasis on "Role." Carole's lighthearted response sprinkled with laughter forever softened his heart. It did not take long for my wife to figure out why Kevin and I so enjoyed each other's company out on the road, and Kevin immediately knew why Carole and I were meant for each other.

I wanted to share some encouraging news about Carole's progress with Kevin that evening, so instead of staring out the window, watching the dry scenery fly by, I picked up the cell phone and dialed his number.

"Hi, Kev," I said with as much cheer in my voice as I could muster.

"Davey!" Kevin exclaimed. "How are you doing?"

"I'm all right, Kevin," I said soberly. "Under the circumstances, things could be a lot worse."

"How's kah-Role?" he asked.

"Actually she's doing all right, Kev, which is why I called. She seems to know what's going on around her."

"Ah, that's great news," Kevin said with a sigh of relief. "I'll be up to visit with her in the next day or two."

"That would be great, Kevin. I know your being there would be a comfort. Nicole and I will likely be there. Kev, has anyone been in touch with Dan?"

"Yeah," he said. "As a matter of fact, I called Dan the morning after your accident. I couldn't get an answer, so I left a voice message on his cell phone. All I said was that you and Carole had been in a wreck, and I asked him to call me back when he had a few minutes."

"Have you heard back from him yet?"

"He called me back later that day."

"I feel bad that I haven't been in touch," I said. "Do you think I should call him?"

"No, I don't think you need to," he said. "I'm keeping him up to date on your progress. Dan was ready to drop everything and come to Michigan, but I told him to sit tight because there was really nothing he could do."

"How did he take the news?" I asked.

"Well, actually it was sort of a strange conversation. I was at Hurley, trying to get my mind around Carole's condition. I didn't know what to say, think, or do, so I went outside to get some fresh air and regroup. While I was standing by the front entrance to the hospital, my phone rang. I thought about ignoring the phone until I realized that it was Dan calling me back. I really needed someone to talk to, so Dan's timing could not have been more perfect."

"So, what was so strange about your conversation with Dan?" I asked playfully. "I mean, isn't every conversation with Danny just a little bit unusual?"

"Yeah." Kevin laughed, and then his voice broke, and there was a brief pause before he was able to continue. When Kevin regained his composure, he replayed the conversation he had had with our friend Dan.

Kevin told Dan everything he knew about the hit-and-run, the extent of our injuries, and where we were with our recovery. He ended his report to Dan with the news that Carole's condition was critical and that she was not expected to survive her injuries. When Kevin finished talking, there was a long pause. He thought he had lost the signal.

"Hello, Dan? Are you still there?" Kevin asked, thinking he had been talking to a dead phone.

"Yeah, Kev, I'm still here," Dan said, "but I have to tell you something, and you're probably going to think I'm crazy."

Dan had been performing with some musicians at a Catholic convention in San Diego when Kevin called and left the message on his cell phone. Just prior to returning Kevin's phone call, Dan had been sitting in a makeshift chapel at the hotel where he was staying.

"I lit a couple of candles on the altar," Dan said, "and was sitting there all alone with a rosary hanging from my fingers, praying for a couple of friends and a family member.

"As I sat there praying, a Trinitarian nun came into the chapel. We had never met. In fact, I had not seen her at the convention prior to that moment. She approached the altar, rearranged some flowers, and then sat down. Within minutes she was back at the altar, fiddling with the flowers again. I wanted to say something because she was really distracting. I just put my head back down and refocused on the rosary in my hands.

"Just about the time I got my concentration back, that nun got up again, went back to the altar, pulled a rose from one of the arrangements, and turned to walk toward me. I thought maybe the nun had sensed my less-than-welcoming attitude and was coming over to scold me. When I looked up, she was standing directly in front of me. As we made eye contact, she leaned forward and handed me the rose. 'The Lady said you were going to need this,' she said. When I thanked her for the rose, she became very upset with me.

"'Don't thank me! I told you, *the Lady* said you were going to need this. *That* Lady!' she said emphatically, pointing toward the statue of the Virgin Mary.

"She really scolded me," Dan said. "I suppose I should have known better than to respond the way I did, but that nun wanted to be sure that I knew the message had come through her spiritually."

It took a few days for me to fully appreciate the significance of Dan's encounter with that nun. It wasn't until I shared Dan and Kevin's conversation with another friend before I began to completely understand what had taken place.

Dan was a devout Catholic. Kevin was Lutheran. Carole and I were two casual Presbyterians. Legalistic die-hards in each of those denominations, as well as many other pious sects, would suggest that theirs is the right way and all others are misguided.

Through that nun, the voice of the Spirit had silently traversed the man-made barriers of three mainstream religious denominations to prepare Danny the Catholic for his conversation with Kevin the Lutheran about the crisis facing their mutual Presbyterian friends, Dave and Carole.

The rose was our reminder of the blood that had been shed for our safety, salvation, and well-being. The message was that we were all in God's hands.

Some may disagree, but as far as I'm concerned, that proves that being a Christian and receiving Christ's message really has nothing to do with what church we attend. It does, however, seem to suggest the raison d'être for attending church in the first place.

CHAPTER 9

PASSWORD

—⚍—

The commute to Hurley in the backseat of my daughter's car had become a daily ritual. Nicole usually put in half a day at work before leaving the office early to swing by the house and pick me up for another trek to Flint. How she kept her home life intact while holding down a full-time job between hospital visits was a mystery to me.

Because I was still unable to comfortably lie down in bed, my morning routine started with maneuvering out of the recliner where I spent my nights and into the wheelchair. Then I would tend to personal hygiene (bathing in the bathroom sink), which required considerable effort and time. Sometimes I would crawl up the stairs and into the kitchen to fix myself something to eat. Most of the time I just parked in the wheelchair by the front door and waited for Nicole to pluck me from the house and stuff me into the backseat of her Pontiac Vibe.

An hour later we would be rounding the curve that encircled the medevac landing pad outside the front entrance to Hurley, where Carole had made her grand entrance. Nicole knew where the best parking spots were, so she never wasted any time in the hospital's public garage. Once I was strapped back into the wheelchair, we headed for the elevators to the fifth floor.

Hospital policy stated that not more than three people were to be in Carole's room at any given time. That discipline was easily maintained. The problem was that from the very first day, there had been a steady stream of visitors filing through. It was flattering to learn that so many people were that deeply concerned about Carole's welfare, but privacy had become an issue. The constant quiet commotion caused by all of that pedestrian traffic had become more of an intrusion than a comfort.

Apparently I wasn't the only one who preferred to see it stopped. Carole's somewhat agitated state alerted the doctors that she was suffering from sensory overload. Her body language was trying to tell people to step away and leave her in peace.

One of the doctors on the hospital's psychiatric staff gently pulled me aside.

"I think it would be a good idea to cut back on the number of people coming to see Carole," she said. "You might want to limit visitation to immediate family only."

That's odd that I am being handed responsibility for crowd control, I thought to myself. *If too many people are coming through the doors, why isn't hospital security getting involved?*

"I agree with you," I said. "It is a little annoying, but aside from feeling as though I have to play host to so many visitors, what's the problem?"

"Excess noise and confusion stimulates unnecessary cognitive activity, which, if allowed to continue, will result in critical increases in brain pressure. Carole's recovery has been put at risk by the constant influx of people moving in and around her room, whispering and discussing her situation."

The doctor was kind and concise, and she spared no effort in sharing her concerns. It had never occurred to me until the doctor brought it up that Carole's recovery was being jeopardized by having so many well-wishers whisking past her bedside.

"In her fragile condition, Carole lacks the ability to segregate and process the noises surrounding her," the doctor said. "This conversation we're having, the beeping coming from the monitors that are hanging all around her bed, that rattling cart that just rolled by outside the door—every sound is coming at her in a confusing clamor of racket, and to her it's all at the same volume level."

The doctor's cautious warnings immediately made sense, but I had not a clue how to restrict the growing herd of onlookers. At that very moment, the lady attending the phones at the nurses' station stepped into the conversation.

"The telephone in Carole's unit needs to be turned on," she said. "There's a woman on the phone who has called several times already, and I cannot transfer the call."

"Who is it?" I asked, struggling to get out of the wheelchair.

"She didn't give a name," the attendant said. "All she would say was that she was a high school friend from California."

Confusing thoughts swirled through my already overloaded brain. The doctor was trying to tell me to cut back on visitation while the attendant was asking me to turn on the phone. Absorbing the rapidly expanding list of reasons Carole should be isolated from outside contact triggered in me an irrational, hair-raising fear. I felt like a teenager standing in my dad's backyard, waiting to be scolded for having made the wrong choices yet again.

I've caused all of this, I said to myself. *Stupid decisions are the reason my wife is lying there dying.*

I was suffering from a surprisingly delicate state of mind, and my emotions were rapidly unraveling. By that time I was standing, balanced on one leg with one hand on the wheelchair for stability.

"That's probably Diane on the telephone," I said in a shaky voice. "She's a close friend of ours, but there's nothing I can tell her that she doesn't already know, and Carole certainly isn't in any condition to take the call."

The attendant lady must have sensed the turmoil boiling up inside me. "I'll handle the call," she said. "We'll just tell your friend that the call cannot be transferred."

A moment later, the attendant lady came back to relay instructions to the staff that the phone in Carole's unit was not to be connected. Then she turned in my direction, gently put her hand on my arm, and let me know that the situation had been handled. Her kindness unraveled the last thread holding me together.

"What am I supposed to do?" I asked. "How do I tell people they can't see my wife?"

I broke down. Unresolved feelings totally took over as I leaned into the lady's arms, burying my face in her shoulder, sobbing uncontrollably. She wrapped her arms around me, gently patted my back, and whispered into my ear.

"Just let it out," she said. "You've been through a lot. Just let it out."

The attendant was a robust lady with a mother's commanding demeanor. Her comforting words found their way to the depths of my soul, helping me regain my composure. I loved that lady for the compassion she shared. On that day, she was my personal saint.

The doctor had already moved on to her next patient.

After a few deep breaths, I thanked the attendant for her help and asked her what she thought I should do.

"A little trick people have used to cut down on the number of visitors is to give the patient a new name."

"You mean like an alias?" I asked.

"Yes," she said. "Choose any name you like, and that will become her new identity. The patient's name will be changed in the hospital records."

"How do you keep her records straight?" I asked.

"We know who she is because we have her real name alongside her alias in our records. The people at the front desk won't know that, though. Your wife's name will no longer appear on their patient roster, so anyone asking for her at the front desk will be told there is no one in the hospital by that name."

"So her alias becomes the password," I said.

"Exactly," she said. "And without the correct password, no one will be allowed through those locked doors down that hallway."

So without further deliberation, Carole became Suzie Murphy.

The necessary forms were signed, and in a matter of minutes, hospital records had been modified. Carole's secret identity was in place. In a manner of speaking, she had been entered into the hospital's witness protection program, which brought excessive visitation to an abrupt halt. I later discovered that at the very moment Carole's identity had been disguised, people were at the information desk near the main entrance, asking which room she was in. The staff behind the counter simply told those visitors that the hospital had nobody by my wife's name registered as a patient.

Restricting visitation effected a dynamic change in Carole's recovery. In a matter of hours, Carole's recuperation seemed to slip into the fast lane. Within a couple of days, Carole was breathing on her own and the convulsions had all but stopped. She seemed to be resting more peacefully, and her legs had begun to move. She was also responding to voice commands and had begun squeezing my hand when I held hers in mine.

Toward the end of Carole's second week in the trauma unit, my sister, Shirl, came for another of her regular visits.

"How's she doing?" Shirl asked.

"She seems to be making progress," I said, "but I think she still has her contact lenses in her eyes."

"You're kidding!" Shirl said. "My gosh, I have to take mine out at the end of the day or my eyes will dry out so badly that I won't be able to wear them again for a couple of days."

"I mentioned something about it to one of the nurses yesterday, but I'm not sure she did anything about it," I said.

"Well, let me take a look and see." She leaned over the rail to get a closer look. "Yep, they're still in there. Let me see if I can get them out." Shirl gently laid her fingertips on Carole's cheek. "Carole, can you turn your face this way a little bit? I'm going to see if I can get those contacts out of your eyes."

Ever so carefully, Shirl popped the lenses off Carole's eyeballs. The color of life literally flushed back into my wife's face. Her eyes immediately turned back to their beautiful blue, and her expression seemed to become once again relaxed and radiant.

The next day an unusually large number of people had been gathering in one of the glass-enclosed units on the opposite side of the nurse's station. It seemed odd so many people had been allowed to crowd into that one little area with a patient in such critically fragile condition. Nicole and I noticed that some of the visitors heading in that direction were quietly sobbing as they rounded the corner and passed Carole's room.

Then we heard gasps of disbelief; wails of agony, stifled screams, and group grief as life support systems one-by-one were reverently unplugged and shut down. Machinery wound its way to a quiet rest as the remaining life ebbed from that unfortunate young man's body.

Family had gathered to witness the end of a loved one's life. I felt twinges of guilt for being grateful that it wasn't my wife's room to which people had been summoned for a final good-bye.

When a nurse came by to close the glass door to Carole's unit and protect us from witnessing the sounds of horror associated with the death of another human being, I asked her to please leave it open. I thought pushing the echo of that family's pain out of earshot to be an insult to the survivors suffering from their loss. I grieved with them.

Once again I thanked God for sparing both my wife and me.

—⁓—

Early one afternoon near the end of the second week, Nicole and I approached Carole's fishbowl room for our daily visit. A group of nurses were crowded around her hospital bed, busily moving tubes and frantically checking the monitors and medical instruments she was plugged into. It appeared as though we had rolled in on an emergency.

Visions of that young man who had recently lost his battle in the unit around the corner swirled through my head. Acid filled my stomach, and my abdomen tightened from fear. We cautiously approached the room, silently braced for the news that all of the progress we had seen in Carole's recovery had been an illusion of optimism.

One of the nurses glanced up just as we reached the doorway. The expression on my face must have exposed the panic. She looked into my eyes and smiled cautiously.

"We're getting ready to transfer Carole to McLaren Hospital," she said.

"What happened?" I asked.

"The doctor is going to see about reconstructing her elbow. He believes she is strong enough now to undergo the surgery."

Once again a dizzying sense of relief coursed through my body, leaving a slight tingling sensation from my fingertips to my toes. My brain was being thrust back and forth between comfort and chaos like a basketball in a game filled with unexpected turnovers. I wasn't sure just how many more episodes of that sort of hockey-puck shock therapy I would be able to handle.

"Is she going to stay at McLaren?" Nicole asked.

"No," the nurse replied. "You can wait here. She'll be transferred back to Hurley after the doctor has finished. The surgical staff at McLaren is better equipped to handle this sort of reconstructive surgery. The procedure should only take a couple of hours."

A few minutes later Carole was rolled out of the ICU, and she disappeared through a set of doors with an ambulance crew walking along both sides of her bed like pallbearers escorting a casket. The rest of the day disappeared while Nicole and I patiently waited.

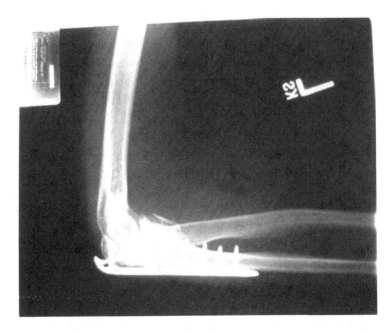

Much like my ankle, Carole's elbow had been crushed. The joint must have been permeated with shards of shattered bone fragments. The genius of yet another surgical expert salvaged enough of her bone structure and the elbow joint to assure a nearly full recovery with a moderate amount of physical therapy. He could just as easily have amputated the entire arm without any need for explanation.

As the nurse had promised, Carole was returned to Hurley several hours later. A fresh bandage wrapped around her left arm covered the stitches that held the skin closed over a permanent titanium elbow screwed securely in place.

—∿—

During one of those long afternoons at Hurley waiting, visiting, and then waiting again, my sister and I sat in the hospital cafeteria, biding our time until the nurses allowed us back into Carole's room. Shirl idly browsed through the Flint newspaper.

"Wow! Look at this!" she said.

She handed me a page out of the newspaper that contained a short article about hospitals and the critical care they provided. Hurley Medical Center of Flint, Michigan, had been ranked among the top-sixteen trauma units in the entire United States. I took that piece of news as yet one more indication that Carole and I were in God's hands. What are the odds that, of all the hospitals she could have been taken to, my wife was at Hurley—one of the best in the nation! I began to understand why we had been taken to two separate hospitals. The way things had been unfolding certainly seemed to be more than just luck or mere coincidence.

My daughter and I were regulars at Hurley's ICU. We had become well acquainted with many of the staff and received friendly greetings and an occasional hug from whoever happened to be on duty as we entered the area each day to visit my wife. Such was our greeting as my daughter and I arrived not long after Carole's trip to McLaren.

The attendant on duty met us in the corridor outside Carole's room with a slight degree of excitement mixed with frustration in her voice.

"It looks like Carole will no longer be fed through a tube," the nurse said with a twinkle in her eye. "This is one strong-willed lady!"

"What happened?" I asked.

"You know how she kept grabbing at the IV and wouldn't leave the oxygen hoses alone?" she asked.

"Yeah, that's why you had to tie her hand to the bed rail, wasn't it?" I asked.

"Yes," she said, "but she still managed to pull the tubes out of her throat. We put them back in and tied her hand a little more tightly to the bed rail, but as soon as our backs were turned, she leaned over, held on to the tubes with her tied hand, and pulled herself away from her clenched fist, and out they came again."

"Okay, so now what do we do?" I asked.

"I had the kitchen send us a tray with solid food," she said. "When it showed up, we set it in front of Carole and handed her a fork. Without hesitation, she started feeding herself."

When Nicole and I entered her room that afternoon, Carole turned her head, looked straight into my eyes, and whispered, "I love you." Those were the first words I had heard from her lips since the day of the wreck.

I was dumbstruck; nothing could describe the unbelievable sensation of relief I felt. Hearing her speak was nothing short of breathtaking.

God's miracle continued unfolding before our eyes.

CHAPTER 10
WHERE'S THE HACKSAW?

—∞—

Two full weeks had passed since the accident before Nicole was finally able to convince me that we needed to see the surgeon from St. Mary's about my foot. Unlike me, she had been paying attention when the medical team pointed out that surgery needed to be performed as soon as possible if there was to be any chance of avoiding foot amputation. So she scheduled an appointment and we made the hour-and-a-half trek to his office on the west side of Saginaw.

When we got there, the doctor from St. Mary's quietly confirmed that my foot was in bad shape. As Nicole and I sat listening to the prognosis in an examining room at his office, memories of Dad's painful struggles with one wooden leg meandered through my mind.

The only remaining decision seemed to be how much of the leg I wanted to save: should the foot be taken off at the ankle, or should the doctor hack the whole leg off above the knee and avoid the potential for problems in the knee joint down the road? Weighing the pros and cons, trying to decide which procedure would produce less of a handicap in the long run, consumed my every waking thought. Either way, amputation seemed inevitable.

"I think it can be saved," the doctor said, "but it's hard to say whether you will ever be able to walk on it again. At the very least, it's going to be painful."

"Should I have it taken off?" I asked.

"Not necessarily," he said.

Surprised by his optimism, the future seemed suddenly brighter.

"I can perform the surgery, but I have a friend who is a specialist in that sort of reconstructive surgery whose expertise would ensure better results. If you're willing to go through the process, I will refer you to him."

With that bit of advice, our St. Mary's doctor sent us home with an appointment to see his guru the following day at the Oakland orthopedic clinic, which is located near William Beaumont Hospital in Troy, Michigan, as well as a prescription to have more X-rays taken of my ankle.

Four weeks was the accepted time limit before the untreated damage to my foot and ankle was expected to become permanent. The doctor was very specific about the fact that circulation to the tissue where the talus had been broken needed to be restored as soon as possible. Otherwise, the bone would die. After that it wouldn't matter how many screws a surgeon installed; the dead bone would eventually disintegrate like a box of soda crackers under the weight of my body. We needed to move fast if there was ever going to be a chance that the vessels, nerves, and bone tissue would properly knit back together.

Nicole scrambled to get me in for the X-ray work at the hospital in Cass City, twenty miles north of Marlette. Then she piled me back into her car and hustled to Troy, seventy miles south of Marlette, to see the specialist for his opinion.

We arrived in Troy ahead of time, sat through the backlog of patients in the waiting room, then met with the specialist more than an hour after the time of our scheduled appointment. He removed the splint and bandages, examined the ankle, and left the room. A short while later he returned to inform us that the digital formatting on the disc with the X-rays taken in Cass City was incompatible with the media his office used. We needed to have another series of X-rays taken, after which his office would reschedule his examination for a later date.

Again, my daughter's emergency medical training intervened to save the day, and maybe my foot. Nicole was not bashful about reminding the doctor that the clock was ticking and got right to the point, throwing in a few impressive-sounding medical terms during her request for him to reconsider the urgency of my need for attention.

I thought we had blown our chances altogether when the doctor left the room looking somewhat disgusted, but he returned a short while later with a technician who went right to work taking more X-rays of my ankle. After another interminably long pause, the doctor returned and informed us that the nature of the injury and the extent of damage to my ankle were more severe than he had anticipated. He concluded that the necessary corrective surgery was out of his league.

Well, that's the end of that, I thought to myself. *I guess we're back to deciding how much of my leg goes into the Dumpster.*

The good news was that he had taken Nicole's remarks seriously and was equally concerned about the length of time that had elapsed since the injury had occurred. With a heightened sense of urgency, he had taken it upon himself to make an appointment for us to see his guru, a top-rated surgeon located in West Bloomfield, Michigan. He then advised us that he would assist that doctor in the operating room if the procedure was deemed feasible.

We left the Oakland orthopedic clinic with a confused sense of optimism. Was there a chance the foot could not be saved? Were we spinning our wheels hoping for the impossible?

Sometime within the next few days, we met with the doctor in West Bloomfield. He was a gentle-spirited, youthful-looking man with a polite, boyish demeanor whose appearance made him look young enough to be my grandson.

His staff took more X-rays, and we waited while the doctor reviewed the condition of my ankle and considered the options. When he came into the examining room holding the X-rays, he had that familiar unsure look on his face. He advised us that the chances of saving my foot were slim, mostly because we were on the borderline of elapsed time since the accident. However, he was willing to give it a try.

Surgery was scheduled to take place the following Monday morning, three weeks and one day after the ankle had been

104

irreparably crushed. I fully expected the surgical procedure to be an exercise in futility, but that drive to survive that had been programmed into me since childhood prevented me from folding the hand I had been dealt.

With Nicole's encouragement, all of my chips were on the table. This was no longer a gamble, because there was nothing left to lose. I was ready to face the scalpel or the hacksaw. The choice of which tool to use was entirely up to the surgeon.

CHAPTER 11
WORD SALAD ON THE SIXTH FLOOR

—◊—

Carole had become the ICU miracle girl. Everyone working in the unit was amazed by her recovery, and they all shared in the joy of our victory over death. Grateful as we were for surviving, however, being alive was only half of the equation. We still had a long road ahead of us, and the outcome included no guarantees.

Near the end of her third week at Hurley, Carole was transferred from the fifth-floor intensive care unit to the rehabilitation ward one floor above. After settling Carole into her new room, Sherrie, the head nurse, pulled me aside and asked for some specific details about Carole's personality, background, interests, and anything else that might help the staff plan a successful therapeutic recovery.

Sherrie, Nicole, and I enjoyed a pleasant, comforting conversation about my wife, sharing personal experiences and comparing individual interests. Sherrie seemed genuinely interested in knowing who Carole was, and her reassuring demeanor provided much-appreciated encouragement.

Sherrie then gave us an overview of the hospital's approach to rehabilitation, referring to literature we had received when Carole had first been admitted to the hospital. I later pulled out the information packet the hospital had provided and found the following explanation:

> Following a traumatic brain injury, there are eight
> stages of mental (thinking) and emotional recovery.

These stages may last different lengths of time, from a few hours to many weeks or months. It is hard to know how long a stage will last, or when progress will stop. At any time, two or more stages may be seen. It is possible to skip a stage completely.

Each stage of recovery is helpful in predicting possible behaviors. Everyone is different and should not be labeled to a certain stage. These stages help staff plan treatment programs for the patient.

Stage 1 patients are unconscious, nearly comatose, barely alive. That pretty much described Carole's condition the entire first week.

Sherrie explained that although Carole had been transferred to the rehabilitation unit as a stage 2 patient—slightly better than stage 1—her initial assessment was that Carole had been demonstrating behavior and awareness more aptly categorized as that of a stage 4 patient: confused, agitated, and overwhelmed, but reacting to surrounding activity.

A stage 5 patient is marginally functional yet capable of wandering off the ward if left unattended. That explained why the doors to the sixth floor were locked from the inside. Typically a patient would be discharged from Hurley's rehabilitation unit once stage 5 had been reached.

Sherrie was optimistic about Carole's condition and seemed confident that recovery would be swift.

Okay, I thought to myself, *Carole skipped right past stage 3. That has to mean that she's coming out of this faster than anyone expected her to, so she must not be in as bad of shape as everyone thought. If patients are discharged at stage 5 and Carole is already showing signs of being stage 4, I should be taking her home in a couple of weeks, maybe sooner!*

In typical fashion I had already started calculating in my head the number of days before my wife and I would be going home to lick our wounds and jump back into our daily routine.

I still didn't get it. What we had been through was not the result of a slip and fall on the hiking trail. Our injuries were far more serious than my brain would accept. The human psyche plays tricks on the imagination, and when that happened to me, reality went right into the trash heap. A little bit of denial had fueled a whole lot of false hope.

Although the effects of TBI vary from person to person, physicians have documented baseline behavior patterns repeated in nearly every TBI patient. In other words, if a person hits his head hard enough, he will likely experience memory loss, disorientation, physical impairments, cognitive impairments, and combative behavior.

If those cowboys actually smacked people on the back of the head with the butt of a pistol the way it's done in the movies, there had to have been a lot of brain-damaged rustlers wandering around on the lone prairie. People don't survive that sort of head trauma in real life.

Carole displayed most of the expected characteristics of TBI, but her response to therapies and rate of recovery perplexed and puzzled her team of therapists. She seemed to defy the norm. She had sporadic memory issues and frequently became disoriented, but that was no surprise to anyone. She also exhibited minor physical impairments, but those were mostly a result of her broken bones and weakened muscles, the latter a result of her having been bedridden for so long. Carole had to relearn how to walk, but as her strength returned, so did her coordination and muscle control.

Nobody had warned me about the potential for Carole to exhibit a changed personality. That aspect of brain trauma was one of the unexplained mysteries of behavioral science. Subtle differences in Carole's character had already surfaced, but I alone recognized those changes because nobody else knew her as intimately. What I had been witnessing generated a dark, nagging fear that stole its way into my subconscious. Displays of impatience and self-centeredness that I had never seen in her had become a noticeable part of the interaction between us. Other less obvious traits conspired to make my wife appear as though she had become a twin sister with a dark side. It was hard to put my finger on any one thing, but overall she reminded me of a third-generation videocassette tape with a resolution that had become a little grainier each time it had been copied.

I passed it off as a temporary condition that would go away as the healing progressed, but my underlying fear was that this was the new Carole I would be challenged to meet head-on. Focusing on being thankful for not having to make funeral arrangements became a saving state of mind and helped me to avoid a total meltdown, but training myself to ignore the obvious also perpetuated an unhealthy degree of denial.

After a week in the rehabilitation ward, Sherrie called me aside and once again quizzed me about my wife's personality.

"How would you describe your wife's behavior prior to the accident?" she asked.

"Normal," I said, not sure why she was asking. "She had a job, raised our children, and did all the stuff a traditional wife and mother would do. Why do you ask?"

"Just trying to get to know your wife a little better, that's all," she said.

"Well, I can tell you one thing for sure," I said. "She got along with everyone. If Carole was in a checkout line at the grocery store for more than five minutes, she would start bonding with total strangers standing in line with her. Hold her there for ten minutes and she would probably be exchanging recipes and phone numbers with them. She had always been a very outgoing people-person."

"That's interesting," Sherrie said with a tone of curiosity.

"Why?" I asked.

"Most patients display uncharacteristic behavior during their recovery from a brain trauma," she explained. "They tend to conduct themselves in ways quite the opposite of their normal behavior."

"So you're saying there is a Jekyll-and-Hyde personality that takes over?" I asked.

"In many cases, yes," she said. "Preachers suffering from TBI tend to turn the air blue with vulgar language. Mild-mannered patients become combative and abusive."

"So if what you're saying is accurate, my wife should be swinging at everyone who walks past her."

"Yes, and that's what is so curious about Carole. She has displayed none of those expected behaviors," Sherrie said. "Your wife has behaved much like the preaccident person you just described."

Going by the book, Carole should have been a prime candidate for the straitjacket. Once again, she had defied the odds.

On the other hand, there were some rather uncharacteristic theatrical posttrauma habits in her behavior, and everyone seemed to notice those. For example, Carole had been displaying a fairly creative sense of humor, and she seemed to know when she was playing for the crowd with her one-liners. Her quips and jabs were usually spiced with colorful adjectives that flirted with profanity without actually using foul language. The first time she revealed that side of her new personality, we were all taken back a little.

Another interesting and somewhat entertaining development was something called word salad—the use of phrases or words out of context. For some reason a traumatized brain often connects thoughts to the wrong words. The conversation makes perfect sense to the patient, but the listener often needs a creative sense of awareness to understand. Carole often kept visitors wondering exactly what she was talking about.

During an afternoon visit with one of Carole's friends sitting at her bedside, the topic briefly turned to details about the accident.

"Do you know what happened?" the friend asked.

"Yeah," Carole said. "We went for a ride on the motorcycle, and some guy driving a pencil sharpener ran over us."

Carole's comments were often hilarious, mostly making sense while sprinkled with colorfully nonsensical remarks.

In spite of those lighter moments, discomfort plagued my wife. Much to her dismay, Carole had been fitted with a mesh vest with straps that could be tied to her wheelchair. She was yet unable to walk under her own power, but that didn't stop her from trying. For her own safety, she had to be strapped in.

Not surprisingly, with all of the ribs on her left side painfully healing, lying still had also become a serious challenge for her. She thrashed around in her bed so actively that to prevent her from falling out during the night, the staff had fitted it with a tent made of nylon mesh. Her little enclosure reminded me of the mosquito netting some of the soldiers had been lucky enough to have around their bunks in Vietnam. The rule was that any time Carole was left alone in her room, the sides were to be zipped closed.

Cautious as everyone was, however, Carole's stay at Hurley had not been without a small degree of unfortunate calamity. After hugging his mother good night one evening, Jason started zipping the sides of her tent closed. The attending nurse told Jason that she would take care of zipping Carole in for the night, so Jason obligingly left the sides of the tent unsecured. The next day we discovered that the nurse had not done as she said she would and Carole had, in fact, fallen out of bed and onto the floor during the night. That same nurse tried to blame Jason for leaving his mother unprotected. We never saw that nurse anywhere on the sixth floor after that.

Perseveration is another affliction common to recovering TBI patients. Like a child in a shopping cart who won't stop repeating what she wants, the patient becomes so focused on staring at an object, touching something, or vocalizing an issue that the only way to end the episode is to ignore or isolate the patient. Perseveration is fueled by the patient's severely compromised ability to reason.

After Carole had finished her meals, the attendants wanted her to remain in an upright position until her body had had ample time to digest her food. There was a high risk of her aspirating on the contents of her stomach if she experienced any indigestion while lying down. To keep her sitting upright and in her wheelchair, the straps on her mesh vest were fastened to the back of the chair. Carole constantly reminded anyone within earshot that she did not want to be tied to her chair. That alone was not unreasonable, but the repetition soon became a challenge to deal with.

"Untie me so I can go over there and lie down on the couch," she would say.

"You just finished eating, Carole," I would say. "You can't lie down for a while."

"Then just let me go over there and sit on the couch for a few minutes."

"We'll help you over to the couch in a little while," I would say to her. "Would you like to play cards or try working on your needlepoint?"

"No, I want to go over there and lay down on the couch for a little while," she would say. "Don't I have some scissors with my needlepoint stuff?"

"Why do you want your scissors?"

"So I can cut these straps."

"Why would you want to cut those straps?"

"So I can go over there and lay down on the couch."

"No, you need to stay sitting up for a while longer."

"Just give me some scissors so I can cut my way out of this wheelchair and go over to the couch and lay down."

There was no anger or emotion in her voice. She simply kept repeating the same thing over and over, becoming increasingly agitated by our lack of response. The more agitated she was, the more persistent she would become.

During one of Rodney's visits, Carole assaulted him with her usual chant.

"My back hurts," she said. "Untie me so I can go over there and lay down on the couch for a little while."

"No," Rodney said. "The doctor says you have to stay in the chair for at least half an hour. After that we'll see what we can do to get you out of the chair."

"Just let me lay down on the couch for a little while," she insisted repeatedly.

Rodney, understanding the rules, refused to give in to her persistence and patiently repeated his answer every time she asked until she finally gave up out of frustration.

"Well, then read between the lines," she said as she held up her hand, giving Rodney a one-finger wave.

From that point forward, Carole referred to Rodney as her foreman.

Post-trauma amnesia had become Carole's most persistent and long-lasting problem. The trauma had compromised short-term memory. Loss of consciousness following the accident had resulted in amnesia creating gaps in the time line. The results were varying degrees of disorientation that mimicked early stages of Alzheimer's.

She suffered through bewildering experiences that were much more intense than simply trying to get her bearings after waking from a nap. Carole frequently asked where she was and why she was there, terrified by the total lack of familiarity with her surroundings.

Sometimes her recall would be dead-on accurate. A moment later, her memory would call back an event from months or years earlier and she would refer to it as though it had taken place the day before. Confusing people, places, and moments in time was a common occurrence. During that phase of recovery, her thoughts skipped across conversations the way a bad telephone connection cuts out syllables or sentences. Her dialogue often gave others the impression that she was hallucinating.

"Hi, Carole!" Shirl said as we walked into her room one Sunday afternoon for our daily visit. "How're ya doin' today?"

"My hands hurt," Carole said.

"Really?" Shirl asked. "Why?"

"I spent the night writing a bunch of checks to pay for all of the supplies I had to buy," she said.

"What supplies?" Shirl asked.

"Your cousins, Dave and Brian Merz, have been downstairs handing out wine and chocolate to the patients on the fifth floor," she said.

"Really?" Shirl asked. "When did they start working here?"

"I don't know," Carole said, "but somebody had to pay for all of that stuff they were giving away."

It was, of course, all in her imagination.

"Some guys broke out of prison," Carole said. "I have to wear this vest until they've been caught."

"No kidding?" Shirl asked.

"Yup," she said. "The reason I have to sleep in this zippered tent is because Dave turned me in, so now I'm in jail."

Wow.

I began to wonder what sorts of drugs we had not been made aware of that the hospital might have been giving my wife!

—∞—

Rehabilitating a brain trauma patient, generally speaking, equates to reteaching the individual to do things he or she once knew how to do. The hope is that the process will help neurological pathways reconnect or reroute themselves as information is processed. The challenge is to get the patient to retain input, and that requires a level of concentration often missing following TBI. Carole's ability to concentrate for any length of time had been noticeably compromised. She had been given Vicodin to relieve pain and Ritalin to help with concentration, but the therapist's greatest challenge was to get Carole to pay attention long enough for the therapeutic methods to stick.

Mental and emotional issues can be tricky to treat. Even the most experienced therapists will admit that fixing the psyche is often a crapshoot. Sometimes a partial return to reality is all the patient's family can hope for.

The outcome from physical therapies, on the other hand, tends to be more predictable simply because the observer can see the injuries and visibly measure the patient's progress. Carole's occupational and physical therapies were aimed at getting her back on her feet and functioning under her own power. To some degree she had to relearn how to eat, speak, and bathe. Eating came naturally, as did speaking—although the therapists had to continue reminding Carole to use her "adult voice" because she kept whispering.

In retrospect, I believe that the whispering may have been an automatic reaction to damaged bronchial tissue from the day the staff at the Marlette ER kept trying to insert the breathing apparatus into her lungs. She may also have been suffering from painful tissue that had been tenderized by vinyl tubes jammed down her throat in the ICU. No examinations for possible injuries to her throat were pursued. Regardless of the reason, speaking aloud required Carole to muster an unusual amount of effort.

Carole had also developed a persistent cough, but nobody seemed concerned until one afternoon Carole let slip a dirty little secret she had been keeping. Nicole was quizzing Carole about what she would do if she could go home.

"Go hang out in the woods behind the house," Carole said.

"Really? What would you do if you were hanging out in the woods?"

"Smoke."

"Whoa, busted!" said Nicole, laughing hysterically.

That night on the way home, I asked Nicole why she didn't seem surprised that her mother wanted to smoke.

"Dad, she's been smoking for years!"

"I did not know that. How did you know?"

"When Jason was just a little kid, Jeremy and I used to send him back in the woods in the morning to spy on her."

"I thought she was back there walking the dog!" I said. "I didn't know she smoked. How long has that been going on?"

"Since before Jason was in school. Really, Dad? You didn't know Mom smoked?"

I did not have a clue. When I got home that night, I opened Carole's purse, and tucked neatly in the bottom was a pack of Marlboros and a Bic lighter.

Realistically, Carole's coughing was likely a side effect from her twenty-year smoking habit that I had known nothing about. That piece of my wife's past became another shocking revelation.

I wonder what else she's been hiding from me all these years, I thought to myself. *Smoking? Really? How could I have not known about that?*

Bathing was surprisingly a ground-up learning experience for Carole. The nurse would tell her how to turn the water on but then had to explain to Carole how to regulate the temperature of the water coming out of the showerhead. Carole would be handed a bar of soap and a washcloth, but she had to be shown how to apply the soap to the washcloth before bathing herself.

Step-by-step, the lessons continued. As each piece of every task was explained, Carole executed the procedures from that point forward exactly as she had been shown. She relearned every normal daily activity from brushing her teeth to sweeping the floor. One of her therapies included trips to the parking lot so she could practice getting in and out of an automobile.

Memory exercises continued the same way. Practicing simple arithmetic problems, reading books, and writing things from memory on a chalkboard all restimulated her brain and helped her to regain the capabilities of a functioning, literate adult.

Carole's response to therapy had been remarkable. Her sessions were not overly aggressive, but she seemed driven to heal herself. Recovery was progressing faster than anyone had expected, and it became a challenge for the staff to keep Carole's charts abreast of her rate of improvement.

Less than one month had passed since the day of the accident. Every visit revealed noticeable progress. Recovery was no longer a question of "if." It had become a matter of "how far." By the end of week four, everyone watched in disbelief. This lady who had not been expected to live appeared to be mysteriously healing herself, and she was getting it done quite handily.

God delivered hope.

CHAPTER 12
THE ATTORNEY

—∞—

When the driver of the vehicle we ran into was finally tracked down, the police read him his rights and took him into custody. During the initial interview, the officers asked him if he knew why he had been arrested.

"Yes," he said.

"Do you remember seeing a motorcycle?" the interviewers asked.

"Yes."

"What were you doing at the time of the collision?"

"I was waiting to make a left turn," he said.

He made it sound as though he had been innocently sitting behind the wheel at the intersection, waiting for oncoming traffic to clear, when we recklessly rear-ended his car.

"So you admit that you knew your car had been hit?"

"I thought a deer ran into me."

"Do you remember seeing two people lying in the road after that?"

"Yes," he said.

The officers were suspicious. The pieces of this guy's story were not fitting together.

"Why did you drive away after the motorcycle had run into you?"

"I was on my way to pick up my uncle and take him to the hospital because I thought he was having a heart attack."

"You knew that a motorcycle had run into your car and afterward you saw two people lying in the road, yet you left the scene of the crash. Don't you think you should have stuck around?" they asked.

"The ambulance guy told me it was okay to leave," he said.

The officers knew it was highly unlikely that any emergency personnel would have given the guy permission to leave the scene of an accident, especially if they thought he might have been involved. One look at his wrecked automobile would have tipped anyone off.

A few days after the accident, our son Jason took extensive photographs of the scene and a few photos of the car we had collided with. A long, black skid mark on the highway left by my motorcycle tire indicated that we had been riding in the center of our northbound lane of traffic when we collided with his car. The photographs also clearly showed that we had not hit him from behind; we had smashed into the side of his car.

There was no doubt we had run into the guy, but the only marks on the rear of his car were bloodstains along with some minor damage to the far left tip of the bumper. If we had hit his car from behind while he was waiting for traffic to clear, the impact from our motorcycle would have caved in the rear bumper and would at the very least have dented the trunk lid on his car.

The major damage caused from the crash started at the left rear wheel well and continued along the driver's side of the vehicle. The only logical explanation for that sort of damage is that the guy's car was sideways in the road when we ran into it. For his car to have been in that position at the moment of impact, he had to have pulled onto the road directly into our path only seconds before we collided.

I am thankful that Jason had the presence of mind to take those photos. The official police report was based upon statements taken from the driver. The report was inconclusive and contained several conflicting versions of what had taken place. The stories that driver had given the police did not match the evidence in the photos.

In other words, the guy was a liar. The fact that he had left the scene also proved that he had no conscience.

Our kids instinctively knew that we were going to need a lawyer to represent us. A hit-and-run accident with no witnesses leaves a lot of room for arguing over who was at fault. Someone capable of running from the scene of an accident that ended with two human beings lying helpless and dying in the middle of the highway would undoubtedly be capable of lying about what had happened, and that was exactly the way it played out.

Over the years both Carole and Nicole had become acquainted with dozens of attorneys through their jobs in the legal system. Most of the lawyers they had met specialized in some aspect of law, so Nicole was aware that their search for the right attorney would probably involve a lot of legwork. Thank God, my daughter knew enough to stay away from the TV lawyers. We needed legal representation, not a cluster of clowns.

While I was still holed up at St. Mary's, Jeremy and Nicole networked their way through a long list of legal contacts, calling law offices and soliciting advice from officers of the court with whom Carole had become acquainted. Following one referral after another, they finally came in contact with a lawyer from Royal Oak, Michigan. The guy was recognized as an expert in Michigan's no-fault law and specialized in crashes involving motorcycles and cars.

A week after I came home from the hospital, Nicole sat me down and told me what she and her brother had been up to.

"I know the guy who was behind the wheel of that car you ran into," she said. "Jeremy and I talked it over and decided you and Mom were going to need a lawyer."

Initially the thought of hiring a lawyer was a little frightening. *Why do I need an attorney if I didn't do anything wrong?* I asked myself.

Having to prove that Carole and I had been injured seemed a little ridiculous. Nicole's advice sounded as though someone might try to blame the whole thing on me. Our having no memory of the event certainly cleared the way for speculation. On the other hand, having an attorney meant that we wouldn't go down without a fight.

The cold reality was that it would take a lawyer to protect us from winding up on the wrong side of blind justice.

"So did you find anyone?" I asked.

Nicole briefed me on the results of their search and then handed over the telephone number of the guy she and her brother believed would be most suitable for the job. She agreed to make herself available when I met with the attorney, so I called his office to introduce myself. His name was Bob, and he was glad to hear from me. Following Nicole's advice, I arranged to have him come to meet with us on Friday, July 13.

Bob was a congenial gentleman. He was comfortable to talk with and seemed willing to spend whatever time necessary to help us decide whether or not he was the guy we were looking for. He went over all of the information he had about our situation based upon what Nicole had told him over the phone, and then Nicole filled in the gaps that helped him get a more complete picture of what we had been through up to that point in time.

We pulled out the stack of photographs that Jason had taken of the accident scene, the car, and the motorcycle and handed them over to Bob for his opinion. He was quick to point out that the nature of the damage to the car and the location of our skid mark on the highway suggested that the car had not been legally positioned for a left turn, as the driver had claimed. Bob's conclusion was that the crash had been unavoidable.

"I don't have all of the pieces yet," he said, "but from these photographs alone I am confident that I can prove you were not at fault."

After the initial meet and greet, he got down to the nitty-gritty.

"In addition to covering the cost of saving your lives," he explained, "no-fault law provides for replacement income based upon your earnings at the time of the accident."

The cap on the amount that we could claim was far less than our income had been, but even the amount that was allowed would have been more than adequate to meet expenses and afford us the opportunity to recuperate comfortably without worrying about losing our home.

"You are entitled to reimbursement for medical mileage and any out-of-pocket medical expenses, co-pays, and deductibles," he said. "The insurance company is also obligated to pay for in-home attendant care and replacement services for as long as you or your wife are unable to handle the chores around the house."

Finally, I can pay those guys for mowing the lawn, I thought to myself—as though yard maintenance were a priority!

"Once your case has been established, all of those benefits are payable and due within thirty days from the time your claims have been submitted." he paused and then said, "You should also know that reimbursement for accident-related medical care and expenses will continue for the rest of your lives."

The news came as though it were a gift from God.

Bob's explanations were thorough and easy to understand. His overview of benefits, entitlements, and the insurance company's legal obligations trumped any notion I may have had about handling it on my own. Without actually saying so, he had made it pretty clear that this was not a job for a do-it-yourselfer.

Bob gave us his recommendations and told us that he would like to handle our case, assuring us that our claims would be dealt with fairly. He knew that we were genuine and that he only had to present the evidence we had already accumulated to prove that our claim was legitimate. I sensed that he believed our situation was cut-and-dried and that representing us would be a matter of routine.

He was confident and up-front about his law firm's fees, and he appeared to be a gifted, understanding, and seasoned attorney. He claimed a success rate of proving fault on the part of the automobile driver in ninety-nine out of one hundred cases involving an automobile and a motorcycle.

After finishing his pitch, Bob excused himself to make a few telephone calls. While he was out of the room, Nicole and I spent a few minutes privately going over what he had told us. We discussed our options and bounced around the idea of taking a few days to think it over.

While we talked, a telephone call came from the doctor's office in West Bloomfield confirming that foot surgery had been scheduled for Monday morning, July 16. That bit of news was huge in comparison to everything else. I was about to find out whether or not my foot would be fixed or replaced by a prosthetic leg.

At that moment, the thought of waiting to sign this lawyer on to our team just didn't make sense. Pieces had been falling perfectly into place, and it seemed as though any further discussion would have put procrastination in place of wisdom. I looked across the room at Nicole and she instinctively knew what was going through my mind without saying a word.

"I think this is the guy you need to hire, Dad," she said. "He seems to know what he's talking about, and as attorneys go, trust me; this guy is for real."

"You're right, Nic," I said.

When Bob came back into the room, I told him that he was the guy we wanted on our side. He pulled out the agreement and showed me where to sign, and just like that, we had our own personal legal representation. There were no fees to pay up front, and there were no strings attached. He was at my disposal, and the feeling was empowering. I felt shielded.

He thanked us for our confidence in his ability to do the right thing, we shook hands, and he left.

The tension drained from every muscle in my body as an almost euphoric feeling of relief filled my mind. All I wanted was to have our life back, and it sounded as though we had found the advocate who could hand-deliver it to our front door. I didn't care about being rich. Nevertheless, my imagination began to spool up images of comfortable surroundings beyond our wildest dreams. Was it possible that Carole and I were destined to wind up independently wealthy as a result of the compensation due us for damages?

Surely, I thought, *if Stella can successfully sue a fast-food chain for millions of dollars after dumping hot coffee into her own lap, we should be financially set for life!*

Suddenly the retirement riddle seemed to have been solved. When this was over, we would never want for anything ever again. That's what I thought, anyway.

Like a driving rain landing on a leaky roof, reality would slowly seep through the cracks and saturate my brain with feelings of desperation and doom. We didn't know it at the time, but what we were facing was a long, drawn-out, bitter battle—one that without a competent attorney we would surely have lost.

I never regretted signing that agreement with Bob. He did as good a job as anyone could expect, and he was fair with us. I cursed the system and thanked that lawyer time and again for his counseling, perseverance, and in-depth knowledge of Michigan's insurance-driven laws. To this day I believe God brought Bob through our front door to stand in the gap against a brazen insurance bureaucracy.

CHAPTER 13

COMFORTABLY NUMB

—ɯ—

I continued losing weight during those first three weeks following the crash. By the time we made the trek to Beaumont for surgery on my ankle on Monday morning, the sixteenth of July, another fifteen pounds had disappeared. None of my clothing fit me anymore. Pain medication and stress had rendered food unappealing to me, and the negative side effects of an anemic appetite had become obvious to anyone who knew me. Staring back at me in the mirror was a gaunt, sickly man with a furrowed brow and the look of desperate intensity. Ironically, weight loss actually lifted my spirits. The bathroom scale had not stopped at 135 pounds for me since the day I received my high school diploma forty years earlier.

Lack of sleep combined with my slim and trim body, however, did nothing to enhance my appearance. My foot ached constantly, and those broken ribs made it impossible to get comfortable. I would sit in the recliner with the bum leg propped up on a chair in front of me and watch TV until I passed out from boredom or fatigue. Pain medication was probably doubling as a sleep aid, but short catnaps were the best I could hope for.

In spite of my weakened condition, nothing stood in the way of me going through with the scheduled foot operation. Or so I thought.

At 7:00 a.m., I was lying on a gurney inside William Beaumont Hospital, being prepped for surgery. The young doctor from West

Bloomfield who had reportedly written a chapter in the book on procedures to fix shattered ankles was supposed to have been preparing to peel back the skin and save my foot. Unfortunately, because of some sort of scheduling error, my doctor was also on call to staff the emergency room that day.

Around two o'clock that afternoon, the young surgeon entered pre-op and sent everyone else out of the room. Then he sat down in a chair next to the gurney and started explaining why it had been such a long wait.

"I'm really sorry it's taking so long to get you into the OR," he said.

"That's okay, Doc. I'm doing all right."

"For some reason," he said, "the hospital scheduled me to cover the ER today. Wouldn't you know, I've been dealing with two patients who seem determined to bleed to death in spite of my efforts."

"Busy day, huh?"

"Yes," he said, "and it doesn't look as though things are going to lighten up anytime soon."

"Do you think you'll still have time to work on my foot today?" I asked.

"There is a possibility we can get you in today, but it's going to be a while," he said. "I'm trying to stabilize those two patients who came through the ER this morning. I can't get started on you until I'm certain they're out of danger. Once we start on your foot, I don't want to be interrupted."

That doctor was obviously under a lot of pressure.

"We have a couple of options," he said. "We can keep you here for a few more hours and hope to get you into the operating room, or we can reschedule your procedure for the day after tomorrow."

The day after tomorrow, I thought to myself. *I wonder how that affects the odds of saving the foot.*

"If we reschedule the procedure," he said, "you can either stay here at the hospital or we can send you home and check you back in on the day of the surgery."

It was going to be at least another four hours before he might be able to fit me in, and I could see that he was already exhausted.

"Well, Doc," I said, "thanks for taking the time to explain the situation. But please don't apologize for the delay."

A tired smile came across his face.

"You've already had a long day," I said. "If you think waiting a couple more days to work on my foot is the thing to do, then let's reschedule."

He seemed relieved. That doctor acted as though he needed my blessing before he could go back to work and save someone else's life.

"Send me home," I said. "As long as I am able to travel, there's no need for me to take up space in a hospital bed. I would feel better about this if you finished taking care of those other patients in the emergency room and then went home to get some rest."

"Thank you for understanding," he said.

I silently thanked God for the doctor's protective hand and then thanked the doctor for having left me alone in a place where I had finally been able to get some sleep. The painkillers and quiet, caring environment had relieved my aching ribs and relaxed the tense muscles in my leg for the first time since I had been released from St. Mary's.

The procedure was rescheduled for Wednesday, two days later. Nicole made a few phone calls and then loaded me into the car and took me back home that night. The pain pump was still strapped to my side with an attached morphine drip inserted into my thigh to desensitize nerves in my foot.

Two days later we relaunched the mission, arriving back at William Beaumont Hospital shortly before eight o'clock in the morning. My sedated body was finally wheeled into the operating room that afternoon. The surgeons spent the next five and a half hours repositioning bone fragments and inserting seven titanium screws at various angles to hold the two sections of the talus together.

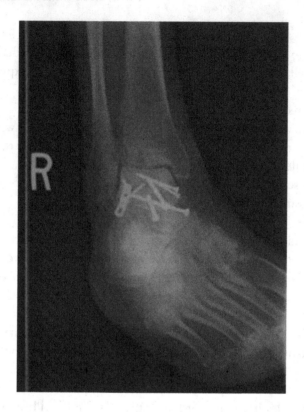

By the end of that day, my foot had finally been reassembled and the waiting game had begun.

When I finally regained consciousness, Roger, one of my cousins, was standing at the foot of the bed. What a welcome sight he was!

Roger shared a lot of detail from his conversation with the surgeon, but the only piece of information that really stuck was that the doctor had expressed concern over the success of the operation. He went so far as to tell Roger that had I been a smoker there would have been a zero chance of saving the foot. Blood circulation in the ankle had been that sparse. The doctor was very worried that damage to bone tissue from lack of blood flow meant the surgery might have been a waste of time. Even if the bones healed, my mobility would be seriously limited. Amputation remained a very real possibility.

Curiously, nothing Roger said sounded all that urgent. It wasn't so much that I didn't care about what the doctor said; I had just lost the ability to comprehend. Because of heavy painkillers in my system that the doctor had prescribed, compounded by the lingering effects of anesthesia, my capacity for grasping the concept of severity or long-term impact had disintegrated. Medication also anesthetized the emotional pain I felt at having been separated from my wife, my life, and everything in between.

As though I were drifting through time, semiconscious thoughts brought back images of dusk on the shores of Lake Huron. In my mind's eye I found myself gazing across a vast, flat body of water void of any landscape. Sky blended with waves, and both disappeared into the haze where a horizon should have been. My tired body had been set adrift without compass or paddle, and my weary mind had become blissfully disengaged.

Like that song by Pink Floyd that tells about a heroin-induced euphoria, I had become comfortably numb. Such was life for the next two days. On Friday, July 20, my daughter brought me back home to stay. I took a couple of pain pills, crawled onto my makeshift chair-bed in the family room, and went down for the count.

CHAPTER 14
LIVING ON MEATLOAF

—◊—

An old high school teacher shared a bit of wisdom just before I headed off for my freshman year in college.

"You will never fully understand what being on your own is all about," he said, "until you run out of toothpaste."

Truer words had never been spoken.

My loss of companionship following the accident created more than an emotional void. Carole's role in our partnership became crystal clear to me when I was forced to fend for myself. I had taken her so much for granted! Learning to live without her was very similar to the way a person continues absentmindedly flipping the light switch during a power outage.

The first real sign of solitude appeared in the form of an empty cookie jar. Almost simultaneously, the last drop of milk was gone, the last slice of bread had been toasted, and the final roll of toilet paper had been used.

I wasn't just running out of stuff, though. Things weren't getting done around the house either. Piles of dirty laundry accumulated, and stuff remained lying where it had been randomly tossed. Cleaning, cooking, doing the laundry, and shopping were things I had never had to worry about. Those were Carole's chores, and she had always done them so seamlessly that it never occurred to me how desperate things could become if she were suddenly no longer around to do them. Without my wife's finishing touch, our home slowly transformed into little more than living quarters. Lord, had I been spoiled!

With all of Carole's responsibilities suddenly dumped in my lap, the concept of survival gave free time a whole new meaning. I discovered the stay-at-home mom's frustration.

"So, what have you been doing all day while I was at work?" asks the man of the house.

"Oh, nothing," responds the wife. "Just polishing my nails and watching the children play."

How insanely out of touch those Hollywood scriptwriters had been! This wasn't TV land, and my name wasn't Ward Cleaver. This was the real deal.

Four weeks had passed since our crash. One by one, most of those friends who had been helping take care of things left me to fend for myself. I went into survival mode. As a crippled man, adapting to a bachelor's life required a little creativity mixed with a lot of compromise.

Food was priority number one. It had become obvious to me that the sink would be caked with soap scum if someone didn't clean it out once in a while, but a dirty sink did not qualify as a life-threatening condition. Gross, maybe, but I could live with a dirty sink. My hands were full just learning how to get through the day without going hungry. Shopping for groceries presented some logistical issues, but the whole idea of keeping the pantry stocked was moot. I wasn't a cook. Bread, milk, peanut butter, and jam defined the extent of my culinary skills. As food supplies dwindled, my daily diet gradually evolved into the one-meal-a-day restaurant plan. As long as I had a ride, I could find a place to eat.

During one of her many visits, my sister had baked a meatloaf and left it in the refrigerator for me to nibble on. That tasty dish would probably have stretched into four weeks' worth of sandwiches if Rhonda hadn't thrown the last quarter of it into the garbage can when I wasn't looking.

"You have food in the refrigerator that is starting to spoil," Rhonda said as she passed through the family room one afternoon.

"Yeah, I suppose I should clean that out," I said.

"I already threw a bunch of it into the garbage," she said.

"You didn't throw out that leftover meatloaf, did you?" I asked.

"Yes, I did," she said. "It had green-and-white fuzzy stuff growing all over the top of it."

"Yeah, I know it did, but all I had to do was scrape that part off before I threw it in the microwave!"

She gasped. "You were still eating that?"

"Sure I was," I said. "I just added a little extra ketchup to cover up the taste."

Rhonda nearly gagged when I shared that little insight. I guess it was just one of those "guy" things. I had eaten a lot of stuff that looked worse than that when I had traveled on the road with other musicians. In retrospect, it was probably a miracle that I had not keeled over from food poisoning.

Losing the use of one leg required some serious mental and physical adjustments. Simple tasks became difficult chores. Balancing on one leg while attempting to brush my teeth or comb my hair, for example, presented an interesting challenge. Although I could put no weight on the right foot, the rest of that leg from the knee up was still useable. Standing on the left leg while using a chair to bear weight on my right knee freed both hands and solved the balancing issue.

Numerous everyday gadgets we have all taken for granted had become minor obstacles. Handles were rarely in the right place. Seats were often at the wrong height. Doors to public places opened hard and inconveniently slammed shut with perilous persistence. Adjusting and adapting to the environment required twice the normal level of energy.

Anyone debating the necessity for handicap-accessible facilities should try making his way unassisted through a buffet line with a pair of crutches and one unusable leg. The experience will provide a whole new appreciation for the aggravation an amputee endures daily. Our family had befriended numerous athletes with missing limbs through Dad's affiliation with adaptive sports and his winter snow skiing activity. Amputees had a name for people who still had all of their limbs attached. They called us TABS: temporarily able-bodied souls. As was the case with my father and his missing leg, I had no choice but to adapt; so in the wake of the example he and his fellow skiers had set, I pressed forward.

Crawling up and down the stairs on my hands and knees was easy enough, but slithering across the floor to get to and from the stairs would not do. Maneuvering through the house in the wheelchair was mostly a matter of making it through the door jambs without accidentally tearing off the molding, but hauling that thing up and down the stairs so I could get around on the other three levels was not going to happen. The wheelchair remained on the ground floor entryway level, providing convenient mobility throughout the family room, bathroom, and laundry room. A pair of crutches or a walker placed at the top of each staircase provided sufficient mobility to avoid being stranded elsewhere throughout the house. Good strategy!

The next challenge was figuring out how to haul things up and down the stairs while crawling on hands and knees. Lifting with one hand while maintaining my balance with the other was tricky. Shifting the load one step at a time was possible so long as the items I carried weren't too cumbersome. Seriously diminished strength coupled with constant pain in both shoulders had become the limiting factor.

Personal hygiene presented the most formidable of obstacles. Prior to the accident, my morning routine had always included a hot shower. With a leg that had become nothing more than dead weight, climbing in or out of the bathtub had proven to be impossible. Balancing on one leg in the shower was entirely out of the question. In fact, just crawling up and down two flights of stairs to get to and from the master bathroom, where the shower was located, had become a ridiculous challenge. Somehow the half-bath on the same floor as the family room, where I spent most of my time, needed to be converted into something with a little more utility.

Rummaging through the laundry room, I found several plastic pans Carole had stashed, and under the sink was a stack of old bath towels that she had relegated to the rag bin. I dragged the stuff out of storage and piled it neatly on the countertop in the tiny little bathroom off the family room. After several trips up and down two flights of stairs on my hands and knees, all of my personal toilet articles were within reach. I made one trip down the concrete steps into the basement to retrieve a folding chair, and finally the new makeshift bathing facility was complete.

With a little experimenting and a lot of mopping up, I learned the art of bathing in the bathroom sink with a washcloth while seated in a folding chair. The first few attempts consumed a lot of towels just in keeping the flood on the linoleum bathroom floor from migrating into the family room carpet. Washing and drying the soaked and dirty rags and towels became a daily ritual. Fortunately the laundry room was just around the corner on the same level as my modified bathroom, so doing the laundry was somewhat convenient.

Washing my hair was a little more of an ordeal. The only place suitable for the task turned out to be the kitchen sink. There was simply no other place in the house where I could put my head under running water while balancing on one leg. The faucet had a detachable wand, so the kitchen doubled as a makeshift hair salon. Every morning I crawled up the stairs with a couple of towels and a bottle of shampoo tucked under my arm. Washing, rinsing, and drying my hair took less than five minutes. Cleaning up the mess afterward was a different story.

One morning while my sister, Shirl, sat on the deck outside the kitchen window with a book in her lap, I worked my way upstairs and proceeded to shampoo my hair. Halfway through the process, the detachable wand came unhooked from the retractable hose inside the faucet head. There I stood, my hair full of soapsuds and the wand in my hand, with water gushing all over the place from the hose. Mercifully I managed to shut the water off before the kitchen flooded. Thanks to my sister's support, both my hair and the kitchen countertops were squeaky clean after the mess had been mopped up. After a couple of trips on hands and knees down the concrete steps and into the basement to retrieve the necessary tools from a box of wrenches, I managed to repair the hose fitting and reattach the wand. If only I could have tackled other maintenance and upkeep issues around the house as successfully!

Because it had been such a hot, dry summer, our lawn required very little attention. Still, the yard was looking seedier by the day from buckhorn and broadleaf weeds sprouting out of control. Helplessly watching my beautiful yard deteriorate was very discouraging. Our neighbor had promised to keep an eye on the fishpond by the patio, but the circulating pump soon burned itself out as a result of neglect. Roger and Leslie, the recipients of the concert tickets Carole and I had purchased, became our unsolicited caretakers. Leslie tended to the flowers, and Roger replaced the pond pump and then kept up a daily vigil to prevent any further damage.

My sister spent many days and nights watching over me. My daughter drove me back and forth to Hurley nearly every day, and Roger and Leslie were at our house at least once a day, every day, keeping an eye on the yard and anything else around the house that needed attention. Friends from around the community stopped by to visit and ensure my needs were being met. The owner of the local country club sent his crew to our house with mowing equipment several times to groom our lawn. Neighbors raked the leaves for me. My brothers and sisters from the VFW and Ladies Auxiliary baked goodies and brought treats to the house. People from several local church congregations dropped off gifts and various dishes. Cards, letters of encouragement, and cash donations arrived daily through the mail.

Living alone was a challenge, but the truth is that I was never truly alone. God, my daughter, my family, and my friends were with me daily. Help came from people and places I would never have dreamed. It was humbling to be the recipient of such support, compassion, and generosity.

Never would it be possible for one person to pay back even a portion of the lifesaving support that was so generously sent my way. I silently vowed to pay it forward every chance I got.

CHAPTER 15
CONFLICT

—◊◊◊—

Carole's stay at Hurley had originally been projected to last six months or longer. In spite of her aggressive rate of recovery, we had heard nothing to suggest that she might have been released sooner, so we were prepared for the long haul. When we showed up at the hospital for our daily visit on Thursday, July 26, a little over four weeks after the accident, Sherrie met us at the door.

"The doctor has asked to schedule a meeting with the therapists and the family to review and evaluate Carole's progress," she said.

We had been asked to pick a time for the meeting, but because I sensed this was going to be a very important session, I wanted to include our son Jason. I needed to find out what would most conveniently fit his work schedule, so I told Sherrie I would get back with her the following day. That night I waited up for Jason. When he returned home from work, I told him about the meeting, but he offered no response. The next morning I asked him again and reiterated the fact that I had to give the hospital staff a decision that day.

Jason appeared to have become uninterested in his mother's condition, although I knew that wasn't the case. Nevertheless, his visits were noticeably infrequent and his mother had begun asking about him. I sensed something was bothering him, but he didn't seem to want to talk. My son never was much of a conversationalist, so when we did talk, the discussions were usually short and one-sided. Jason rarely shared his feelings, plans, or experiences with his mother or me, and even when he did, it was typically only after one of us had goaded it out of him. There was a distance that had developed between the two of us that I had never quite been able to understand. The accident seemed to have widened that gap.

I pressed Jason for an answer, trying to explain that his sister and I wanted him to be a part of the decision process. That only seemed to annoy him all the more. Finally he told me that going to a meeting at Hurley in the afternoon would interfere with his work schedule and attending a morning meeting would interfere with his workout plans at the community exercise room.

Interfere with his workout plans! I thought to myself. *He sure doesn't seem to care much about his mother's future.*

Under unbearable stress and totally out of patience, I went ballistic. My inept attempt at including our estranged son in the decision-making process ended in a serious disagreement. I said angry things to Jason that should never have been said, and there was no taking those words back. Worse yet was the notion that he seemed okay with the fact that I was upset and gave no indication that he was hurting too. It seemed as though he had made up his mind that a relationship with his father wasn't worth the effort.

All I could do was retreat, sobbing like a spanked child, crawling backward on hands and knees down the stairs and into the family room. I was light-headed, nauseated, and lost in an emotional free fall while blind bitterness and pain consumed the cavernous emptiness inside. I had failed miserably in my attempt to bring Jason into the decision process. Everything I had said to him in anger had effectively severed the few remaining strands that held together any semblance of a relationship between us.

Why didn't they just leave me on the highway to die? I thought to myself. *There wasn't any pain. Why did I have to wake up?*

"Distraught" does not come close to describing the way I felt. Jason's raw, humiliating rejection had left an indelible scar. Later that day, on our way to visit Carole at Hurley, I shared that horrible experience with Nicole.

"I feel as though I have become more of a burden to you and your brothers than any of you care to handle," I said.

"That's not true, Dad," she said.

"Regardless, Nicole, you've made some serious sacrifices to take care of me. I totally understand if you need to move on with your life and leave me to take care of things on my own."

"Dad, how are you going to do anything on your own? You can't drive, and you can't walk. You need someone to help you. I'm not going to just walk away and abandon you."

"Thanks, Nic," I said, looking away to hide the tears in my eyes.

"If Jason doesn't want to be a part of the process, we'll just pick a time to meet with the hospital staff and go without him," she said. "I don't agree with the way he's handling this thing, but there's nothing either of us can do about it."

Regardless, Jason's cold detachment had killed something inside me, and my heart ached. After that demoralizing episode, he became even more distant, coming in late every night and going straight to his room without saying a word. The following morning he would rush out of the house without so much as a good-bye. I felt like the unwanted roommate. Any attempt to reach out felt like crossing the line, so I simply gave him his space and left him alone.

Thank God, my daughter stood by me. As difficult as it must have been for her, she did her level best to meet my needs and accommodate my every wish.

—⁂—

On Monday, July 30, during the family meeting with the doctor and his staff, Nicole and I received the news that Carole was scheduled for discharge from the hospital on Tuesday of the following week, August 7, only six weeks after the accident. We were elated. It was a miracle Carole was even alive. Now she was being released after a few weeks instead of the six months that had been predicted. I felt like calling everyone and having a celebration, but the doctor was quick to point out that Carole's imminent discharge did not mean she had been cured.

"Your wife is still suffering from posttraumatic amnesia," he said. "She really isn't ready to be set free."

"Then why is she being released from the hospital if she's not cured?" I asked.

"Because your medical insurance does not cover neurological care," he said.

My mood slipped from euphoric to panic-stricken. And I was livid. The insurance company, not the physician, was dictating the extent of Carole's care. Suddenly I was faced with either taking my wife home with me or having her transferred to a brain rehabilitation facility at the expense of everything we owned. The medical insurance company—the money side of the medical care system—was forcing the hospital to throw Carole into the street before she had been healed. She could walk and talk, but she could not function as an independent individual. Injuries not visible to the naked eye were obviously insignificant to those responsible for making her whole.

That was my first prickly encounter with the gangs that identify themselves as the medical insurance industry. Fortunately I had no idea what bureaucratic nightmares were in store, or I may have imploded from fear, anxiety, and depression, spinning helplessly toward that black hole of surrender.

"Isn't there something you can say that will convince the insurance company that releasing her is the wrong thing to do?" I pleaded.

"They already know that she cannot function without someone attending to her needs," he said. "Physically there is nothing further the hospital needs to do. Her injuries are healing nicely. As far as your medical insurance company is concerned, they've fulfilled their obligation."

"Then what am I supposed to do?" I asked. "I can't take care of her in my condition."

"You can either take your wife home or follow our advice and have her transferred to a neurological rehabilitation center," he said. "Either way, she cannot stay at Hurley."

The thought of meeting Carole's needs while confined to a wheelchair became instantly overwhelming. I had no qualms about selling everything if necessary to pay for her recovery, but taking care of her on my own presented a real dilemma.

Our attorney had briefed us about in-home attendant care, but the information was useless without someone to walk me through the process. Asking for help had always been so foreign to me that the concept never clicked. In retrospect I know that the no-fault insurance carrier should have assigned someone to oversee our case and ensure that our needs were being met. I never clearly understood why our attorney did not go to bat for us.

If not for my sister, daughter, and anyone else willing to pitch in and help, I would have been totally at a loss. Where were the people who should have been responsible for such details? Where was the expert advice when we needed it most? Even though we were both eligible for assistance, there was clearly none provided.

I reentered the conversation as the psychiatrist continued through his list of neurological rehabilitation centers located around the state of Michigan. His presentation was intended to put us at ease and to offer alternatives for Carole's continued care. The trouble was that every place he referred to was more than a two-hour drive from home, and I was unable to drive.

Our daughter interrupted the doctor's recitation.

"What about the Lighthouse?" she asked.

There was a moment of silence as though the doctor had never heard of that facility.

"I'm talking about the Lighthouse Neurological Rehabilitation Center, located in Caro," she said. "Is that on the list of approved facilities?"

Well, of course! I had been so preoccupied by this latest twist of events that the Lighthouse as an option had never crossed my mind. Had Jason's job search not landed him a position on their staff, we would likely never have been aware of that facility.

"As a matter of fact," the doctor said, "the Lighthouse would be an excellent facility for Carole."

"Then why don't we take her there?" I asked.

"They have quite a waiting list for inpatient care," he said. "Honestly, you'll be lucky if you can even schedule an interview with them, let alone have your wife admitted. You're certainly welcome to try, but I have to remind you that regardless of where your wife is taken for continued neurological care, you will still be faced with the responsibility of paying for it."

Walls were closing in. The doctor's report came as a warning to brace for impact. Already reeling from physical trauma, it seemed as though the situation was plummeting toward emotional and economic ruin as well.

Another collision was looming, and just like the motorcycle crash, this too appeared to be unavoidable.

CHAPTER 16
THE LIGHTHOUSE

—⁂—

The doctor's news regarding Carole's discharge and recommendations for ongoing care left me with the feeling that I was about to be dragged through another detour I would have preferred to avoid. Little by little, any scrap of control I imagined I had was being eroded by someone else calling the shots, and it had become obvious with each passing day how insignificant my input was. It felt as though an invisible force was pushing us toward an unavoidable crash landing.

The salt in the wound was the battle line beginning to appear on the horizon. It was amazing how an insurance company could be so callous. To limit their financial exposure, those bean counters and adjusters representing our medical insurance carrier actively asserted their authority over my wife's welfare. It suddenly became apparent that there was, in fact, a dollar value secretly placed on human life, quality of life, and the extent of care to which we as policyholders were allowed, regardless of the degree of care needed to effect the cure.

Proper medical care simply costs more than insurance companies are willing to spend, but they sure don't tell that to the policyholder while they're collecting the money in premiums! The real likelihood of going broke and losing everything while Carole was stashed in some faraway facility had seriously dashed any hope I had of getting through the ordeal unscathed. It was a desperate situation.

The day after receiving the news of Carole's impending release, I tried contacting our lawyer for an opinion. His receptionist said that he would be out of the office for the next two weeks.

"He usually checks in every day or two," she said. "I'll be sure to tell him that you called."

"If he does," I said, "please tell him this is urgent."

Ten minutes later, Pastor Michael Hollenbeck stopped by the house for a visit. We talked about the dilemma—my fear of losing my wife altogether in a system run by a bureaucracy that seemed unable to do the right thing.

Michael suggested we call the Lighthouse anyway. Without a moment's hesitation, he picked up the telephone, dialed the phone number from memory, and in less than a minute was talking to Connie, the Lighthouse's administrative director. To my surprise, he was able to arrange a meeting with her for that very afternoon.

Michael cancelled his afternoon engagements, piled my wheelchair and me into his van, and off we headed to the Lighthouse in Caro. It happened so fast my head spun with thoughts, questions, and a nagging fear of rejection.

Around four o'clock that afternoon, I sat in the conference room at the Lighthouse with Michael by my side, sharing my story with Connie. It was extremely difficult for me to maintain my composure while sharing details of the accident, the injuries, and the medical and financial crisis we faced.

To confirm some dates during the meeting, I pulled out the wall calendar I had been using as a date book. Connie's eyes went wide, and she gasped.

"Where on earth did you find that calendar?" she asked.

"My car insurance agent gave it to me last December," I said. "Why do you ask?"

"Look at the photographs on that calendar," she said with amazement.

Until that very moment I had not realized that next to each month were photographs of lighthouses from the Michigan shores of the Great Lakes.

Connie then asked me to spell my last name. She opened her folder and began running her finger down a list of names.

"You must know a lot of people," she said. "You and your wife have been on our prayer list since your accident occurred in June."

I told her that our youngest son, Jason, had started working at the Lighthouse in March, five months earlier.

"He's probably the one who put our names on the list. We didn't even know this place existed prior to Jason finding a job here. If he had found a job somewhere else, I might be having this conversation with someone in Dearborn or Grand Rapids. Those places are more than two or three hours from our home. It has been hard enough finding transportation to Hurley to visit my wife, and that's only a one-hour drive. The Lighthouse is twenty-five minutes from my front door. My son works here, and my daughter works at the courthouse a mile down the road, so finding a ride to be with my wife would certainly be no problem if she were to be admitted here."

Again I swallowed the lump that had formed in my throat. It seemed childish to be so emotional, but the thought of my wife being taken somewhere that was too far away for regular daily visitation scared me to death. I was concerned that she might be traumatized by yet another strange environment where the care she was supposed to receive might not be so good if someone from the family wasn't there regularly to observe.

I also had visions of months or maybe years spent alone at home. More than once the thought had crossed my mind that this might have been God's way of preparing me for the inevitable end. Carole was not out of the woods. Her life-threatening injuries and her neurological rehabilitation were projected to take six to eight months, maybe longer. Her release from Hurley was happening several months sooner than anyone had thought, but that was because the insurance company, not the doctor, had dictated the end of her stay.

Connie probably sensed that my emotion had been heavily spiced with desperation. She was reassuring and supportive, but I was so distressed by the end of the interview that I was begging for help.

"There should be no problem paying for Carole's treatment," I told her in a quavering voice. "Our medical carrier has informed us they do not pay for neurological rehabilitation, but with a line of equity on our home already established, there should be no problem coming up with the money to make this work. I'll sell the airplane and the Corvette if that's what it takes. I just want to make sure my wife has every possible chance to get well."

Connie set down her notebook, sat back in her chair, and calmly folded her hands on the table in front of her. Turning toward me with a look of comforting compassion, she looked squarely into my eyes and smiled.

"Let's not worry about how we're going to pay for this right now," she said softly. "Let's just see what we can do to get your wife the help she needs."

Then she closed her files and rose to her feet, politely signaling that our meeting was over.

"We don't have any beds available at the moment, but we may soon have a vacancy at one of our houses here on campus," she said with confidence.

Turning toward an associate who had attended the meeting, she asked, "Isn't one of our patients about to be discharged from Mission Point?"

"I'll have to check to be sure," the staff member responded, "but I think you may be right."

"If you have a few minutes," Connie said as she turned back toward Michael and me, "I'll take you to Mission Point and introduce you to the team that runs that house."

It sounded as though we were taking a drive to visit an outpost somewhere in the marshlands of the Saginaw Bay. I had mixed emotions regarding the thought of taking my wife to a rehabilitation facility. It was a relief to have found a place close enough to visit, but it also felt like trying to find a good home for an unwanted pet. We left the conference room, piled into our vehicles, and followed Connie around the administration building and onto a paved street that took us through the center of forty acres of mowed hayfields. I later learned that those hayfields were part of the Lighthouse campus.

Next to a large grove of trees on the opposite side of those hayfields was a small subdivision of single-story ranch-style homes situated along both sides of a winding, paved side street. Any unsuspecting visitor driving through that section of the grounds may have thought he had wandered into a small housing development. There was nothing to suggest those houses were anything but another private residential section of Caro, Michigan.

We pulled into a parking spot next to the home that had been named Mission Point. After I crawled out of the vehicle and into my wheelchair, the three of us followed the sidewalk leading up to a large porch built onto the front of the house.

From the porch, the view overlooked a freshly mowed lawn that gently sloped down and away. Near the bottom of the slope, where the grass met with the weeds along the edge of the vacant lot next door, was a small garden plot. Some of the residents had planted vegetables to eat and flowers to decorate their rooms. An elderly gentleman was standing next to the garden with a hose in his hand, and a young man was standing at his side. The scene could have been a life-size re-creation of a Norman Rockwell painting portraying a guy helping his grandfather water the garden. The old guy was a resident. The young man at the gentleman's side was a staff member assigned to watch over him that afternoon.

The porch had been partially enclosed with hip-high planter walls along the perimeter and a roof with large, overhanging eaves to protect visitors and residents from the sun and rain. A two-man gliding bench sat at one end of the porch. Comfortable outdoor chairs situated in groupings had been interspersed throughout the remaining area, allowing ample room for wheelchairs to maneuver among the furnishings. From that vantage point, everything within our view gave the impression that we were walking into Grandma and Grandpa's house.

Once inside, I noticed a distinct change in atmosphere. It was a pleasant environment with a warm, homey feel, but the spacious layout was definitely designed to accommodate special needs.

The front door opened into a large, open living room. All of the residents could gather in that room to watch the big-screen TV or to be entertained by musicians, speakers, or most any other sort of group activity. The room had been comfortably furnished with couches, upholstered chairs, and recliners, and there was plenty of space among the furnishings for those residents who were confined to wheelchairs.

The kitchen and dining facilities occupying about a third of the front half of the house had been partially separated from the living room area by a dividing wall. The house staff included a nutritionist who prepared the meals for each individual patient's diet. At designated times during the day, all of the residents gathered together around the community dining table for breakfast, lunch, supper, and a bedtime snack. Between meals the dining table doubled as a place for residents and guests to play checkers or board games, or just sit and visit. A hallway dividing the house into two halves led from the rear corner of the living room area to a door that exited out the rear of the building. Along that hallway, the house staff maintained an office next to a large commercial-grade laundry room.

To the best of their individual abilities, with assistance from staff members all residents were expected to take care of their own laundering and share in the housecleaning chores. Interestingly these living conditions were an extension of the daily therapy each of the ambulatory residents underwent. All of the residents shared the hope, however remotely possible, that someday they would graduate to living on their own.

Located in the rear central half of the house were two huge handicap-accessible bathroom facilities. They had been designed for efficient cleaning and sterilization as well as accessibility and had been equipped to accommodate every conceivable physical disability. Private bedrooms were situated along the outside walls on both ends of the house, with windows overlooking the outdoor landscape. Each of those rooms had been custom furnished according to individual residents' needs.

The cozy room Connie had in mind for Carole was located in the rear of the house and had its own private closet, chest of drawers, desk, and chair. The furnishings included a comfortable lounge chair for visitors who wanted to spend time with her in the privacy of her room.

Mission Point wasn't home, but as group home environments go, it was about as close to home as anyone could wish for. The noninstitutional atmosphere was comforting, and the staff was accommodating almost to a fault. It certainly dispelled any images I might have had about a brain-rehabilitation facility.

Okay, I thought to myself. *The worst-case scenario is a temporary stay at some place too far away to see my wife until the Lighthouse can make room for her.*

That day marked a turning point in my life. What had started out as a morning filled with overpowering discouragement ended with a sense of satisfying victory. With Mike's help I had launched a little damage control and, in the process, had begun to learn some things about myself. Although the stuff we owned was near and dear, I had no reservations about liquidating everything to have my wife back home, even if home turned out to be somewhere other than the one we called our own. A slow change in priorities had begun to leave a trail that seemed to indicate that I was well on my way to a clean, fresh start.

If only my wife could join me, I thought to myself.

CHAPTER 17

ANNIVERSARY 37

—◦◦◦—

Wednesday, August 1, the day after my conference with Connie at the Lighthouse, I shared with Carole the details of our meeting, the visit to Mission Point, and everything I had learned about the facility. She seemed remotely interested but was probably unable to comprehend.

That same afternoon, Nicole, Rodney, and our friend Kevin rendezvoused with my sister Shirl in the day room at Hurley to help Carole and me celebrate our thirty-seventh wedding anniversary. Carole was pleased to see all of us, but she was about as interested in having a party as she was in the news of her possible transfer to the Lighthouse. She did not care about events or milestones.

Like a distracted child in her own little world, my wife zeroed in on the food my sister Shirl had brought with her. Carole may have lost the ability to express hope or experience joy, but she certainly had not lost her appetite. After gorging herself on fried chicken, Carole devoured the chocolate cake Shirl had baked. A short while later, we were politely informed by one of the hospital staff that chocolate cake was not on Carole's diet plan. We were told the chocolate conflicted with her medications. Oops! Oh well.

Shirl had also brought some homemade zucchini bread, so she sliced it and served it as a second dessert.

"This is amazing," Kevin said. "It tastes more like cake than bread."

"It's zucchini bread," Shirl said.

"Kah-Role," Kevin said, "you've made zucchini bread before, haven't you?"

"I think so," Carole replied.

"So what's in zucchini bread?" I asked.

Kevin and Carole looked at each other wide-eyed and openmouthed. Together they burst out laughing hysterically and answered my question in unison almost as though they had rehearsed their response.

"Zucchini!" they said, and then they laughed even harder.

A preadolescent behavior had surfaced. It was almost as though parts of my wife had reverted back to the mannerisms and sensibility of a nine-year-old girl.

I had hauled our dominoes to the hospital that day in the event Carole might enjoy a game. After Shirl and Nicole cleared the food away, my wife seemed eager to play, so we gathered our chairs around the table and set up our racks. Before the end of the first round, it was obvious that we would be playing by a new set of rules that Carole was making up as we went along.

Carole had adopted a rather blithe attitude. Nothing seemed to make her genuinely happy or sad. It was refreshing to watch her laugh about things, especially those things that otherwise might have been soberly serious issues. But it wasn't the real Carole we were seeing. Her emotions had flatlined. Regardless of the topic, Carole's colorful replies were the same—probably best described as reflexive responses. It was obvious that her interaction with other people, albeit pleasant and humorous, was mostly autonomic, not necessarily logical. She never gave a blank stare. Random comments from anyone in the room would generate a rejoinder from Carole. Her level of comprehension had been dampened, but she could still carry on a conversation.

This new version of the woman I had dated in high school and then married was curiously disturbing. There was nothing threatening or particularly challenging about this strange twist in Carole's character, but I did wonder if this was the person I would be caring for through the rest of her days—a young grandmother

151

with an adolescent's intellect. Had I been involuntarily recruited for adult daycare?

It didn't matter. She was alive, we were still married, and life would go on.

The morning following our anniversary party, an associate from the attorney's office phoned to assure me that the other driver's no-fault insurance company would be responsible for paying all accident-related medical expenses not covered by our medical insurance carrier. That meant Carole's neurological rehabilitation was not going to cost us our home after all. His report brought immeasurable relief. It was like a wedding anniversary gift.

It still didn't make sense that our motorcycle insurance wasn't paying for any of the medical care, but that was the least of my concerns. The clock was ticking, and Carole's discharge from Hurley was only a few days away. I was still hoping for available space at the Lighthouse, but regardless of where the next move took us, at least I no longer had to concern myself with how I would pay for the care she needed. I was cautiously optimistic.

Unfortunately the information from our attorney's office only served to establish a false sense of security. Our attorney's associate kept hinting that we were expected to cover the cost of medical care until the auto insurance company got around to paying us back. What I did not know was that the rules, probably written by insurance lobbyists, allowed an insurance company up to two years to pay what they owed. Even if we had somehow liquidated all of our possessions at a fair price and handed over every penny collected, we would have been unable to pay off the enormous debt that had already accumulated. The total owed exceeded our material worth several times over, and ongoing medical care was far from finished. Our credit and credibility were on the line, and there wasn't a thing I could do to prevent total financial destruction.

I prayed a lot.

Father, if it is your will that our world be destroyed, please grant me the strength to bear the pain and burden of the losses we are about to suffer. Amen.

On-time payment in the mysterious world of medical funding is a radically misleading concept. The word "delinquency" is not in an adjuster's vocabulary. That would explain why so many of the cases coming through Carole's office at the courthouse involved people suing their insurance companies for nonpayment. Laws protected the insurance companies from having to pay fines, penalties, or damages for taking their sweet time coughing up the cash. The worst case for the insurance companies was a court order forcing them to pay the claim plus interest, and that didn't even equate to a slap on the wrist. In other words, the adjusters were allowed to drag their feet, and they did so with impunity.

Unbeknownst to me, everything we owned was skillfully being exposed to the vultures waiting to pick over whatever could be found to satisfy financial appetites. Battle lines were drawn between the insurance company who refused to pay, the lawyers who were taking a piece of what was being paid, and the medical billing authorities who were waiting to be paid. Those we owed had no patience for those who owed us. I sat in the middle of the war zone while collection notices piled up and creditors became increasingly impatient.

A little while after our attorney's office had called that day bearing news about medical funding, Connie called from the Lighthouse. There were still no vacancies at Mission Point, but the good news was that Carole had been approved for inpatient care and would be admitted as soon as a bed became available.

"Don't give up," she said. "A lot can happen in a week's time."

A lot has already happened, I thought to myself. *What more should I expect?*

On August 6, the day before Carole was to be released from Hurley, I received a phone call from our attorney's associate informing me that the no-fault insurance company had hired a case manager to monitor medical expenditures and oversee our recovery process. That tiny shred of optimism I had gained four days earlier vanished into thin air.

Oh, great, I thought to myself. *The insurance company won't pay for our medical care, but they sure don't have a problem hiring someone to follow us around and tighten more screws!*

CHAPTER 18

THE CAVALRY ARRIVES

—〜—

I could feel my temples start to throb from anger as I listened to the associate tell me over the telephone about this case manager person who was about to invade our lives.

"Why do I get the feeling that nobody trusts me?" I asked the associate. "I don't need somebody looking over my shoulder. Why can't the insurance company just leave us alone and focus on doing what they're supposed to do? I just want to get healed so I can get on with my life."

I was still holding my breath, waiting to hear where my wife was going to wind up once the nursing staff had involuntarily wheeled her out of the hospital in less than twenty-four hours. Having an insurance company's representative following my every move just seemed like one more obstruction thrown onto the wreckage-strewn obstacle course that I had already been forced to pick my way through.

The case manager was the person who technically should have been at our side from the very beginning, and it was the insurance company's responsibility to fill that position. In retrospect, however, I believe God had stalled the process to prevent the insurance adjusters from getting in the way of the critical care Carole and I needed in the early stages of our survival.

Officially, a case manager's job is to ensure proper care and treatment by serving as liaison between the insurance company, the medical providers, and the patient. In reality, the case manager represents an insurance company's front line of defense. Under the guise of patient care, the case manager's prime responsibility is to bend to the wishes of the one writing the checks. The insurance industry's talking heads will deny any such allegation, but my firsthand exposure suggests that the case manager's job performance is measured in terms of how deeply spending cuts can be executed without noticeably undermining the doctor's recommendations.

It seemed a bit peculiar, however, that our attorney wanted to know if there was going to be any conflict of interest with having this particular individual assigned as our case manager.

"I don't understand," I said. "What do you mean by conflict of interest?"

"Well, we have reason to believe that you already know the lady who has been assigned to handle your case," he said.

"Really?" I asked. "What's her name?"

He repeated the lady's name, but it didn't ring a bell.

"What makes you think I know this person?" I asked.

"Because she's related to the circuit-court judge your wife works for," he said. "The lady handling your case is his sister."

I didn't recognize the lady's name because the associate had given me her married name.

Of over four thousand pending cases with that insurance company, this lady, a friend of our family and sister to Carole's boss, had been randomly assigned to oversee our care, acting as an agent for an insurance company determined to minimize its expenses.

"No," I said, "I can't see any reason for concern. If anything I would think having her as our case manager would be somewhat of an advantage."

"That's what I figured," he said, "but I thought it would be a good idea to check with you to be sure."

"Do you mean we have a choice?" I asked.

"In a way, yes," he said. "But normally you just go with whomever they assign and learn to live with the decisions. If problems arise, we can file an appeal for a replacement."

"I can't imagine that happening," I said. "I sure don't see anything wrong with having a personal friend handling our affairs."

I had no sooner hung up the telephone than it rang again. This time it was Connie calling me from the Lighthouse, informing me that the room at Mission Point had just been vacated and that the staff attendants were at that moment preparing the space for Carole's arrival. Connie also informed me that because of Carole's medical condition, the folks at the Lighthouse had decided to dispatch a team with a vehicle early the next morning to transfer Carole from Hurley to the Lighthouse. Everything had fallen perfectly into place, and I was thanking God for having provided guidance for the people who had made it happen.

"By the way," Connie said before hanging up, "we just hired a new nurse to work on our night shift at the Lighthouse. She said she knows you personally and knows all about your accident."

"Really?" I asked. "How would she know me?"

"She was your attending nurse when you were at St. Mary's Hospital in Saginaw," Connie said. "You might be interested to know that she will now be assigned to care for your wife while she is residing here."

Coincidence?

CHAPTER 19
WAKING UP LONELY

—ɷ—

At eight o'clock in the morning on August 7, 2007, Nicole and I headed out the driveway for one last trip to Hurley. The drought that had turned everything to a crispy brown was finally ending as the dark, towering, cumulonimbus clouds opened up. The first rainfall we had seen since before the accident in June was coming down in buckets. It had been a long, dry, painful six weeks.

We had already cleared most of Carole's personal belongings from her room at the hospital, so there wasn't much left to do but sign the release forms and wheel her out the front door. As we rode the elevator one last time up to the sixth floor, Nicole and I exchanged comments on how strange it was going to feel visiting her mother somewhere other than at the hospital. Although it had only been a matter of a few weeks since the accident, it felt as though we had been living that daily routine for years.

The team from the Lighthouse showed up shortly after we walked into Carole's room. To my surprise, they had already orchestrated the move. I sat on the sidelines in my wheelchair, watching the crew gather my wife and her few remaining things. I then followed the entourage to the elevators, into the main lobby, and out through the front entrance, where the Lighthouse vehicle was parked.

That was the day Carole's flameout ended and her brain started recording again. I could almost see the transformation in her level of awareness taking place as she was rolled out the double doors and onto the sidewalk in front of Hurley and loaded through the side door of that little bus headed for the Lighthouse. It was as though the change in scenery had turned her memory switch back to the "on" position. Carole gazed up at the sky as though she were seeing it for the first time. She then turned her head slowly from side to side, studying the landscape around the entrance to the hospital. She lifted her arms, looked down at the wheelchair she was sitting in, and then looked up at her attendants as if to ask them what was going on. There was a look of wonderment in her eyes and her expression was that of someone trying to figure out exactly where she was and how she had gotten there.

The staff asked if I needed help getting on the bus. I had no idea family was allowed to ride along, so their question gave me pause. That moment's hesitation was interpreted as a yes, and the two Lighthouse staffers went straight to work helping me aboard.

Well, this is a fresh experience, I thought to myself.

"I'll see you at the Lighthouse, Nic!" I said to my daughter as I disappeared through the door.

Up the steps I crawled, grabbing onto anything within reach to keep from losing my balance. Sliding into the seat next to Carole, I felt like a schoolboy sitting with his girlfriend on a class field trip.

"Do you know where you are?" I asked her.

"Yes, I'm sitting here right beside you on this little bus!" she exclaimed.

"Yes, but do you know where you have been for the past month and a half or why you were there?"

"I've been in a hospital, and from what you've told me, I was brought here because we were in an accident on the motorcycle."

She had a look of curiosity mixed with resolve as she tried to piece things together. Posttraumatic amnesia continued to inhibit her ability to totally process her surroundings or circumstances, but she knew she was leaving the hospital, and that appealed to her.

"We were the victims of a hit-and-run accident," I explained, mostly for the benefit of the Lighthouse staff. "The police have caught the guy who left us on the highway. The motorcycle was wrecked, and you were airlifted from the Marlette hospital to Hurley, here in Flint."

Carole reacted as though she were hearing it all for the first time. She seemed startled by the news.

"Were you hurt?" she asked, still sounding a little puzzled.

"Yes," I replied patiently. "I was airlifted to St. Mary's. I almost lost my foot. I might still lose it. It all depends on whether or not the bones heal back together. Meanwhile I can't put any weight on it. That's why I'm using a wheelchair and crutches."

As we pulled away from Hurley, I shared details of the accident with the staff to help them better understand who Carole was and what they would be dealing with. That wasn't the first time Carole had been told where she was and how she had gotten there, but that was the day the details started to sink in. A look of mild panic washed over Carole's face. She acted as though she needed time to process the events unfolding before her eyes, so I quit talking.

Hurley Medical Center disappeared in the rearview mirror with my wife and me sitting side by side, swaying back and forth, silently watching the inner-city neighborhoods go by. The little bus with its stiff suspension rattled and bounced over the expansion cracks and potholes littering the streets as we wound our way through Flint and onto I-69. The rain had let up, and the sunlight poked through the broken layer of clouds overhead. Freshly washed landscape radiated under patches of deep-blue skies. I leaned back in the seat, contented and eager to get on with the next phase of recovery that promised to bring my wife one step closer to home. Carole seemed a bit more relaxed, so it seemed like a good time to break the silence.

"Do you remember anything about being at the hospital?" I asked.

"The only thing I remember is that Jason told me he bought Rhonda an engagement ring," she said. "Is that true, or was I just dreaming that?"

The *ring!* Of all things, Carole remembered Jason telling her about the engagement ring he had picked out for Rhonda. Six and a half weeks in the hospital and the only thing she could remember was something our son had told her that first week while she was still in a coma! Suddenly I realized that those stories about a comatose patient's level of comprehension were true. Carole's brain had been absorbing the activity around her even though she was unconscious. Recalling details related to all of that commotion might have been a whole different issue, but nevertheless she knew, albeit subconsciously.

I shared the revelation with the Lighthouse attendants, and they looked at each other without changing their expressions. Whether or not they believed Carole's recollection about Jason and the ring remained a mystery. It didn't matter. I knew her tale was true.

Carole and I spent the rest of that day's journey happily sharing light conversation with the two Lighthouse staff members, but her first night at the Lighthouse was not easy for either of us. Shortly after Carole was settled into her room at Mission Point that afternoon, Nicole and I had to hit the road. It broke my heart to leave my wife in yet another strange environment. It felt as though we were abandoning her.

As we headed for the parking lot, I turned to wave good-bye. The scene reminded me of those first days of school for each of our children as they climbed aboard the bus, found a seat, and peered back at us through the window with hesitant fear in their eyes. There sat my Carole, waving to us from her wheelchair, looking lost and forlorn. I so wanted to stay with my wife!

Around six-thirty that evening the phone rang. The call was from Carole.

"Dave," she said in a hushed tone, "come and get me."

I nearly panicked.

How in the world did she get her hands on a telephone? I wondered. *Who is supposed to be watching her?*

"Carole, I can't come and get you," I said. "I can't drive."

"I need to come home."

"I'm sorry, but you can't come home yet," I said. "I know you don't want to be there, but that's the best place for you right now."

"All right," she said.

"Are you okay?" I asked.

"No, I want to come home," she said.

"We can talk more about this when I come to visit with you tomorrow," I said.

"Okay," she said, "I'll see you tomorrow."

What a helpless feeling!

Two hours later the phone rang, and it was Carole again. She sounded anxious and a little bit scared.

"Dave, I need you to come and get me out of here," she pleaded.

"How did you get your hands on a telephone?" I asked her.

I had visions of her hiding in a closet, secretly talking on the phone like a child fearing for her life.

Don't panic, Dave, I told myself. *There has got to be a perfectly logical explanation for this.*

"My attendant gave me the phone so I could call you," she said.

"Aren't you supposed to have someone with you at all times?" I asked as calmly as possible.

"Yeah," she said. "My staff attendant is standing right here next to me. Here, you want to talk to her?"

Without hesitation, Carole handed the phone to her attendant.

"Hello?" the attendant said.

"Hi," I said. "I'm a little confused. Is there a problem?"

"Nope, everything's fine," she said. "Your wife and I are just sitting here visiting."

What's going on at that place? I wondered suspiciously. The terrified child scenario kept playing back through my mind. The brain rehabilitation phase of her recovery was either going to be really good or really bad. I was floored by the fact that my wife had been able to simply pick up the phone and call home long-distance. It caused me to wonder if anyone had been keeping an eye on her.

"Why is Carole on the phone begging me to bring her home?" I asked.

"She asked if she could call home, so I gave her the phone," the attendant said in an understanding voice. "A lot of our residents call their family members, especially when they first arrive. She's a little homesick, and we know that she would really rather be there with you. I thought it might help her get past her fear of being here if she could talk with you. She's gonna be all right. It's just going to take her a little while to get comfortable. Would you prefer not to have her call you?"

"No, of course not!" I said, backing away from my abrasive tone of voice. "Thank you for letting her call me. I just didn't know that she even had that option. Nobody told me about that part of the arrangement."

That was when I began to realize just how personalized Carole's treatment at the Lighthouse was going to be. My wife was being cared for as a resident, not as a patient. When Carole first arrived at the Lighthouse, she had been prescribed one-on-one attendant care around the clock, seven days a week. She was certainly not being neglected! As a matter of policy, the Lighthouse staff attendants were trained to accommodate a resident's every reasonable wish. Handing Carole the telephone was simply their response to her simple request.

Again I thanked God for this latest turn of events.

I choked back the tears once more as I lay in bed that night, smoothing the blankets where she should have been sleeping beside me. My ribs had healed enough to graduate from sleeping in a chair to lying flat on a mattress, but I was still alone. Saying good night to an invisible silhouette had become a nightly ritual.

Jason was nowhere to be seen, even though we were still living under the same roof. It would have been comforting to have him around to talk to during those long, lonely hours in that big, empty house, but I couldn't blame him for keeping his distance. His dad hadn't been the most pleasant person in his life.

The Lighthouse approach to patient care was the reason for Carole's accelerated rate of recovery and for my not going completely off the emotional deep end. The staff took a personal interest in both Carole and me and the life we had shared. Carole and I felt as comfortable and at-home as could be expected under the circumstances.

To my surprise, the personnel at Mission Point had also been secretly keeping a watchful eye on me. I noticed that everyone showing up to visit residents at Mission Point had been required to sign in on a visitor's log except me. On one occasion I glanced at the sign-in sheet and noticed that the staff had been signing me in and out as I came and went, but there were notes in the margins next to my name. A couple of those comments were observations that had been made regarding my activity and behavior. Judging from those comments, I believe they sensed trouble.

Carole's recovery continued in the fast lane. On the fourth or fifth day of her Lighthouse therapy sessions, Carole climbed down out of the shuttle bus and headed into the main building, dragging her walker behind her. Her therapists looked at each other, laughing. One of them turned to my wife and said, "Carole, you can probably leave the walker in your room at the house. It doesn't look like you really need it anymore."

Within a couple of weeks after her arrival, the 24/7 attendant care had been relaxed to one-on-one attendant care during waking hours. A short time later, Carole was reclassified to "group" status, which meant that she was able to get out of bed on her own and tend privately to her own personal hygiene and care. Before long she was plodding out to the kitchen in her robe and slippers in the morning, pouring her own coffee, and sitting around the table, casually visiting with the staff members.

In a repeat performance of what the staff at Hurley had experienced, Carole continued making unbelievable progress. The people at the Lighthouse could not believe what they were witnessing firsthand.

Over the course of the first couple of weeks following her transfer from Hurley, Carole commented on Jason having stopped by to pay her a visit on his way to work at one of the youth houses down the street from Mission Point.

At least he's spending some time with his mother, I thought to myself. *I sure wish he would make time for me.*

A few weeks after her arrival at the Lighthouse, Carole was taken to her neurosurgeon for a follow-up examination. When the doctor opened the door to the examining room where Carole was waiting, he apologized for interrupting her quiet conversation with the nurse. The doctor thought he had entered the wrong room until he had confirmed Carole's identity.

After a thorough examination, the doctor sat down in the chair across from Carole and let out a deep breath.

"This is amazing," he said.

The doctor leafed through Carole's file one more time and then looked her straight in the eye.

"In medical terms," he said, "I cannot explain your recovery. I didn't expect you to live, let alone walk and talk."

"Well, a lot of people have been praying for me," Carole said. "God has been taking care of me."

"I have to agree with that," the doctor said. "I can't see any reason for you to return for further examinations."

With that, the doctor whose care had been focused on Carole's most critical, life-threatening injury closed his file and, to his own amazement, signed her release and sent her back to the Lighthouse to complete her therapies.

Chapter 20

Fighting for Independence

The greatest discovery of any generation is that a human being can alter his life by altering his attitudes.

—William James

In spite of the miracle of having survived a near-death experience, I had developed a lousy attitude. Altering it had become an insurmountable task. It had always been easy to spot flaws in other people's reasoning, make suggestions, and offer ways to improve their quality of life. Why was it so difficult to follow my own advice?

There was more than enough reason to have a positive outlook. The medical care we both received had been second to none. Support from friends and family was saving us from financial ruin. Carole's recovery continued progressing at a remarkable pace, and although there was no guarantee my foot could be saved, it was nevertheless still attached to my leg. It was all great news, but not great enough to dispel the dark cloud of desperation that blocked every ray of hope as I watched the life that Carole and I had worked so hard to build slip through our fingers at an increasing speed.

Living expenses continued to pile up, and we were rapidly running out of resources. The business had been closed for nearly two months. Carole's paychecks continued to come through, but her unused paid days off were rapidly being used up. Generous gifts and donations continued arriving, but they were not enough to keep us from losing ground. Meanwhile, there had been no word from the insurance company regarding lost wages compensation, reimbursement for out-of-pocket expenses, or any of the other settlement privileges we had been promised. Our attorney only seemed mildly concerned that the wheels under the insurance machine had not yet started turning.

The growing mountain of unpaid medical bills made me laugh out loud. Even if we had sold everything we owned at fair market value, there was no way we could have covered even the cost of our stay at Hurley or St. Mary's. I had been unable to put a price tag on any of the other services rendered, so there was no way to know how many thousands of additional dollars had been spent toward our care. Without the benefit of any sort of orientation or training, the overwhelming task of deciphering medical jargon and sorting through the paperwork transgressed from taking care of unfinished business to simply trying to keep track of unfinished business.

A small, still voice in the back of my mind kept telling me to have faith that everything would work out. But the whole concept of relying on God to provide remained difficult at best. Like a cold virus that just wouldn't die, depressing thoughts hung on with a vengeance. There was no single solution because there were so many unresolved issues. Financially I was anxious, emotionally I was a wreck, and physically everything I tried to do had become a challenge.

While in Southeast Asia I came across a bronze plaque with what I assumed to be an old Chinese proverb engraved across the front. That saying pretty much described my basic philosophy on life:

> All things come to he who waits
> so long as he who waits
> works like a slave while he waits.

In other words, God could provide the shovel, but I still had to do the digging.

I was not accustomed to waiting around for things to happen, but in my physical condition, all I could do was wait. Working was out of the question. An overwhelming feeling of helpless dependency grated on my nerves. Having been raised to fend for myself, I found nothing comforting or therapeutic about surviving on someone else's charity. Sitting with my leg up all day long without doing something to earn a living was so far out of my comfort zone that sleeping through the night without nightmares became a rarity.

The unsettled confrontation I had had with Jason prior to Carole's discharge from Hurley ate away at my conscience. Mild shock waves triggered by random thoughts of our disagreement were wrecking my body. What I perceived as irreparable damage to our relationship made the muscles in my shoulders tense and caused acid in the pit of my stomach to erode any semblance of an appetite. I had slipped into a very dark place and sensed that it had become unbearable for others to be near me.

My gyro was tumbling. It felt as though I were in the cockpit, stuck in a holding pattern, low on fuel, circling the airport while waiting for air traffic control to finish their coffee break while a storm rolling in threatened to close the field. I had abandoned household chores. Transportation had become a daily challenge for me. I felt literally no sense of accomplishment or closure. Simply taking care of myself filled my every spare moment. More discouraging was the fact that nobody seemed to grasp the magnitude of such an insoluble environment. I was doing it all alone.

This cannot be happening, I thought. *Other people have gone through this and survived. Suck it up, Dave!*

While Rhonda's father, Bill, sat visiting with me one Saturday afternoon, he asked if I had any interest in attending Sunday morning worship services.

"Might not be a bad idea," I said. "Where do you suggest I go?"

"Well, we've been going to Grace," he replied. "You're welcome to come with us if you like."

"I've been thinking about attending Grace since before our accident. Maybe it's time for me to quit thinking and start doing."

"Do you want me to pick you up in the morning?" he asked.

"If you don't mind," I said. "I don't know how else I would get there."

"Okay," he said, "we'll be over to get you in the morning on our way to church."

As I rolled myself in the wheelchair around the corner and into the church sanctuary that Sunday morning, my friend Pastor Mike Hollenbeck, standing at the pulpit, interrupted himself in the middle of an announcement.

"Everybody, turn around and say hello to the guy we've all been praying for!" he said.

I was speechless as the entire congregation stood and applauded. It felt as though I had finally found a home. The timing could not have been more perfect. Compassion provided a remarkable sense of relief. The outside world remained full of peril, but I had found safe sanctuary in God's house.

—⁂—

Since Carole's new residence was at the Lighthouse, visiting with her no longer involved traveling to Flint. The trouble was that without a ride from someone, I had no way of getting to her no matter where she was. She could have been in Marlette, three miles down the road, and visitation without a chauffeur would have been out of the question.

Jason worked at the Lighthouse, so I tried hitching a ride with him to visit with my wife. That didn't work out.

My daughter worked in Caro, two miles from the Lighthouse, but her day started at seven o'clock in the morning and ended at four-thirty in the afternoon. Because of Carole's morning therapies, we wouldn't be together until after lunchtime. Catching a ride home with my daughter meant leaving at four thirty in the afternoon. Waiting for my son to finish his shift meant that I would be stranded until after midnight. Lights out at Mission Point was nine o'clock. Neither Jason's nor Nicole's work schedule coincided with visiting hours.

None of my friends were in a position to provide a taxi service, and there was no way I could afford to hire someone to haul me around.

The bottom line was that unless I figured out a way to drive myself around, I was marooned.

Why couldn't I drive? I thought to myself. *Dad drove, and he only had one leg!*

Dad had come home from the war without his right leg, and he seemed to have adapted quite nicely. Things had often been awkward for him, but that did not keep him from driving.

I was a licensed driver, and there were three roadworthy vehicles sitting in our driveway. All three of them had automatic transmissions, so I only needed one good leg to handle the stopping and starting part of driving. The only issue was that my right foot needed to be elevated. That was going to take a little ingenuity.

If I can sling my right leg over the center console without getting in the way of the steering wheel or the gear shifter, I might be able to make it work, I thought to myself. *Maybe I can sit sideways and rest my right leg on the passenger seat.*

Then I remembered that the old pickup truck didn't have a console; it had a bench seat!

I can do this! I said aloud. *I know I can do this!*

The idea was exhilarating. I was like a guy sitting in jail who suddenly realized he had been holding the key that would unlock his cell door.

I laid the crutches across my lap and rolled the wheelchair out to our old 1976 Chevy pickup truck to survey the possibilities. The truck had a spacious cab with a bench seat. Years earlier I had retrofitted the truck with cruise control. That meant my left foot wouldn't have to stay plastered to the gas pedal once the vehicle was up to highway speed.

It was obvious that sitting sideways while driving would have been a little radical, but without a center console to contend with, I didn't have to turn my body so far. I did, however, need to find a way to keep my right leg propped up, so I wheeled across the gravel driveway and into the workshop to find an empty milk crate. Two small pillows stacked on top made that makeshift footrest on the passenger-side floor the perfect height for my right leg to rest comfortably. There was plenty of room left to operate the brake and gas pedals with my left leg.

Balancing on one good leg while leaning against the tailgate afforded me plenty of leverage to hoist the folded wheelchair into the back of the pickup. Hobbling around to the passenger-side door on crutches and then sliding backward across the seat and into the driver's side of the cab was a cinch. I dragged the crutches into the cab, pulled the door shut, and was in like Flynn. I had been liberated!

The Lighthouse was a thirty-mile drive over paved country roads with light traffic, but that first trip turned into a hair-raising experience. I flinched every time a car passed in the oncoming lane. Staring wide-eyed into the rearview mirror as vehicles approached from behind while I was sitting at an intersection, waiting to turn left, made me feel as though I was about to be rear-ended. More than once I had to fight the urge to smash the gas pedal to the floor and head for the ditch.

On one of the country roads, I came across skid marks on the pavement that led through the ditch and ended at the base of a huge elm tree where bark had been peeled away. Those tire tracks and the missing bark sent a chilling panic through me. That naked spot on the tree had been the scene of someone's trauma. The very thought of broken bones or worse conjured up seriously unsettling images. I had to pull off the road and sit for a few minutes before the jittery tension finally subsided.

It was too bad someone didn't have a camera to catch the look of disbelief on everyone's face the first time I pulled into a parking spot in front of Mission Point.

"You shouldn't be driving!" one of the staff members said. "You can't use your right foot. How can you possibly control that vehicle?"

"Look," I said with a little more attitude than necessary, "my dad only had one leg, and I watched him drive a stick shift. How many feet do you need to operate an automatic anyway? And you'd better not tell me two or you'll give yourself away as one of those people on the highway with their brake lights flashing every four or five hundred feet!"

"But it can't be safe," another person said. "You've never used your left foot to operate the gas and brake pedals, have you?"

"As a matter of fact, I have!" I said. "Not only that but I'm also a professional musician. I have played a drum kit for more than forty years. I have no trouble making both feet and both hands function independently while I'm singing into a microphone. I'm not going to have any trouble driving a vehicle using my left foot."

Our attorney had an entirely different take on the issue.

"You need to get your doctor's written permission before you drive another ten feet," he said. "If you have an accident without a doctor's approval to drive you could be sued for everything you're worth, and the insurance company will disallow any claim or coverage."

Yeah, right, I thought to myself. *Like the insurance company is cooperating with me now!*

As much as I hated to admit it, the attorney's advice made sense. If I had learned anything from the motorcycle crash, it was that accidents happen even when you're doing everything right. I was in dire straits from the accident we had already been in, and I hadn't been doing anything wrong. I could only imagine how I would be thrown to the wolves if I were to be involved in an accident while driving under questionable circumstances.

His advice had been disheartening, but I was not discouraged. I planned to slide behind the wheel of my own vehicle whether it was legal or not. Nobody was going to force me to sit around any longer and wait helplessly for permission to move on with my life.

Still, I wanted to do the right thing, so I called the foot surgeon's office and asked for a prescription that said it was okay to drive. To my surprise he didn't bat an eye.

"Sure," he said. "There's no reason you can't drive a vehicle with your left foot. Just make sure you keep your right foot elevated."

Just to be on the safe side I called my friend, the Sanilac County undersheriff, and requested that he stop by the house to survey my situation.

"So what's your opinion?" I asked him after demonstrating my ability to get in and out of the pickup truck.

"The mailman sits on the wrong side of the car," he said, "and nobody seems to have a problem with that!"

"So you don't think there are any safety concerns with the way I'm approaching this thing?" I asked.

"Nope. Obey the laws and drive safely," he said. "You won't have any trouble."

Four days later the mailman—sitting on the wrong side of the car—delivered the doctor's prescription legalizing my driving privileges.

What I did not realize was that reaching that milestone of independence also gave the insurance adjusters the perfect excuse to drag their feet while they reexamined the validity of our claims. I actually started imagining there might be someone sitting in the bushes outside the house waiting to catch me on film doing anything that the insurance company could use—like driving my own vehicle—to prove that I had been faking my injuries. My cynical side imagined conversations taking place in that mythical insurance adjuster's conference room.

He says he can't walk and he says he can't work, but he can drive. Are we sure there's really anything physically wrong with this guy?

I didn't care anymore. Our attorney said not to worry. According to him we would not be held responsible for any of our unpaid medical expenses. Frankly I didn't believe him. A stack of collection notices was growing next to the pile of unpaid bills. I figured that at the very least, our credit rating would be ruined by such delinquency.

Silly as it sounds, the only thing of importance to me at that point in time was that I could drive again, meaning that my days of begging for rides were over. That was a major victory in my fight to reclaim independence. Being able to crawl into the pickup and go anywhere anytime was empowering.

Regardless, maintaining a positive outlook remained a challenge. We had the best attorney, but I had really begun to wonder just how successful he was going be as long as he continued trying to reason with an unreasonable bureaucracy. Visions of overpaid, undermanaged paper shufflers sitting in their cubicles, sipping coffee, and taking their sweet time thumbing through our case files fueled the flames under a cauldron of seething anger. There was absolutely no sense of urgency on anyone's part. If someone had been forcing accountability upon those responsible for the grief that their lackadaisical behavior caused, maybe things would have moved along a little more expeditiously.

The bottom line was that avoiding total disaster meant someone was going to have to get our ship moving, and it needed to happen soon. Red flags were going up all over the place. Losing our home and everything we owned was looking more probable with every passing day.

What's more, I had no idea if or when Carole would be able to come home.

CHAPTER 21

FIRST HOME VISIT

—◊—

Finally I could come and go as I pleased without help thanks to the convenience of that old pickup truck. Driving to visit my wife in Caro provided a welcome change in scenery from the stark, boring expressway that connected us to Flint. I felt as though I could reach out and touch the wildflowers and trees as I cruised along the two-lane roads through Michigan's rural Thumb.

I had graduated from the wheelchair to a Roll-A-Bout, a raised padded platform on casters with a pair of handlebars to hang on to. That little gadget resembled a child's scooter with a miniature monster-truck lift kit installed. I could support my weight with the right knee on the platform, push myself along with the left foot, and move around in a near-standing position.

Aside from those minor improvements in my quality of life, daily survival remained a test of patience and endurance.

Peace only came during visiting hours. Each day, I would arrive at the Lighthouse midafternoon and sit with Carole until around ten o'clock in the evening, when I would quietly roll out the front door after everyone else at Mission Point had been tucked in for the night. Thursday nights were designated movie nights, and I was privileged to ride the bus with my wife and the other Lighthouse residents to the theater in Bay City. Occasionally I would join Carole and the group for supper around the big table in the kitchen at Mission Point. Most of our evenings were spent side by side on the front porch or sitting in Carole's private room watching a movie on the portable DVD player I would bring with me.

Friends came to visit during the weekends. Occasionally, just to break the monotony, one of the staff members would reserve a company car during the week and take the two of us to a restaurant for a private evening out. The Lighthouse went to great lengths to provide a relaxing, therapeutic environment for its residents.

Near the end of August, Carole's therapists arranged for her to come home for an afternoon. The plan was to have Carole try her hand whipping something up in her own kitchen with trained supervision at her side. Multitasking was one of the rehabilitation techniques used to measure cognitive skills, and the therapists needed to test Carole's abilities somewhere outside of the test kitchen they had set up at the Lighthouse. Home seemed to be the perfect climate for such an experiment.

The day before Carole was scheduled to come for her first visit home in more than eight weeks, our friends Roger and Leslie came by the house to spruce things up. Roger cleaned out the fish ponds and got the waterfall up and running while Leslie replaced dead plants around the patio with baskets and pots filled with fresh flowers. A couple of hours before Carole's scheduled arrival, Leslie started a small campfire in the woods behind our house.

I called Carole's friend Bonnie to see if she would like to join us while Carole was home for the afternoon. Then I contacted my friends from the Christian Motorcyclists Association and invited them to pay a visit as well.

Everything was set for the perfect homecoming. The weather was ideal, the house felt lived in, and friends would be there to greet her.

When Carole arrived home, her attendant was very accommodating. She let Carole explore her own home by herself for a while and then went inside and asked Carole to show her how to bake a cake. Carole had no trouble finding the supplies and utensils she needed, and in no time she had the cake in a pan, baking in the oven.

Bonnie showed up a short while later, and we all went to sit by the fire in the woods. Something came up that prompted Carole, Roger, and Leslie to return to the house. I was comfortable where I was, and Bonnie didn't appear too eager to move, so the two of us stayed by the fire to visit a while longer.

"She doesn't need to be there," Bonnie told me as though she were an authority on the subject of neurological rehabilitation. "I don't see anything wrong with her at all."

I was mildly taken aback by Bonnie's comment. She was noticeably confrontational, and I could feel the anger rising, making it extremely difficult to remain cordial.

"There are a lot of things having to do with brain trauma that the untrained eye will never see, Bonnie," I told her. "Unless you're with her around the clock, there's no way you or anyone else can accurately draw that conclusion."

"I still don't see it," she stated in an authoritative tone of voice. "I just don't believe she needs to be locked up in a rehab facility."

"She's not exactly locked up, Bonnie."

I struggled to keep her disagreeable opinions from luring me into an unpleasant debate, but Bonnie continued laying down the gauntlet.

"Well, she can't come and go as she pleases, can she?"

"No, but she's not ready to be turned loose without someone there to help her."

"What makes you think she needs help with anything?" Bonnie asked.

"You don't think Carole needs help?"

"Nope," she said conclusively. "She's the same Carole I knew before the accident. She needs to be right here at home."

Bonnie continued to express dissatisfaction over my decision to keep Carole "incarcerated" and scolded me for not bringing her home to live. Much like Carole's father, Bonnie disagreed with most everything I had to say. She seemed to have a chip on her shoulder and argued unwaveringly.

Continuing the discussion threatened to ruin the milestone occasion of my wife's first trip back home. Nothing I said seemed to sway Bonnie's thinking or get her to drop the subject altogether, so I suggested we go back to the house to join the rest of the group. Hobbling along on my crutches with Bonnie carping at me the whole way across the yard, I wondered why I had even asked her to come for the visit. I found it extremely challenging to keep a civil tongue. Bonnie finally realized that I was trying to ignore her and dropped the subject as we reached the back door.

While we were standing around the kitchen, visiting with Roger and Leslie, Bonnie started in on me about something else I had allegedly done that she was unhappy about. That was when everyone in the room discovered just how short my fuse had become and just how loud the explosion was when the lit fuse reached the powder keg in my head. I unloaded on Bonnie mercilessly. When I had finished saying my piece, she turned and walked out the door, never to return. Being handed a dose of her own verbal venom was apparently more than she was willing to bear.

After Bonnie left our house, Roger and Leslie tried to placate me by agreeing that Bonnie's comments had been abrasive and uncalled for, but the truth was that I had lost the ability to tolerate any degree of displeasure. Ordinarily, I would have either tried reasoning with her or given her credit for having an opinion, and then tactfully changed the subject. Instead, something snapped. I was simply not going to be challenged.

The whole episode was unnerving and a little embarrassing.

Half an hour after Carole and her attendant departed for the Lighthouse, my friends from the CMA showed up. We stood around visiting, and I did my best to be cordial, but the episode with Bonnie had seriously darkened my already miserable disposition.

A dismally dark side of me had surfaced. It was taking over, bringing with it a consuming, nearly uncontrollable anger. Unfortunately those unsavory characteristics were with me to stay.

CHAPTER 22

JOUSTING WITH THE ADJUSTERS

—⁓—

Late in August a phone call came from our attorney's associate asking for copies of our tax return for the current year plus returns for the two years prior to the accident.

Geez, I thought, *am I going to be audited now?*

Paranoia strikes deep. My parents' experience with the tax collectors during the late 1970s had taught me to be suspicious of anyone asking to see my books, tax returns, or anything else related to personal finances. Their encounter with the IRS had put an end to the family-owned manufacturing operation, and I wasn't about to let that happen to me.

Something told me that this insurance company was not above soliciting help from the government to avoid paying what they owed, the same way a bully hides behind his dad to keep from being beaten up by the kids he has been pestering. No-fault laws had already been written in the insurance company's favor, but a bottom-line mentality fueled by greed knew no boundaries.

"Why do you need that information?" I asked with hesitant skepticism.

"The insurance adjusters are trying to determine your lost wages compensation," he said.[2]

"Isn't that supposed to be determined by our earnings at the time of the accident?" I asked.

"Yes" was all he would say.

"Well, I don't have a tax return for the current year," I protested. "All I have is a profit-and-loss statement for the first six

179

months of this year, and I have already sent you that information. That is all they should need to develop a trend."

I was angry and discouraged. *Haven't we already been through enough?* I asked myself.

"This feels like a precursor to receiving the royal shaft," I said.

"I don't know what they're trying to prove," he said. "We'll just cooperate with them and see where this takes us."

"Well, I can tell you one thing. If they wait for my current year's tax return before making a determination, we'll probably lose our house. It's only August, for crying out loud! My taxes won't be completed and filed until next January or February. That's five months away. What are we supposed to do for the next five months?"

"I don't know what to tell you," he said. "We are obligated to provide them with whatever information they request. They can take as long as they deem necessary to make a decision."

It had occurred to me that this guy was a lawyer, not an accountant. *Maybe he just doesn't understand the principles of bookkeeping,* I thought to myself.

"Why would they want to know what my income was for two years prior to the accident?" I asked, pressing for a logical explanation.

"I'm not really sure what they're thinking," he said.

My confidence in this associate's initiative was beginning to waver. It did not make sense that he would so willingly roll over and let the adjusters dictate such clearly inappropriate and unacceptable terms.

"Well, the past two years have nothing to do with what I was earning at the time of our accident," I said angrily. "My business was growing. I hope they don't plan on averaging my earnings to reduce their exposure. While those people dillydally around, my wife and I are going to lose our house and everything we own!"

I was livid. Demanding to see tax returns that wouldn't even be prepared for another five months spoke volumes. The insurance adjusters did not have one bit of concern for the financial hardship that they were creating.

"What about Carole's compensation?" I asked. "There should be no question what she was earning. Her employer has already had to file a second affidavit, and we still haven't seen a dime."

Then, punctuating my tirade with sarcasm, I added one last challenge.

"Do I need to send you copies of all her pay stubs again?" I asked sternly.

"No," he replied. "There should be no reason for the delay in her lost wages. I'll call them and see if I can find out what the holdup is."

The stress resulting from our situation was steadily intensifying. I was scared to death that we were going to lose everything. The insurance adjusters were taking their sweet time while we were caught in the middle between providers and collectors. It was only a matter of time before our money ran out, the bank ran out of patience, and we were run out of our home.

Helplessly waiting for the inevitable crash landing was brutal.

Carole's boss, the circuit judge, stopped by the house for a visit one evening, concerned that we might be running short of cash and wondering if we had seen any relief from the insurance company. I shared with him that we had been living on Carole's unused vacation and sick days while we continued pouring horrendous amounts of money into our truck's gas tank. We both knew that source of income had nearly been exhausted.

The judge was not surprised to hear about the bundles of unpaid medical bills that continued arriving in the mail. A significant percentage of lawsuits that came through his courtroom involved people suing their insurance companies for nonpayment. He was not optimistic.

—⚭—

On another battlefront, the war was in full swing with our motorcycle insurance adjuster. The guy assigned to handle our claim was being a mild-mannered jerk.

Unfortunately we really don't know how good our insurance policies truly are until we try to file a claim. Our independent agent had apparently never had to handle a claim through this company and was floored by the difficulty we were having.

We had purchased that motorcycle for two-thirds of what it should have sold for, yet this guy wanted to send it to the scrap yard for a little over half of what we had paid for it. I was still making payments on our bike, and I would have sold the machine to pay off the bank loan, but there was no way the sale of that motorcycle in the shape it was in would have brought enough to cover the balance we still owed. The settlement offer wasn't even enough to get the motorcycle repaired.

We were definitely on the short end of the stick.

Michigan no-fault law also states, "Motorcyclists cannot sue negligent motor vehicle operators for damages to their bikes."[3] In other words, we had no legal recourse.

So there we were with a wrecked, unusable motorcycle that was worth less than we owed on it, an adjuster who refused to cooperate, and laws that prevented us from recovering our losses.

That was about the time that I was informed by our attorney, "Motorcycles are specifically excluded as a motor vehicle under Michigan's no-fault law."[4]

Michigan required motorcyclists to be licensed drivers with a motorcycle endorsement, and their bikes were to be registered, titled, licensed, and insured. Motor vehicle insurance coverage on our motorcycle, like every motor vehicle insured in Michigan, also included compulsory fees paid into Michigan's catastrophic claims and uninsured motorist funds.[5]

Because our two-wheeled motor vehicle was not considered a motor vehicle under Michigan's no-fault law, I was not considered a motorist. Therefore, as far as Michigan's no-fault law was concerned, my wife and I were simply two pedestrians who got run over by a car, and medically speaking, our motorcycle no-fault insurance company didn't have to pay for so much as a Band-Aid.

That is how far our negligent, dull-witted legislators had allowed Michigan's laws to be twisted in favor of the car insurance companies. What a rude awakening to learn that legislation had been written and passed requiring motorcycle riders to pay for insurance that did not provide protection! With the help of our elected officials, the automobile insurance industry had been transformed into a slick shell game.

Talk about extortion!

CHAPTER 23
THE DARKEST DAY

For we walk by faith, not by sight.
2 Corinthians 5:7 (KJV)

—⚏—

Anger issues had rendered me unapproachable. Unresponsive insurance adjusters and insensitive people further inflamed my already sour disposition, and it showed. People distanced themselves like rats jumping off a sinking ship. Meanwhile, my youngest son was packing his suitcase.

Jason had been talking to his mother for some time about moving out of the house and living on his own. Understandably, he wanted and needed his independence. At the age of twenty-four, he was certainly old enough; and he had already been on his own, living in a rented house on the other side of town with friends while he commuted to college. He had only come back home to live because his friends had moved on and there was nobody left to share the rent and utilities on the house they all lived in together.

What didn't make any sense to me was that he was talking about heading for Arizona to live with a friend who had camped out in an aunt's spare bedroom, played the guitar, and was unemployed. Jason had no job prospects and no money to speak of. He was old enough to do as he pleased, but he certainly wasn't heading for anything that represented stability. Visions of hippies living on the streets in the Haight-Ashbury district of San Francisco during the sixties came to mind. I was apprehensive about the direction he was leaning in and not at all impressed by the people who were influencing his decisions.

Although Jason had been making the payments on his pickup, the vehicle was titled in my name and my signature was on his car loan. To keep his insurance rates affordable, we had him listed on our auto insurance policy. I told him that if he intended to take that vehicle across state lines, he would first need to have it refinanced and retitled in his name. I also told him he needed to get his own car insurance coverage while he was at it.

I wanted my son to show some initiative, but I was more concerned about protecting our interests. As the cosigner of his car loan I would be responsible for picking up the tab if he missed a car payment. Because my name was on the vehicle's title, everything I owned could be attached to a lawsuit if he was involved in a fender-bender. And if his driving record was less than stellar, my insurance rates would rise. I explained those things to Jason, and he was clearly not happy. He protested, but I stuck to my guns. Financially, we were in no position to help him. Moreover, he needed to learn how to be on his own. At one point I nearly backed down from my demands, but something kept telling me to stay out of his way.

A few days passed, and he started complaining that he needed a cosigner before any bank would talk to him about borrowing money. I wasn't surprised. I figured that sooner or later he would come looking for a reprieve.

"Welcome to the real world," I said. "You want to be grown up and independent, this is the way you do it. Find someone willing to cosign a loan for a vehicle that's going to be driven to the other side of the United States by a guy who has no source of income. The rest should be a breeze."

Even though he knew I was right, his antipathy toward me ratcheted to a new level. It was amazing how callous I had become.

Among the possessions he had planned to take to Arizona was his drum kit. When he started making comments that sounded like he was going to pack his drums into my road cases for the trip, I intervened.

"How do you plan to get those cases back to me after you get to Phoenix?" I asked. "The shipping is going to cost you almost as much as a new set of road cases!"

"Fine," he said with disgust. "I'll leave the cases here. It's not like you're using them, but whatever!"

"Whether I'm using them or not, Jay, those cases are expensive and they're mine. If you want a set of cases to haul your drums around, maybe it's time you went shopping for your own."

I handled my son the way I had been handled by my elders when I was growing up in spite of the fact that I hated the way they had dealt with me. Anger was oozing from every pore. I was uncooperative and unkind, and I sounded very spiteful, and I knew it. I had convinced myself that forcing him to take responsibility was the best thing for him.

Secretly, the last thing I wanted was for my son to go to Arizona, so I sure wasn't going to make it any easier for him to split. The whole time he was packing, I prayed that he would reconsider his move and stick with me through his mother's rehabilitation. Both he and his fiancée, Rhonda, had good jobs. It seemed to me that instead of leaving home because he needed to find a job, he was leaving his paying job to get away from home. More to the point, it felt as though he were desperately trying to get as far away from me as possible.

Finally, the day came.

On Saturday, September 1, 2007, about a month after our terrible disagreement over his seeming lack of interest in helping with his mother's care, Jason hugged his mother good-bye as she lay in her bed at Mission Point and then left his job at the Lighthouse.

At eleven-thirty that same night, I sat in my wheelchair at the edge of the parking pad in front of our garage and watched his taillights disappear over the hill as he drove out of my life.

Dealing with Jason's departure was undoubtedly the most difficult and darkest day of my entire life. The heartache I felt was mostly due to his having left home with so many things between us unresolved and headed for Arizona without so much as a job opportunity. With precious little experience in the music industry and no ties to any particular musical group, Jason took off for Phoenix to play music with a friend who had painted what seemed to me a rather unrealistically rosy picture. I feared for his well-being. Watching my youngest son drive away was more heartbreaking than watching my oldest son head off to the war in Afghanistan.

I rolled myself over the threshold back into the house, closed the door behind me, and slipped into a deep, suicidal depression. All of the things I would never have the opportunity to do with my son came to me in a torrent of painful memories. The model railroad I planned to build with him would never be pulled out of its packaging. That radio-controlled airplane would never come down from the loft. My son would never get his pilot's license, and I would never again have the opportunity to watch him play hockey. Everything his mother and I had given him had been left behind. The Bowflex was still in the basement, his stereo equipment was on a shelf in the garage, and the clothing his mother had filled his closet with had been abandoned in a pile in the middle of the upstairs hallway.

Like a moth shedding its cocoon, Jason had stripped himself of everything that even remotely connected him to his family and literally disappeared into the dark of night. That was the silent finale to the disagreement between us from a few weeks earlier, and nothing remained but the raw memories of an argument that ended with a father/son relationship bleeding to death.

I sat sobbing uncontrollably until finally dropping off to sleep in our family room, slumped in the seat of the wheelchair. I was alone and lonely. Never before had I felt such emptiness, and it left a bitter aftertaste that I knew would never leave me.

My life changed dramatically that night. It seemed as though I had traveled through time thirty years into the future. I had a vision of me, an eighty-eight year old widower, alone in the family room of our quad-level home, unable to get up and down the stairs on my own. I was sobered and depressed. Admittedly, a significant part of the agony existed because Jason was the last child to leave home, but there was nobody to help me get through the pain of final separation. When he disappeared into the dark of night, our house suddenly became the emptiest of nests. His departure was not a healthy one, because this nest had been broken, and he drove away while the pieces were still scattered.

I don't believe I am capable of suicide, but that night was likely as close as I will ever come to finding out. Had I not had such a strong faith in God, I believe I would have swallowed a bullet. Something spiritual seemed to temper my grief. Not only was I terrified at the prospect of having to face God after ending the life of one of his creatures (me), but visions of my kids finding me dead at my own hand caused a fear worse than the pain of loneliness to well up within me. They had already been through hell, and I was not going to put them through any more grief. This was my pain, and I wasn't about to let it seep into anyone else's life.

The promise I had made to take care of my wife as she lay comatose in the ICU haunted me as well. I could not abandon that promise, regardless of the pain. I had *promised* her! That commitment would not leave me alone.

Once again I tried turning everything over to God, but my heart was no longer in it. All I asked for was to be taken without any further pain to anyone. That night I believe I subconsciously gave up hope. If everything was lost, so be it. Nothing anyone could say or do from that point forward could hurt any more than the physical and emotional agony I had already suffered. I simply handed in my resignation.

The moment Jason's taillights went out of sight, I realized just how much my life had relied on the presence of my wife and children. Their peace, happiness, and safety had been my reason for living. I thought again about the little speech that I had given the kids shortly after being brought home from St. Mary's hospital in July. I gathered them together and thanked them for proving that their mother and I had raised them right. I told them that we had no desire to run their lives. All we asked for was a front-row seat so their mother and I could watch. Two months later, there I sat, desperately alone, my family scattered to the wind. The roof may as well have caved in. Jason's timing could not have been worse.

It seemed taking care of Carole was all I had left to live for, and nobody had any idea where that stagecoach was headed. As far as serving any further purpose, I felt neutered and useless. There seemed to be no reason for me to recover and return to work other than to earn enough money to pay the mortgage, buy food, pay off the medical bills, and pay the insurance and taxes on a big, empty house.

The next morning I woke and sat in my temporary bedroom, pondering the situation. It was clear that I could not and would not survive if I allowed this depression to maintain its grip. I had to make a conscious decision to be positive. The episode exposed a very significant reality: a healthy mind cannot simultaneously entertain misery and happiness.

After Jason left home, basic survival mode kicked in. All that mattered to me was my wife's safety and happiness. I no longer cared if the bank took our house. I gave up hoping for any word from either our attorney or the insurance adjusters. Financial ruin seemed inevitable. So, resigned to defeat, I braced for the impending doom and narrowed my sights on the here and now, focused on making it to the other side of this insane expedition. I would do it with or without any possessions left to my name.

I knew Carole was increasingly stressed over being forced to reside with patients who had little chance of ever leaving the Lighthouse because of their debilitating injuries. Being housed with those patients made her feel as though she had been branded unable to lead a self-supporting lifestyle. She didn't feel incompetent or incapable, but her surroundings caused her to seriously doubt her own self-worth.

A week after Jason disappeared over the horizon, Carole began to show some somber emotions. Tears welled up in her eyes every time I kissed her before going home for the night, which made it doubly difficult to leave her there. I needed to do something that would make her feel important—something intimate and private that involved just the two of us.

On my drive to the Lighthouse that Sunday after church services, I hatched a plan to make a getaway to a quiet little clearing in the woods across the street from Mission Point. We had gone there a couple of times prior to that day, and each time, the peaceful break from the group at the house seemed to lift her spirits. I figured we could sit and dream about our future together with nothing but the birds singing in the trees and the breeze blowing through the canopy of leaves over our heads.

Cruising along on my knee scooter, I rolled through the front door at Mission Point, entered Carole's room, and whisked her out of the house, heading for the sanctity of the grove. Just as we were stepping off the porch, her attendant came out and asked where we were going.

"To the woods across the street to spend some time alone," I said.

"I'm sorry, but Carole cannot leave the porch without an attendant at her side, and at the moment, there is nobody available to accompany her."

"I'll be with her," I said.

"I'm sorry, but Carole cannot leave without someone from the Mission Point staff to accompany her."

She had lit my short fuse, and the explosion came without warning. First I read her the riot act, and then I went inside to the manager's office to challenge this change of rules.

"Carole and I have been over there several times already without a chaperone," I said. "What makes today any different from every other day?"

My voice rose and drew the attention of every staff member and resident inside the house. The manager calmly explained that policy specifically stated an attendant was to accompany any resident leaving the house. I knew I wasn't going to win the argument, and I had already created a serious ruckus. Hanging my head, I turned and went back out to sit with my wife on the porch.

I turned around and discovered that Carole's staff attendant had followed me out the door. I fully expected her to give me an earful and order me to leave the premises. On the contrary, she expressed her sympathy and apologized that we had not been allowed to seek the privacy we so desperately needed. As quickly as my fuse had been lit, the fire went out. I apologized for such unacceptable behavior and thanked her for taking care of my wife. Then I stood up and, balancing myself on my good leg as best I could, gave her a hug and told her that I would leave if it would make things any better.

"Oh no!" she said. "You need to be here with your wife, and she needs you here with her. We'll just try to keep people from bothering you while the two of you are here on the porch together."

A short while later, I pushed myself over to the pickup, pulled out two folding lawn chairs, and dragged them to a private spot on the lawn behind the house. Back on the porch, I took Carole by the hand. I was determined to bend the rules and show someone that I still had the power to make up my own mind.

"Come on," I said, "we're going somewhere private even if it's only around the corner."

Carole and I spent the rest of that afternoon and early evening sitting alone in the yard behind Mission Point while I acted out in childish defiance. Fortunately this was not the Lighthouse staff's first rodeo. The Mission Point attendants simply kept a compassionate, watchful eye on us from a distance.

CHAPTER 24

WHAT, NO HANDRAILS?

—𝔪—

During the first week in September, shortly after my confrontation with the staff at Mission Point, I decided it was time to take the next step toward recovery. Carole's therapists and counselors called a team meeting at our request to explore the possibility of arranging an overnight home visit for Carole. Although one of the staff members had already been inside our house, she had not been sent for the express purpose of evaluating home safety issues or handicap accessibility. So a formal home evaluation plan was discussed.

I found the "handicap accessibility" issue humorous. A quad-level home is about as handicap inaccessible as a house can be. What in the world did these people think they were going to convert to make our house more livable for my wife and me?

The insurance company's case manager was at the meeting and seemed a little more than eager to have Carole released from the Lighthouse and sent home permanently.

Here we go again, I thought to myself. *The medical insurance company booted Carole out of Hurley, and now the no-fault insurance company has sent their agent to expedite her removal from the Lighthouse.*

I sensed the staff's hesitation to let Carole out of their sight as they came up with several hypothetical what-if scenarios that might pose a threat to her safety. The implication was that I could not provide the necessary care at home, but the underlying concern was that they were equally concerned about my state of mind. I later learned that they had been briefed concerning my recent confrontation with the caretakers at Mission Point.

Carole was certainly a long way from completing her therapies to everyone's satisfaction, but nobody would explain why her treatments could not be continued as an outpatient. I interrupted the discussion with my own Neanderthal approach to logic, probably proving that there was sufficient reason for them to be concerned about my mental stability.

"You all seem to be worried that I won't be able to handle a crisis," I said. "If I'm capable of living alone in my condition—and everyone here apparently has decided that I am—what makes you think that I would not be able to take care of my wife?"

They silently looked around the table at each other. I think it finally occurred to everyone sitting in that room that all of the attention for personal safety had been focused on my wife. Nobody ever gave a second thought to the fact that I was crippled and had been forced to figure out how to survive on my own.

Someone spoke up, suggesting that a date be set for a home evaluation to take place in the very near future. Although the visit was officially being planned for my wife's benefit, there was a subtle undertone that suggested this evaluation should have been conducted several months earlier for my benefit. Out of the corner of my eye, I believe I caught the case manager squirming nervously in her chair.

On Wednesday, September 12, one week after that eye-opening team meeting, Carole and I attended a joint session with the psychologist in Flint who had been assigned to watch over Carole after she was released from Hurley. That afternoon we separately underwent the first half of a two-part psychiatric evaluation. Carole completed the second half of her testing on Friday of that week, and my tests were finished two weeks later.

Carole's evaluation was intended primarily to establish a baseline for future comparison so the analysts would be able to measure her progress. Testing on me was being conducted at my request.

I was concerned that my pilot's license might be suspended should word about our accident get back to the authorities at the Federal Aviation Administration. If challenged, I wanted to be able to wave the test results in the authority's face as proof that I was still fit to fly an airplane. Privately, however, for personal safety reasons, I wanted to know whether I would still be able to handle the workload in an aircraft cockpit or, for that matter, behind the wheel of an automobile. My confidence had been seriously shaken. I had already decided that if I was not comfortable with my test results, I would ground myself before I took a load of passengers down in flames.

Two weeks after the team meeting at the Lighthouse, the therapists arrived at our house for an inspection with the case manager in tow. I opened the front door and cordially invited everyone in for a home tour. Starting in the family room, I showed everyone the temporary living quarters. They all seemed amused by my ingenuity and commented on the unorthodox bathing facilities.

The bug-eyed gasps of disbelief only began when I escorted everyone up the stairs to the second floor and into the living room, crawling on my hands and knees, hauling the Roll-A-Bout behind me one step at a time. I showed everyone where I had stacked the crutches so they would be within reach when I needed them. I also pointed out the walker at the top of the stairs on the third floor, explaining that, as inconvenient as that thing was to use, I still needed something to help get around whenever I went up to the bedroom for anything. Feigned or genuine, the case manager's expression appeared to be one of shock; she was amazed at the way I had adapted to the environment.

"I can't believe you have been living like this," she said. "These conditions are unbelievable!"

I found the case manager's show of concern annoying.

"Well, what choice did I have?" I asked her. "Nobody was here to help me. I had to either figure this thing out on my own or starve to death waiting for help. Everyone seemed shocked when they saw me driving for the first time too. Put yourself in my place and tell me what you would have done!"

The Lighthouse staff remained silent. They knew someone had neglected to do his or her job on my behalf, but they were not there to point fingers. Everyone stood shaking their heads as though they couldn't believe what they were witnessing.

"My dad only had one leg," I said to them. "I've just been doing things the way I thought he would have done them."

Although by that time it made little difference, I finally felt as though someone with authority was listening. I believe the case manager was finally convinced that neither she nor her employers, the insurance company, had been looking out for my best interests the way they should have been.

Whose responsibility was it to see that my needs had been met? I wondered to myself. *Was it the case manager's? Should our attorney have alerted someone? Was I somehow supposed to have known that help was only a phone call away?*

The questions raced through my head. Somebody had obviously dropped the ball on my behalf, but nobody in that group of visitors would either accept accountability or point a finger. I believe the responsibility fell at the feet of the insurance company's representative, the case manager. After that mild confrontation, the case manager's mood softened noticeably. Any further debate would have solved nothing, so the team completed its home evaluation and returned to the Lighthouse. Based upon their findings, arrangements were made to install handrails in the front staircase and handicap apparatuses in the bathtub enclosure. They banned throw rugs as a tripping hazard. The rest of the house remained unchanged.

In-home attendant care never materialized.

On Friday, September 28, we returned to the psychologist's office in Flint to review our test results. Carole's tests revealed typical posttrauma issues—most, if not all, of them curable with continued counseling and cognitive therapies.

My test scores revealed far better results than I had expected. I was comforted by the thought that my piloting, navigating, communication, and cockpit management skills were intact. Memory and recall assessments indicated higher-than-average capabilities. I went home that day thankful that although I might be one angry individual, at least I had not been pronounced incompetent. The psychologist released me with the opinion that there was no further need for testing. Carole was recommended for continued counseling and therapies. No length of time was discussed. We just knew that we were in for an incessantly long haul.

About that time, our case manager started making some strong suggestions about putting Carole back to work. She supposed that going back to the courthouse part-time in December might be a suitable goal. At first I agreed, thinking it might be a good way to jerk Carole back to reality.

"Absolutely not!" was our psychologist's response.

She tactfully told our case manager there was no way Carole would be able to return to work for at least another year, much less another month. Carole's posttrauma amnesia was still an issue, and she was not yet emotionally stable or physically strong enough to handle such a fast-paced, strenuous environment. The psychologist's proclamation made sense and forced me to do a little soul searching.

It suddenly occurred to me that I had been selfishly trying to shove Carole back into her work environment in an attempt to find a shortcut through the healing process. In so doing, I had been playing right into the insurance adjuster's hands, and the case manager was more than willing to accommodate my reckless wishes. I dropped that plan like a hot potato as soon as the truth slapped me in the face. We all needed to be reminded that brain injuries take time to heal.

I thanked the psychologist for looking out for Carole's best interests, but I had an eerie feeling the allied ranks were thinning. It felt as though people were misinterpreting my eagerness to end the trauma as an indication that we were both ready to let go and cross the street on our own. All I had accomplished was to further compromise our status with the insurance adjusters by making it sound as though the medical community had exaggerated the extent of our injuries.

By that time it felt as though I could do nothing right.

I had, however, secured permission from the Lighthouse to take my wife home with me to spend the weekend. So after we finished our appointments at the psychologist's office in Flint, we piled into our daughter's vehicle and rode with her back to our house in Marlette. Although we were both crippled and far from being healed physically or emotionally, that weekend spent under the same roof with my wife was a milestone. For the first time in over three months, I spent a night in my own bedroom, and I had my wife back at my side. That night, before I went to sleep, I silently vowed we would never again be separated.

When Monday morning came around, we rose, had breakfast, and went to the Lighthouse for Carole's therapies. We both fully expected an argument from the staff when I asked about taking my wife back home with me. The manager at Mission Point handed me a form to sign. It was just that simple.

Three days later we attended another team meeting at the Lighthouse. Everyone who held a position to give a thumbs-up or thumbs-down regarding Carole's release was seated around the table in that conference room. Each person was asked for an opinion regarding Carole's progress. To our surprise, all of them applauded our accomplishments and gave us their blessing.

On that day, October 4, fourteen weeks and four days after being left for dead in the middle of M-53, my wife finally came home to stay.

Carole walked through the front door of our home that afternoon with a look of disbelief on her face and tears in her eyes. She hugged me and thanked me for bringing her home, and she then told me that she was excited about finally getting her life back. We had both experienced firsthand what it felt like to have had everything we cherished taken from us without reason, so this homecoming was an especially gratifying occasion. My wife was happy to be back in her own house, and I was relieved to have her back at my side.

A lot of those people who had witnessed my wife's recovery referred to her as a walking miracle. In human terms that may be true, but to those who truly believe in God, it was just another one of His wonders of grace. I told people that God kept Carole alive so that He could keep an eye on me through her.

CHAPTER 25

SO, WHAT'S ON YOUR MIND?

About a week before Carole came home to stay, I was sitting in the corner of the therapy gym at the Lighthouse biding my time between sessions. Dan, a psychologist at the Lighthouse, casually approached and asked how I was doing.

"Okay," I said.

"You feel like talking?" he asked. "I have a couple of things I want to ask you about."

"Sure," I said. "What's on your mind?"

"Let's go down the hall to my office. There's too many people sitting in this room to have a private conversation."

Dan closed the door behind us, and we both sat in his cozy little office, sipping coffee. Dan broke the ice.

"How are you feeling?" he asked me.

Not sure exactly how to respond, I shrugged and made a feigned expression as if to suggest that he needed to clarify the question.

"I'm told you have some anger issues, and the staff at Mission Point has indicated that you are repeating yourself a lot," he said.

Sitting there in front of Dan with the door closed made me feel like a little kid who had been sent to the principal's office. I replayed the confrontation with the staff at Mission Point and tried to pass it off as frustration. Yes, I had been angry and was embarrassed about the outburst.

"I can understand how that would have made you feel," Dan said, leaning back in his chair.

"As far as repeating myself," I told him, "let me give you an example of what I've been dealing with."

I was hoping an explanation might soften the punishment I believed I was about to receive for having behaved inappropriately that Sunday at Mission Point.

"To avoid running into friends and acquaintances in Marlette, I decided to go to the grocery store in Sandusky to buy some things. Carole had always done our shopping, so I wasn't really sure whether I could write a check at that store in Sandusky. On my way into the store, I stopped to ask the cashier about using a personal check to pay for the things I needed. I told her that my wife was in the hospital so I was going to be buying the groceries for a while.

"'It doesn't look like you're doing all that well yourself,' the clerk commented as she looked over the counter at my Roll-A-Bout and my bandaged foot.

"'We were in a bad hit-and-run motorcycle accident in June,' I told her.

"'You were? Where?'

"'North of Marlette on M-53'

"'Do you mean that accident that happened just north of Marlette where the guy left the scene and two people were airlifted to the hospital?' she exclaimed. 'That was you and your wife?'

"'Yes, that was my wife and me,' I said. 'Can I write a personal check here?'

"'Hey, Mary,' she yelled to the girl at the other end of the counter. 'You remember that accident north of Marlette where that guy took off and left two people layin' in the highway?'

"'Yeah,' she said.

"'This is the guy. His wife is still in the hospital.'

"By that time, Dan," I said, "everyone in that section of the store was staring at me as though they all knew who I was. I put my head down and went looking for the stuff I needed, hoping I would be able to write a check when I made it to the final checkout counter."

I continued through the rest of that particular episode, sharing how I kept running into people in that store who knew me and how I found myself having to explain over and over what had happened and how we were doing. I told him that I didn't want to be rude to anyone so I kept talking, politely making my way through the crowd of curiosity seekers.

"Dan," I said, "by the time I made it back to the car, I had been forced to repeat the same story so many times that I had forgotten what I had said to whom. So now when someone asks me how Carole and I are doing, I just automatically tell the story beginning to end. Wouldn't you know it—now the people who have already heard the story are saying that I'm repeating myself, and that kind of pees me off!"

Dan threw his head back and laughed. It was a real belly laugh. His lighthearted response truly eased my tension.

"You and I are going to get along just fine," he said.

Then he took a sip from his cup, and his mood sobered.

"Have you had any thoughts of suicide?" he asked.

I shared with Dan what I had gone through the night Jason left home. It was difficult reliving that episode, and I found myself wiping away the tears as I told him about losing my son.

"Thoughts? Yes," I told him, "but I don't believe I'm capable of ending my own life. Besides, I have too many people that I care about to leave them with the painful memory of my life having ended that way. Committing suicide would hurt my kids and probably devastate my wife. I also made a promise to take care of my wife, and I can't do that if I'm not around. Why do you ask?"

He shared with me his darker concern about a comment I had made to Kristie, one of my physical therapists.

"Do you remember saying something about wishing you were dead?" he asked.

"After what we've been through since the accident," I said, "I have often wished I had just been left on the highway to die. I think I remember saying that same thing to Kristie. So far this entire ordeal has been extremely painful and discouraging."

"Why do you feel that way?" he asked.

"Dan," I said, "we're alive, and I should thank God for that miracle. But nothing I was promised by my attorney has materialized, and I can't get anyone to tell me how much longer I'm going to have to wait. I don't know how far my wife is going to progress in her recovery or whether she will ever be able to return to work. I don't know if or when I will ever be able to reopen my repair shop, and the longer it stays closed, the closer I am to having to start it back up from scratch. Honestly, I don't know if I have it in me to start my business all over again.

"I'm fifty-eight years old, and I'm not a wealthy man, so I still need some sort of an income. Neither Carole nor I are old enough to retire, and our money is running out. If I can't get my business going again, I'm going to have to find a job, but who is going to hire me? I'm overqualified to be a greeter at Walmart, and I'm too far over the hill to get a job anywhere else.

"My youngest child has left for Arizona, and there were issues between us that were not resolved before he drove away. I'm home alone, can't walk, and have been forced to figure out how to take care of myself with a bum leg. I don't even know if I'm going to be able to keep my foot. I am in an extremely desperate place right now. If I didn't have a strong faith in God, I believe I could have ended my own life."

I don't recall specifically what Dan said after that, but I left that first session relieved from simply having had someone to talk to. I looked forward to every session with him after that first meeting. There was nothing he could do that would resolve any of the legal or financial issues I faced, but it was sure nice having someone's shoulder to cry on for a change.

I believe I became Dan's surrogate dependent that day.

CHAPTER 26
A WORD ABOUT PTSD

—ɷ—

A couple of fellow veterans had been dropping subtle hints that they recognized signs of post-traumatic stress disorder (PTSD) in my behavior after our accident.

I had never paid much attention to PTSD. I always assumed PTSD was just the official title for one more socially acceptable ploy by creative bureaucrats to dig a little deeper into my pocket to fund entitlement programs used to buy votes. Not anymore! I did a little bit of research and discovered that PTSD is as real as a heart attack and can be just as crippling.

Shortly after the Vietnam War, the American Psychiatric Association formally identified PTSD as an anxiety issue. PTSD is considered by the experts to be a normal response by normal people to abnormal situations. War, rape, abuse, and automobile accidents are typical examples of events so extraordinarily stressful that almost anyone experiencing such an event would be distressed. Extreme traumatic events often overwhelm a human's ability to cope.

People experiencing PTSD have described their feelings with words like "shattered," "violated," "going crazy," "doomed," "derailed," and "dead inside." Sufferers have said that they suddenly felt different from everybody else.

Stress or violence caused by another human will likely cause the victim to lose faith and trust in humanity, love, and himself. Irritability and outbursts of anger, nightmares, feelings of vulnerability, anticipation of disaster, and overprotective or overcontrolling behavior are among the symptoms displayed by someone suffering from PTSD.

Coping with PTSD includes something referred to as "psychic numbing," which is a way of trying to escape painful memories. Trauma can cause victims to feel disconnected from others, their careers, and the future. In short, a traumatized person will simply shut himself down to block out the past. The irony is that blotting out painful memories usually blocks out the present and the future.[6]

I had no idea that I had been coping with the cumulative effects of traumatic stress from events dating back to childhood, the Vietnam War, and other seriously anxious moments throughout my life. I had become so adept at hiding feelings that every trauma experienced had simply been stuffed into a vault in the back of my brain. Banging my head on the pavement shook those memories loose. They all leaked uncontrollably into my conscious mind and mixed with the stress of dealing with life-threatening injuries, changed behavior, and an unreasonable insurance bureaucracy.

When a friend and fellow Vietnam veteran finally dragged me to the VA hospital in Saginaw nearly five years after our motorcycle accident, I discovered the truth about the disorder, my denial, and myself. The first counselor I saw asked a very provocative question: "Why is it taking you Vietnam veterans forty years to realize you have a problem?"

I responded with a large dose of hostility. "Well, maybe that's because when we came back home, everyone told us to quit complaining, get over it, and just move on," I said.

My tone of voice surprised even me.

Understanding the symptoms helped me to appreciate the fact that my wife had most likely been suffering from PTSD from the time she started getting her memory back on the day she was discharged from Hurley. Her entire personality and disposition had changed in very subtle, almost indiscernible ways. A more comprehensive awareness of PTSD four years earlier while we were still in the middle of the developmental stages of the trauma would have been handy.

—◊—

Three months after the accident, Carole and I were like a couple of people who had emerged from the jungle, still catching our breath and wondering how either of us had survived the plane wreck. It felt as though we had been away for an eternity. We were happy to be alive and glad to be home, but we both knew something wasn't right. I couldn't put my finger on it. For some reason, nothing felt the same. We had once dreamed about taking trips and diving into projects and things we wanted to do for fun and adventure. By the time we finally made it back home to our own living room that October, all sense of pleasure had literally disappeared. We had been traumatized.

It was not simply a matter of what we had already been through that had us cowering in the corner. Constantly having been told to back away and let the experts handle things had been discouraging and intimidating. Frustration over loose ends fueled a sense of hopelessness. Unresolved insurance issues, unpaid medical bills, dwindling reserves, endless appointments and therapies, the potential for additional surgeries, the expected amputation of my foot—all of those things were extremely unsettling for both of us. There was never any sense of closure. My anger escalated, and my attitude worsened by the day. The wait-and-see approach those experts insisted we follow had me wringing my hands out of exasperation. I didn't shy away from social interaction, but there were a lot of sideways glances whenever I expressed an opinion.

Carole had become consumed by her physical, emotional, and imagined mental limitations. She was afraid to do anything for fear of doing it wrong, constantly saying that she didn't measure up.

"To what?" I would ask her. "What is it that you think you should be doing that you are not capable of doing?"

"I don't know," was all she could say. "I can't explain it. I just don't feel like I'm doing anything right."

She wasn't doing anything wrong; she just couldn't get herself settled into a comfortable, fulfilling routine. Nor could I. We had never been people who could be told what to do or how to do it, yet there we were, forced to do as we had been told by people who didn't really know anything about us.

We both struggled with unnecessary stress, always waiting for the other shoe to drop. Neither of us had a clue what was coming, but we had both been sufficiently conditioned to expect the worst.

Carole remained an outpatient at the Lighthouse. I too had become an outpatient, undergoing physical therapy on my shoulder. Every day, we climbed into the old pickup truck and drove to Caro for our appointments. At the end of the day we came home and hid in our house until it was time to go to bed. Our daily routine had become a demoralizing substitute for normal living, and each trip to the Lighthouse served as a reminder that neither of us was able to function without assistance.

Time spent at home wasn't all idle time. Carole fixed supper, and I stayed out of her way. After loading the dishwasher, she would start another load of laundry and fold the clothes as she pulled them out of the dryer. By eight o'clock in the evening, she was usually either in bed or sitting in front of the TV snoring through another episode of CSI. Most of my activity revolved around assembling and copying documents and forwarding them to our attorney's office while trying to track the progress of our claims. That in itself was a full-time job and it was painfully boring work, especially when there was no indication of progress being made.

From the outside looking in, we were just another normal married couple privately making our way through the day. What nobody could see was that we had become entangled in a blizzard of emotional turmoil. Being back together in our own home provided no relief from the strain of our situation. The stress had become oppressive, and we had seriously begun to grate on each other's nerves.

CHAPTER 27
CAMELOT CRUMBLING

*And now abideth faith, hope, charity, these three; but
the greatest of these is charity.*

1 Corinthians 13:13 (KJV)

—⟋⟍—

Personal experience had proven to me that there is nothing
automatic about maintaining any relationship, especially a
marriage partnership. Staying happily married requires a lot of
work and self-discipline. Through the years, our union had seen its
fair share of effort from both of us.

It had occurred to me that syndicated Christian family radio
talk shows consistently emphasized the importance of love in every
relationship. Appropriately so. Love is the main ingredient for
peace and harmony between two people. I found 118 references to
love in the Holy Bible before I quit counting.

Friendship without love is nothing more than a pleasant
experience. A business relationship without the respect that
comes from love will never grow beyond the check-and-balance,
accountability phase. Even a dog will turn tail and run if you fail
to give it your love.

Someone once made the statement that if you want to lose
a friend all you have to do is room with him for one semester at
college. He was right. Even best friends rarely endure such a trial
when their ties are not founded in love.

There were times Carole and I did not like each other or
want to be together, but we knew we loved each other. All things
considered, we had been best friends, and after thirty-seven years of

marriage, we had beaten the odds. We had our share of arguments during that time, and some of them had been real barn burners. On more than one occasion we had considered calling it quits, but after retreating to our separate corners to get the pouting out of the way, we always came back together, agreeing that we really did not want our marriage to end.

But things had changed. What Carole and I faced was something neither of us had ever encountered. I couldn't put my finger on it, but I knew that basically our compatibility had somehow taken a turn. Brain trauma changes a person's personality, as does dealing with those changes. Neither of us was the same person we had been before the accident, and we were not equipped to handle that strange new twist in individuality.

While casually browsing through a pamphlet handed to me by one of our counselors, I came across a statistic stating that fewer than one in ten marriages survived the aftermath of brain trauma. After staring into the jaws of the monster, it was not difficult to see why the documented failure rate had been so high, especially in a society that coddles people who choose to give up and give in. I was convinced that we were the exception. Statistics were interesting, and they revealed a lot about other people's behavior, but we were two people who had always bucked the odds. Those summaries simply did not apply to us. I just said a prayer for those other nine marriages that would become casualties, counted our blessings for being in the one that survived, and pressed on.

The truth is that we both continued feigning happiness as Carole's disposition collided with changes in my attitude, producing relational issues that we had never experienced. I continued hoping that soon my wife would smile and that eventually I would see color once again in the scenery that surrounded us.

Consumed by feelings of vulnerability and impending disaster, nearly every night of sleep was fitfully filled with frightening dreams. A sense of paranoia prevailed. During the day I was irritable and exploded in irrational outbursts of anger while exhibiting dominating, overprotective, and controlling behavior. I had become an insufferable fool.

Carole was in full-blown denial. She displayed all of the typical aftereffects of TBI, including compulsive eating, compulsive spending, and withdrawal. Although none of her counselors or psychoanalysts ever mentioned it, she was also dealing with PTSD. Emotionally flatlined, Carole had no enthusiasm for anything. She had no self-esteem and constantly degraded herself. Thanks to her total lack of confidence, she withdrew and shied away from any interaction with other people. My wife was progressively becoming a recluse. Frankly, I think I scared the grit out of her with my dominating temperament, and she no longer possessed the skills to handle me. Hiding had become her only defense.

Curiously, a willful stubbornness that defied explanation had surfaced in Carole. I went overboard encouraging her to work together with me as a team, but she was determined to prove her self-sufficient independence. To help out around the house, I started doing the laundry occasionally, prepared a few meals, and ran the vacuum, but Carole reacted as though I were trying to send the message that she was not doing her part. She may not have been carrying her share of the load, but the intent was to cut her some slack by helping to maintain tolerable living conditions, not rub her nose in the chores that needed tending. Without realizing what was happening, I had taken on the role of her father, and her reactions were that of a rebellious, sometimes snotty, teenage girl. After having been on the receiving end of her mutiny for the umpteenth time, I withdrew, afraid to help and disgusted by the accumulation of neglect.

My wife's unsavory attitude became noticeable a few days after she was discharged from the Lighthouse. Shortly after Carole had come home to stay, I became bedridden, sick with a nasty flu virus. Although her driver's license had been suspended until she could be retested—another law addressing drivers who have suffered TBI—Carole was determined to drive to the store and pick up some medication for me. She stubbornly refused to take no for an answer, and I wasn't about to let her go alone, so I dressed myself and crawled into the passenger's seat while she drove to the store and back.

When Nicole found out about our little jaunt, she climbed all over me for allowing her mother to drive. I simply told her that her mother was determined to go regardless and that if she was going to die behind the wheel, I might as well have been in the car with her.

Our daughter was not impressed.

Even though she was not legally able to drive, my wife continued arguing with me when I told her she could not get behind the wheel. When we went shopping, she would get out of the car, grab a shopping cart, turn her back to me, and walk away. I began to feel like her chauffeur. Her behavior cut deeply and brought back the nightmare of watching our son run away from home without leaving a forwarding address.

Why doesn't anyone want to be with me? I wondered. It was hard not to hide in a corner and feel sorry for myself.

I hung with her. The phrase "for better or for worse" echoed in my head as a reminder that, regardless of the circumstances, I was committed.

Divorce is not an option, I kept telling myself. *I made a promise to Carole, and I intend to keep it.*

Carole said that she stayed with me because she loved me. I was convinced that she stuck around because she had nowhere else to go, which was a reflection of my own destroyed self-esteem. We were slowly drifting apart.

Like rival gang members staking out their territory, Carole and I engaged in what would probably best be described as trench warfare, both of us making a spectacle of ourselves through childish, divisive behavior. Her stubbornness stretched my patience beyond the limit, and I forced my hand upon her will. She countered with passive aggression. To avoid conflict, she simply learned how to lie to me.

I soon realized that the rebellion had not been confined to our personal relationship. In a seditious attempt to put an end to the therapies, counseling, and doctor appointments, she began lying to the doctors and therapists about medical and physical issues. When I intervened, she became even more defiant by hiding the truth from me, pretending she was all right when I could clearly see that she was not.

When the October bank statement arrived in early November, I sat down to balance the checkbook and discovered that my wife's spending habits had gone totally out of control. I confiscated the checkbook only to learn when the next bank statement arrived that she had simply grabbed a stack of blank checks from the desk drawer and started writing them out of sequence. I realized at that point that I was dealing with calculated subversion. If the no-fault insurance adjusters did not succeed at ruining us financially, my wife's spending habits certainly would. Carole was not lacking in skill, but there seemed to be a serious void in her ability to reason.

The crippling blow came one afternoon when I walked outside and caught her off guard with a lit cigarette between her lips. Startled, she spun around and, with smoke drifting away from her face, stuffed the cigarette butt into a wet paper towel that she clenched in her fist.

"What are you doing?" I demanded

"I wasn't smoking," she announced, looking straight into my eyes.

Wasn't smoking?

I was stunned; speechless.

She's trying to tell me that I didn't see what I just saw with my own two eyes?

That episode marked the beginning of the end.

This isn't the woman I married, I thought to myself.

Our daughter was not surprised when I later shared the smoking incident. As she had indicated during that revealing conversation we had had while Carole was still in the hospital, all three of our kids knew that their mother had been smoking for more than twenty years. With so many things going on around us at the time, I had simply dismissed it as a minor issue and focused on the tasks at hand. But actually seeing the cigarette hanging from her lips and then having her look me straight in the eye while denying the very thing that she had been caught doing, grabbed my attention the way a dog handler forces an animal's obedience by reeling in its leash.

There was no turning away from what I had just seen and heard. The staggering reminder of my wife's secret smoking habit shook me on several levels, the first being the startling realization that my wife had successfully deceived me about her smoking habit for so long. The next epiphany was that I had apparently been so disconnected from my wife that I had not noticed the smell of tobacco or cigarette smoke on her or on her clothing.

How could I have been so detached? I wondered. *Have I really been that self-centered?*

For whatever reason, Carole had simply learned how to live a double life.

A chronic cough that Carole had developed years earlier had been blamed on allergies. She had been seeing an allergist prior to the accident on the premise that inoculations could cure her cough. Truth be known, she was simply in denial about her smoking habit.

After the accident, her cough gave rise to the possibility that there may have been tissue damage caused on the day of the accident when the EMT had to jam a breathing tube down her throat to keep her alive. That specific trauma may have aggravated the compromised condition of Carole's bronchial airways, but in reality, her smoking habit had been the root cause of her chronic cough all along.

Realizing that Carole had so completely and successfully hidden her smoking habit all those years brought the issue of trust front and center in our relationship. I could no longer know whether my wife was telling me the truth or feeding me a convincing lie.

That was the first time that I consciously began searching for an escape.

With each confrontation between us, Carole's disposition continued to decline, and her stubborn attitude darkened. She became depressed and melancholy and regarded every one of her medical issues as a personal failure. There was no reasoning with her, and she would not listen to anyone attempting to provide the help she needed.

I felt responsible for what had happened to us on the highway, which subconsciously accelerated my efforts to take care of her. That simply caused her to recoil even further. Counselors kept telling me to back off, and I bristled at their advice.

What do they know? I would say to myself. *They aren't the ones living with this woman.*

Edging closer and closer to the ultimate marital disaster brought about a whole new brand of nightmare added to the ones that had already been startling me awake in the middle of the night. I had become consumed with thoughts of being abandoned by the system that was supposed to be helping me while I was living with a woman I could no longer trust.

Disillusion dissolved hope, and depression sank deep. Fantasies of stuffing a few essential items into a duffel bag and disappearing into the Rocky Mountains had become a tantalizing temptation.

Our marriage of thirty-seven years was crumbling.

CHAPTER 28

THE BLACK HOLE

—⁂—

November ushered in the cold, bitter Michigan winter that year with overcast skies and frozen ground. Thanksgiving 2007 was just around the corner.

According to my gloom-and-doom calculations, we would be lucky if we didn't have to spend Thanksgiving in separate homeless shelters. I figured we had a month or two before the utilities would be turned off and the eviction notice would be nailed to our front door. I predicted Carole and I would be finished living together as a couple long before we lost our home.

The self-pity part of me privately welcomed a dramatic ending to this twenty-first-century version of *Gone with the Wind*.

Bring it on! I selfishly thought to myself. *What better way could there be to show the system what their negligence has created?*

In one last-ditch effort to avoid slipping into bankruptcy, I telephoned our attorney. His receptionist told me that he was out of town again for a few weeks, so I hung up and dialed his cell phone. To my surprise, he answered.

"Hi, Dave," he said in a cordial voice. "How are you doing?"

"Bob," I said soberly, "you're talking to the captain of a sinking ship."

"What's going on?" he asked, as though he didn't have a clue how desperate our situation had become.

"We're out of money," I said. "We are out of patience, and we are just about out of our minds. I feel as though we should have

215

done the insurance companies a service by dying on the road so the adjusters wouldn't have to deal with our claims."

"Oh, don't say that," he said.

"I don't know what we're going to do. I'm not going to be able to cover this month's utilities or make our November mortgage payment. I'll be thankful this Thanksgiving if we still have a house to cook a turkey in."

"Hang on," he said. "Let me make a few phone calls."

It didn't matter anymore. I really didn't expect to hear back from our attorney, and I was sick of begging and fighting for what was rightfully ours.

I was throwing in the towel on my marriage to Carole, and I didn't care if I no longer had a home to live in. I had already begun planning my getaway. I was ready to just take what was left of my life and live it one day at a time on the streets of America until the end finally, mercifully, came.

If I can get enough cash together to put gas in the car, I can drive to a warmer climate, I thought to myself. *Carole can stay here or go live with one of her friends. I don't care. I'll just move from one rest area to another and sleep in the back of the car until I can get myself either arrested or reestablished somewhere.*

I imagined myself running away and hiding like that guy in the movie *The Fugitive*. How someone who had done nothing wrong could wind up in such a pickle totally escaped me. All of a sudden I was that guy.

The twilight zone had turned into a black hole.

CHAPTER 29

SOMETIMES CHRISTMAS COMES EARLY

—⁂—

Two days before Thanksgiving, I received a phone call from our attorney's associate in Royal Oak. Checks from the insurance adjusters in amounts sufficient to maintain our home and keep us safe from the bill collectors for a while longer had arrived at their office. I remained skeptical, but the news allowed me to exhale and relax for the first time in months. Although we had been seriously wounded and scarred, it appeared as though we had somehow survived another wave of skirmishes.

In one pile of checks, we received Carole's back pay for five months. It came as no surprise that the amount awarded was exactly what our attorney claimed we were owed. Why it had taken the adjusters so long to figure that out remained a mystery.

We had also been granted an allowance for every mile we had logged going to and from hospitals, doctor appointments, and therapy sessions. Compensation included reimbursements for out-of-pocket medical expenses, along with a retroactive daily stipend for replacement services and attendant care.

There was no mention of lost income from my side of the table. I would not be preparing and filing my income taxes for another two months, so I knew that the adjusters weren't even thinking about calculating my replacement wages. I remained hopeful that when they finally saw the light, we would receive a huge amount of money for retroactive compensation.

A heightened sense of optimism lightened the mood. I felt sheltered and safe for a change. It was time to balance the scales and reward those whose encouragement and help had kept us from facing total disaster.

I estimated the number of days that our friends Roger and Leslie had spent taking care of things at our house and multiplied that by the daily replacement services allowance. They were speechless when we handed over a check for around sixteen hundred dollars. It didn't feel like anywhere near enough compensation for the comfort they had provided through their caring compassion.

Although we had received compensation for in-home assistance, the attendant care part of the services we had been promised never materialized. Regardless, we decided that we owed our daughter for all of the days she had spent doing what a hired nurse should have been doing. The money we gave her helped put her finances back on track and gave us a sense of closure.

We paid household bills and had reserves to cover a few more months' worth of expenses if we remained conservative with our spending habits. Financially we were out of harm's way, albeit temporarily. God willing, Carole's monthly income would continue, but there was no guarantee the adjusters hadn't closed the checkbook for another six months.

I simply ignored the growing stack of unpaid medical bills and collection notices.

The long-awaited injection of cash was also sufficient to temporarily postpone my exodus. Waiting around to see what happened had suddenly become affordable for the time being, and sitting tight represented the path of least resistance. So I unpacked my emotional baggage and stuffed my damaged ego back into the underwear drawer.

Thanksgiving came and went that year without any further calamities.

I had begun to accept the bitter fact that after having been shut down for five months, my little repair business might as well have been liquidated. Closing the doors had definitely created a void in the market, but my customers soon found other sources for the work that I had been doing. Buying habits are difficult to change, so I knew that once my customers had found alternate suppliers, it would be difficult to lure them back.

It was disheartening knowing that nearly twenty years of effort had been flushed down the drain and that reopening the business would be like starting all over again. I wasn't sure I had the gumption to go through that. All that remained was the shell of a once-lucrative enterprise, and there was no guarantee my market would even exist once the doors had been reopened. In our throw-it-away culture, repair shops like mine were disappearing faster than vacuum-tube TVs.

I had always wondered how my little fix-it business would finally end, but not in my wildest dreams had there ever been a vision of the scenario that had unfolded. The entire operation had been taken from me by default.

The question remained: what exactly was retirement supposed to look like?

Physical therapists had been improving mobility in my right shoulder, but the pain was not going away. While in therapy I started visiting the chiropractor again, and he detected unnatural movement in the shoulder joint. Both the therapist and the chiropractor suspected something more serious than misalignment or muscle trauma.

Following advice from the physical therapy department at the Lighthouse, I arranged for a medical examination from the doctor who had been overseeing Carole's care. By that time, I was in the habit of contacting our case manager whenever anyone so much as recommended aspirin, so I asked her to join me for the appointment.

I explained to the doctor in Saginaw why he had been asked to take a look at the shoulder, referring to the chiropractor and therapists' opinions. After a cursory examination, the doctor, in spite of everything I had told him, addressed the request with skepticism.

"What makes you think this pain in your shoulder is tied to an accident-related injury?" he asked.

"It started bothering me shortly after I was released from St. Mary's in July," I said.

"I don't understand why nobody caught this before now," he said.

The doctor's challenging remarks immediately got my hackles up.

"Well, neither do I!" I replied tersely. "It aches constantly, and I've mentioned it to several people, but nobody seems to care."

I explained how my shoulder hurt every time I tried to use the crutches and that using a walker was nearly impossible.

"I can't even play my guitar for more than three minutes without unbearable pain. And I might add, Doc, that the Lighthouse therapists would not have been working on my shoulder if they hadn't found something wrong with it!"

Once again it felt as though I had been forced to prove that there had been an accident.

Why not! I thought to myself. *I'm beginning to wonder if I didn't just fall off a ladder and this whole series of events has just been one long nightmare. Even the doctor doesn't seem to be taking me seriously.*

The doctor reluctantly conceded and wrote a prescription to have an ultrasound performed on the shoulder. When the results came back, even I was surprised.

The incurable pain in my shoulder was partially a result of misalignment in the joint, but the majority of the discomfort was due to a tendon that had been separated from the bone. Another tendon had been torn, and a third tendon stretched to the point of separation. That explained why chiropractic adjustments wouldn't hold and therapies had only provided temporary relief. The joint would not stay in alignment because parts inside my shoulder had come unhooked.

When we met back at the doctor's office to review the results of the ultrasound, he seemed enlightened and displayed a much less stern attitude. We discussed the condition of my shoulder and came to the conclusion that unless the damage was surgically repaired, there would be no significant improvement. The news was liberating and, at the same time, frightening. Even though I was destined to return to the operating room, I had been vindicated.

—⁓—

The eighteenth of December, the day of reckoning, had finally arrived. We headed to the surgeon's clinic in West Bloomfield to learn the fate of my foot.

As I fidgeted nervously at the doctor's clinic while seated in the chair next to my wife, our daughter, and the case manager, the thirty-minute wait felt more like hours. Finally the door opened and a nurse culled us from the growing herd of patients that had gathered in the outer waiting area. An X-ray technician escorted me down the hall and into another lab while the rest of my entourage waited in an examination room. I climbed onto the table and assumed the position for another series of pictures of the ankle—the fourth in as many months.

A short while after being escorted back to the examination room, the doctor arrived with a clipboard in his hand and a sober look on his face. Although I had planned to ask the doctor about my shoulder during the appointment, that was the furthest thing from my mind at the moment.

"Well," he said slowly as he examined my records.

I went numb. It might have been his somber expression or maybe the way he looked at the charts instead of me when he spoke. Somehow I already knew that he would be scheduling the surgery to remove my foot. The pain in the part of my foot that was not numb had never quite gone away, and I was convinced that it was because the bones had not knitted back together.

I was prepared to ask the doctor to modify my leg for the most convenient adaptation of a prosthetic device. It no longer mattered if he had to saw off bones halfway to the knee. The time had come to end the waiting.

The doctor continued speaking while my thoughts drifted. Bits and pieces of what he said sifted through the haze as my mind wandered.

Suddenly something he said grabbed my attention.

"Pardon me?" I said, not sure that I had heard him correctly.

"I said it looks like you'll be able to start bearing weight on your foot."

There was a long pause as his words sank in.

It looks like you'll be able to start bearing weight on your foot.

"Really?" was all I could say.

He smiled patiently and then continued.

"I think you'll be able to put all of your weight on it in about four or five weeks. Start out at about twenty-five percent the first week."

I looked at my wife, then my daughter, and then the case manager, who was wiping a tear from the corner of her eye. Then I reached out to shake my doctor's hand and thanked him for having performed a miracle.

He looked at me and smiled.

"You're welcome," he replied humbly.

The doctor's words echoed in my head.

It looks like you'll be able to start bearing weight on your foot.

"Do you think I'll be able to play my drums again?" I asked him.

"Oh, yeah!" he said rather enthusiastically. "That would be great therapy for your ankle. Just take it easy and don't get carried away. It's gonna hurt for a while, and it's probably going to be stiff, but you should be able to put the crutches back in the closet in a few weeks."

"What about therapy?" our case manager asked.

"I'll write a prescription to handle that," the doctor replied. "He's going to need some help getting that foot back into working condition."

As the doctor was preparing to leave for his next appointment, our case manager brought up the issue of my shoulder, explaining the therapies I had been through and the results of the ultrasound examination.

"Is that something you do?" she asked the doctor.

"No," he replied, "but my brother does. Tell the girls at the desk before you leave, and they can make an appointment for you. Since you're already a patient here at the clinic, you should have no trouble getting in to see him."

With that he shook my hand, smiled a boyish smile, and turned to leave the room.

"Thanks again, Doc!" I said as he walked out the door and on to his next patient.

"Anytime!" he said over his shoulder.

I was jubilant! Not only was I going to keep my foot, but the genius who saved it had a brother who could repair my shoulder as well. I felt blessed as another ray of hope finally shone through the darkness that had so consumed the world around me.

On our way out of the clinic, we stopped at the front desk and scheduled an appointment with the foot guru's brother. We wouldn't be able to see him before the middle of February, a couple of months away, but I was certainly willing to wait.

Christmas was only a week away, and Nicole and Carole wanted to stop at a couple of stores at a mall on the way home from the clinic in West Bloomfield. It felt as though Christmas had come early and the gifts had already been opened. Like a kid itching to try out my new toy, I was excited for the opportunity to start putting weight on my foot. Doing a little shopping sounded like a great opportunity to use the gift just received.

As we headed toward the mall, I called my cousin Roger to share the news.

Roger had waited at Beaumont while I was in surgery that day in July, and he had taken the time to talk to the doctor while I was still in recovery. When I woke up in the hospital room, Roger was standing at the foot of my bed, waiting for the opportunity to explain what the doctor had said. He explained that although the surgery had been successful, there was still the strong possibility the procedure might not have been enough to save my foot. He was trying to brace me for the worst possible outcome.

My cousin, also an all-around musician who played the drums, was fully aware of how potentially devastating for me it would have been to lose my right foot. When I called him with the news that I could start walking again, he genuinely shared my joy and was doubly excited that the doctor thought using the drum pedal would be good therapy. What a pleasure it was to be able to share that news!

The parking lots all around the mall were jammed full. By the time we made it from our parking spot in the outer reaches of the lot to the front door of the store, I was huffing and puffing and struggling a little with the crutches. Not wanting to dampen their shopping excursion, I tagged along, laboriously trying to hide the increasing level of pain in my foot. My shoulder had also begun to ache unbearably from using the crutches. I began to wonder if I was going to make it back to the car unassisted. I bit my tongue and followed Nicole and Carole through the store, trying to act as though nothing was wrong.

When we finally made it back to the car, I climbed in and let out a heavy sigh of relief. I had already decided that if they planned to stop anywhere else, waiting for them in the backseat of the car would be the smart thing to do.

The next day, the physical therapists at the Lighthouse wasted no time going to work on my foot and ankle. I knew from the first moment when I had tried to put weight on my foot that learning to walk again was going to be a painful process. I swear the therapists found joy in locating every tender spot from the knee to my toenails.

The first thing we discovered was that my foot had stiffened up so badly from lack of use that the Achilles tendon, which wraps around the heel and extends through the arch, was as tight as a banjo string. The foot had developed plantar fasciitis, a painful inflammatory process of the plantar fascia—the connective tissue on the sole of the foot.

The ball of my foot was swollen, and the toes had atrophied. When I stood flat on the floor, those curled-up toes would not touch the surface without someone pushing down on them. They were as stiff as a board and mostly still numb. The calf muscles on my right leg had also shrunk from lack of use. It was difficult to bear weight, because of the pain and weakness. I was amazed by how quickly my body had lost muscle tone.

In spite of the discomfort, it was a fantastic relief knowing that I wasn't going to lose the foot. Strumming the guitar for more than five minutes still caused unbearable pain in my shoulder, but we had a cure for that. Meanwhile I had regained the ability to play the drums.

Those small steps on the road to recovery had lightened my mood, which somewhat eased the tension between Carole and me. She seemed happy for me and appeared willing to concede, demonstrating an awareness of the conflict between us that she had not previously shown. It was an encouraging sign.

With renewed hope I even began to dream about reopening the starter repair business.

CHAPTER 30
FROM ONE LIMB BROKEN TO ANOTHER

—✠—

Therapies continued on my foot, ankle, and leg for the duration of December and January and into February, and the drive to the Lighthouse continued three days a week with Carole at my side.

The doctor's prediction was that range of motion in my ankle and foot would recover to less than 10 percent inversion and eversion (side to side) and about 30 percent dorsiflexion and plantar flexion (up and down). I'm pretty sure the therapists misinterpreted the doctor's estimate of final mobility as their *starting* point for therapy!

My team seemed determined to force the ankle joint to move in directions that would have made a gymnast envious. Scars from surgical incisions on both sides of the foot were massaged and manipulated to release the tendons from the scar tissue that had formed under the skin. Gently but relentlessly (if that's possible), therapists stretched, bent, twisted, and kneaded my foot through each session until everything from the knee down had turned numb from vigorous stimulation.

Strengthening exercises were introduced to build and condition the muscles in my leg. Balancing drills were surprisingly difficult, as I had lost the ability to stand on one leg, but the therapists knew exactly what they were doing and how far to push the limits of every muscle, tendon, and joint.

Each therapy session ended with my ankle being packed in ice. I had no doubt that those personal fitness Nazis would eventually tear my foot from my leg at the ankle joint, completing the procedure I had originally expected the doctor from Beaumont to perform surgically. Their approach, however effective, introduced me to a whole network of sensitive nerves that I never knew existed.

Eventually, as therapies on my foot, ankle, and leg continued, I was limping into the workout room without the use of the Roll-A-Bout, crutches, or even a cane. My foot continued to tingle as nerves slowly knitted their way back into various parts of damaged tissue. I could literally feel the healing as startling stabbing jolts reintroduced various parts of the foot that were coming back to life.

Late in January I called for an appointment with the surgeon who had worked on me in the ER that first night at St. Mary's. When I explained to the receptionist who I was and why I wanted to see the doctor, she immediately put a priority on my visit and set me up with a time slot to see the doctor in early February.

When the doctor walked into the examining room with his assistant, I stood up, reintroduced myself, and shook his hand. He immediately recognized me and grinned from ear to ear. I handed him the photograph taken from an X-ray of my ankle that revealed seven screws holding it together. Then I sat on the edge of the examining table and stripped off my shoe and sock so he could get a closer look.

He got a little choked up and thanked me for coming to see him.

"I really didn't give your foot a prayer," he said, shaking his head and examining the scars. "I don't think there was a bone that hadn't been jammed out of place or broken. How does it feel?"

"It's still mostly numb, but I'm getting my strength back, and the nerves are painfully knitting themselves back together. My therapists have helped me recover to over ninety percent side-to-side movement and almost seventy percent up-and-down."

"Who did the surgery?" he asked. "Was it the doctor I sent you to?"

"No," I said. "The doctor you sent me to referred me to his guru in West Bloomfield; he then assisted in the procedure."

When I shared the West Bloomfield doctor's name, he was floored.

"You're kidding!" he said in disbelief. "How did you manage to get that guy to do your surgery? That man wrote the book on your type of injury!"

"Well, Doc," I said, "your guru at the orthopedic clinic knew that guru from West Bloomfield, and the rest is history. His brother is going to be doing the surgery on my shoulder to repair tendon damage."

"That's unbelievable," he said. "You sure had the best of the best working on your behalf."

"Well, thanks to you I did. I hope you're counting yourself as one of those best of the best. You could have just as easily pulled out the hacksaw while you had me in the ER at St. Mary's, and that would have been the end of it."

He shook my hand and thanked me again for stopping to see him. I told him that thanks to God's guidance and a lot of prayers, I still had a foot. He agreed, gave me a warm smile, and we parted as friends.

About a week later we traveled back to West Bloomfield to see the foot guru's brother about my shoulder. The brother appeared to be a little older, but he was just as gifted. He examined my shoulder, took a look at the ultrasound results, and gave me two options.

"A shot of cortisone into the joint will take away the pain for about six to eight weeks," he said, "but surgery is the only way you will ever experience a permanent recovery."

Oh, Lord, I thought to myself, *I've heard that before. Please, not more surgery!*

"How long will I be out of commission after the surgery?" I asked.

"You will have four to six weeks of complete immobility in your shoulder before you will be able to start therapy," he said.

"Let's try the cortisone," I said.

Ten minutes later, while the needle was still entering the joint, I reconsidered my options. Wow, I had no idea a shot could be that excruciatingly painful. I'm pretty sure he injected enough fluid into my shoulder to baste a turkey. As much as I dreaded the probability of being incapacitated by surgery for another six weeks, there was no way I was going to spend the rest of my life choosing between the pain of cortisone shots or the equivalent of a toothache in my shoulder.

"I think we should schedule the surgery, Doc," I said as soon as I had quit grimacing from the pain.

"Okay," he said. "I'll alert the staff, and we'll get you scheduled for the procedure."

As quickly as he had entered the room, he was gone. He didn't have the bedside manner his brother had perfected, but I was confident that I had the other pro from Dover lined up to fix my shoulder.

Once again I found it remarkable how God had provided the people who were at the right place and at the right time. His hand continued cradling us.

CHAPTER 31
THE EAGLE CRASHES

Behold, thou hast made my days as an handbreadth;
and mine age is as nothing before thee: verily every man at
his best state is altogether vanity. Selah.

Psalm 39:5 (KJV)

March 2008 came in like the grim reaper. Nearly nine months had passed since the wreck, and we still had no idea if or when either of us would be able to return to work and earn a living. Thoughts of a comfortable, relaxing retirement had long since disintegrated along with all of our hopes and dreams for the type of recreation that normally adds spice to healthy partnerships. It had become difficult for either of us to find purpose.

Closing in on what I had hoped would be the final chapter of therapies and counseling triggered thoughts of getting back to the way things had been before the accident. It made me shudder to think about hitting the floor on a dead run every morning just trying to maintain the things we owned. Any drive to reengage that daily hamster-in-the-wheel grind had disappeared.

Around eleven-fifteen on the sixth of March, I sat watching the evening news, my mind wandering from one unresolved issue to another, hardly paying attention to the talking heads on TV. From out on the highway in front of our house came a loud boom, followed by a noise that sounded something like rubber repeatedly slapping the pavement. I thought a semitruck tire had exploded. The startling blast rattled the windows. Thinking there may have been a trucker in distress I put on my coat and went outside to investigate. Just as I opened the front door, a car coming from the south was completing a U-turn in the highway at the end of our driveway. When its lights flashed across the neighbor's front yard, I saw a pickup truck sitting in the shadows on the grass by the road. A lady screaming hysterically had climbed out from the passenger side of that twisted pickup and was running toward the U-turn car as it pulled to a stop a few feet away.

What is going on? I wondered. *And why is that pickup parked in the middle of the neighbor's front yard?*

There had been an accident. I hobbled back into the house and dialed 911, and I then went back out into the cold, dark night to witness the entire scene unfold, sensing the traumas that lay ahead for the survivors. As vehicles arrived and lit the darkness, I spotted a second vehicle lying on its side a few hundred feet to the south.

I felt a numbing sensation creeping up the back of my neck.

Those poor people are in the opening minutes of what we have been going through for the past nine months, I thought to myself. *God have mercy on what they are about to endure!*

I later learned that the driver of the vehicle lying on its side had crossed four lanes of traffic and collided head-on with the pickup truck that had landed in the neighbor's front yard. The man behind the wheel of the wrinkled pickup sitting on the grass had died upon impact, and the lady running hysterically from the passenger-side door was his unsuspecting widow. Their family had been riding in the car that made the U-turn on the highway after witnessing the horrifying collision.

The family of the deceased man maintained a small wreath in the neighbor's front yard for several years following the accident. I shuddered every time I saw it. A memorial like that could have appropriately been placed alongside the highway to mark the spot where our lives had metaphorically ended.

Holding my breath while waiting for a solution to our financial turmoil and then witnessing the aftermath of a fatal crash left me with the strange sensation that my days on earth were numbered. Nothing in particular suggested how much time was left, but I had an eerie feeling the end was near, almost as though I had been diagnosed with a terminal illness. That fatalistic frame of mind put me in a panic. Every minute had to count for something, which made decisions much harder to face. Negative thoughts poisoned my brain like a festering wound, and the wait-and-see marathon had me geared up for the worst case scenario.

We had been receiving Carole's lost wages compensation along with a daily allowance for in-home attendant care since December. We were not losing ground financially as rapidly as we had been during those first five months of survival, but we were still slipping backward. As it turned out, anxieties caused by the fear of losing were more than far-fetched premonition. Instinctively I theorized all along that we were going to be compromised, and I was right.

On March 7, my birthday and the day following that horrible head-on collision in front of our house, our attorney finally broke the logjam that had been holding up my lost wages compensation. When he called to give me the news, he did not sound pleased.

"Because you are self-employed," he said, "your compensation is based upon your business's net profit."

"Okay," I said, "so what did they say my net profit was?"

"Just over eleven thousand dollars," he said.

"Eleven thousand dollars a month?" I asked.

"No," he said slowly, "eleven thousand five hundred a year."

"That's impossible! Where did they come up with that figure?"

Profit-and-loss statements for the first six months of business for that year revealed net earnings nearly seven times that amount. I assumed the insurance adjusters had been reviewing three years' worth of tax returns for the purpose of lowering my average earnings figures and totally expected them to cheat me out of as much as they could get away with, but this was incredible!

I did the math in my head.

"That comes to around nine hundred dollars a month," I said. "That won't even cover the mortgage payment on my house, let alone the fixed expenses on my business. How am I supposed to pay my bills with that?"

My little repair business had been generating enough revenue to cover more than its overhead. At the end of every month, there was usually enough cash available to pay over seventeen hundred dollars toward our home mortgage, plus the motorcycle loan, all of our household expenses, and still have enough for dining out and entertainment. All of that money withdrawn for nonbusiness expenses—more than fifty-five hundred dollars every month—represented the real net profit that my business had been producing. No-fault law limited the insurance company's exposure to four thousand dollars per month.

I had been awarded nine hundred dollars. The news was devastating.

It was impossible for me to fathom how the numbers could have been skewed so radically in the insurance company's favor. The adjuster's determination would not even cover the business expenses, let alone withdrawals for personal and household expenses. Avoiding bankruptcy meant totally dismantling the business: disconnecting the telephones, canceling all open contracts, turning off the utilities, and suspending all formal agreements with customers and suppliers. Expenses would have to be virtually eliminated, which would have been impossible without paying someone to make the whole operation literally disappear.

"That's not all," he said. "Because our law office had to fight for the settlement, our attorney fees will have to be deducted."

I was speechless. I had been forced to settle for less than 20 percent of what I had been earning. As though that bit of news had not been sufficiently stunning, one-third of that pitifully small amount would be going straight into the attorney's pocket.

"We intend to appeal their decision," he said. "I don't know how they arrived at that amount, but it's obviously an unfair settlement."

The fight had gone out of me. I had been trying to roll with the punches, but that one was a knockout blow. Every bit of Norman Vincent Peale's positive thinking power, along with Dale Carnegie's principles of being influential, had been neutralized.

"Fine," I said. "I can't say I'm surprised. Those people haven't done the right thing yet, and we've had to fight them tooth and nail every step of the way. Why should this be any different!"

"I know it's disappointing," he said, trying to comfort me.

"You have no idea!"

A week after receiving the disastrous news about my compensation settlement we received a letter from Carole's employer. She had been away from her job at the courthouse for so long that the county would no longer cover the cost of our medical insurance. Our options were to either start paying the premiums out-of-pocket or allow the policy to be terminated.

That little bomb landed in our lap to the tune of just over nine hundred dollars a month. If we dropped the insurance, we would have been without any hope of finding a medical insurance carrier who would write a policy for us with our recent medical history. Without health insurance, we would undoubtedly have spent the rest of our days hoping we would never have to visit a doctor again.

Paying for the insurance out of pocket would carry us nine hundred dollars a month closer to financial disaster.

"We have enough to cover this month," I said to Carole. "We can't afford to be without medical insurance, so we'll just have to take it one month at a time."

I said a prayer and then sent a check to the county treasurer's office.

After procrastinating for nearly nine months, the motorcycle insurance adjuster finally came through with a settlement check. The motorcycle had been totaled, yet the amount of money we received wasn't even enough to pay off the bank loan. The bank had not loaned us more than the motorcycle was worth; the insurance adjuster simply refused to acknowledge its true market value.

By then I was so beaten that I just looked at the check from the motorcycle insurance company and tossed it on the pile of unpaid bills as though it was a piece of scrap paper. Eventually I dug the check out of the pile, deposited the money into the savings account, and used the proceeds to continue making monthly payments toward a debt we owed on a machine that nobody could use.

I found it remarkably discouraging to be on the receiving end of what can only be described as wholesale extortion. We had been forced by law to purchase a product that was unavailable when we needed it and that fell miserably short of our expectations when delivery had finally been made.

My repair shop, like the insurance industry, was in business to provide a service. If I had demonstrated the same disregard for customer satisfaction as those underwriters had demonstrated for our well-being, my operation would not have survived its first year.

The irony was that my business did not have the benefit of government legislation forcing people to purchase my product.

CHAPTER 32

BEAUMONT—SURGERY #2

—◊—

I was strangely pessimistic the day we returned to Beaumont near the end of March for the surgery on my shoulder. There was no question that the operation would correct the damage to the tendons and that when the tissue had healed, my shoulder would function without pain. All the same, I dreaded the thought of being on the disabled list again.

The return trip to the operating room was a step back in time to my days spent in a wheelchair and nights in a recliner. I envisioned being surrounded by a sea of red ink and bureaucratic balderdash with an exponentially taller stack of unpaid medical bills and collection notices stemming from yet another expensive hospital stay.

Carole was still unable to drive, so Nicole was once again my private chauffeur. After the number of trips we had made, she had become very familiar with the best routes to and from Beaumont. She also knew the most convenient place for loading and unloading, as well as the best place to park the car while we were there. The trip to Beaumont, the hospital's check-in procedures, and the pre-op ritual moved me along like the river's current carrying debris over Niagara Falls. It felt as though I were back at the Armed Forces Induction Center, saying good-bye for the last time, being processed into a war from which I was not expected to return. It was comforting to have our daughter with her medical background at my side as we walked through the front doors and into the hospital's main lobby.

During the presurgical preparation, the same anesthesiologist who had prepped me for the foot surgery eight months earlier entered the room. He recognized me from the first visit and recalled the fact that my scheduled procedure then had been aborted and postponed for two days.

"So, how's your foot doing?" he asked as he inserted an IV into my right arm.

"Well, I'm walking on my own again, which is a good thing, because after today I don't think I will be able to use crutches for a while."

He laughed and connected a hose to the IV. Then he smiled and released the clamp from the hose, allowing liquid to flow. I never saw him again.

When I woke up in recovery, my shoulder was wrapped in bandages and my arm was in a sling that had been strapped around my waist. The hospital gown was my designated attire for the ride home.

Two days later we returned to the doctor's clinic in West Bloomfield. His demeanor was just as abrupt as it had been during our first visit.

"Everything went very well," he said. "I want you to keep your arm immobile and in the sling for six weeks. Take it out of the sling only when you have something to rest it on for support. Avoid rotating your arm more than ten degrees in any direction. I'll write a prescription for therapy to start in six weeks. Go and have a good life!"

"Do you need to see me again for any reason?" I asked.

"Not unless you have complications. If you follow my instructions carefully, you will have no trouble."

Then he was gone.

No driving and no physical activity while my arm was in the sling—doctor's orders. Carole couldn't drive, and I had nobody available to haul us around. There was no money to pay for transportation, and the insurance company had done nothing to provide assistance.

I had no choice but to ignore the doctor's orders, thumb my nose at liability, take the risk, and cheat.

For the next six weeks, I drove my wife and myself to and from therapies with my right arm in the sling and my left hand on the steering wheel. I never told another soul. Following the rules had simply become too complicated.

CHAPTER 33

FLOATING THE BALLOONS

Take therefore no thought for the morrow: for the
morrow shall take thought for the things of itself. Sufficient
unto the day is the evil thereof.

Matthew 6:34 (KJV)

—ᴍᴍ—

Spring 2008 was largely uneventful. My shoulder healed as predicted, and after a few weeks of physical therapy, I had regained full, painless mobility. Although my foot and ankle ached constantly, I was walking on them.

Oddly my left shoulder had begun giving me trouble. I wasn't surprised, since that was where I had made contact with the highway, as evidenced by the Pop-Tart-size scar from the road rash on the top of my shoulder. The puzzling thing was that there was no pain in the joint until I tried lifting things and doing physical labor around the backyard.

Once again the doctor challenged me when I told him that I thought the pain in my left shoulder was a result of the accident. I tore off my shirt and pointed to the scar on my shoulder.

"That's where I hit the highway, Doc! Now how about a little cooperation here!"

Sheesh. How many more battles are there going to be, anyway? I thought to myself. *Like being left for dead on the highway wasn't hard enough to deal with already!*

I'm not sure whether it was sympathy, logic, or intimidation that finally persuaded him, but the doctor agreed to order an ultrasound on my left shoulder. Thankfully, the results showed evidence of stress correctable with therapy. No surgery would be required.

I breathed a sigh of relief.

Therapies and counseling for both Carole and me continued at a patronizing pace, which further discouraged any sense of independence. We both felt dutifully trapped in recovery mode.

Our relationship remained guarded. It was anybody's guess where Carole and I would be with our marriage in six months, or six days for that matter. Nevertheless, we stumbled along, trying to make it work.

Our common goal, without question, was to finish this unpaid excursion through the matrix as expeditiously as possible. The major difference between my wife and me was that I was not about to take any shortcuts to make that happen. Carole seemed to want it to end at any cost.

—⚅—

The one-year anniversary of our accident was fast approaching. It felt as though we should have been planning something special to observe the day, but I also knew it was obviously not going to be a graduation celebration. We still had a long road ahead of us.

Dan, my counselor, asked if we had any special plans to celebrate having survived the first year of our near-death experience.

"It's crossed my mind," I said, "but honestly I don't know what to do that would be appropriate. Got any suggestions?"

"Float some balloons," he said.

"You mind explaining that in a little more depth?" I asked.

"Some friends of mine were having problems," he said, "and they decided to just give them over to God. In a symbolic gesture, they each wrote all of their concerns and disappointments on slips of paper, tied them to helium balloons, and let them float away as though they were giving their problems over to God."

"Well," I said, "that makes more sense than anything I might have come up with."

Tuesday morning, June 24, 2008, Carole and I called a truce, and then I shared Dan's idea to float some balloons. Carole agreed it was a good idea, so we wrote our personal concerns on little slips of paper, purchased a couple of helium balloons, and tied the little pieces of paper to the strings attached to the balloons. That afternoon we went to the intersection of M-53 and Frenchline Road.

I parked the car in the turnaround drive in front of the old abandoned one-room schoolhouse that occupies the northwest corner of the intersection. As we climbed out of the vehicle, the man who owned the schoolhouse and surrounding property came walking toward us, muttering something that didn't sound nice. I figured he was going to tell us to move our vehicle and go somewhere else to gaze at the landscape. As he approached, I introduced myself and extended my hand.

"Have you lived here long?" I asked him.

"Why do you ask?"

"The guy who once owned this property lived next door to us a mile and a half to the north. Did you know him?"

"He must have been a couple of owners before me," he replied gruffly.

The man didn't seem too interested in small talk.

"Hmm. I was just curious," I said.

No response.

"My wife and I were the victims of a hit-and-run accident at this intersection one year ago today," I said.

"Oh, yeah," he said. "I remember that."

The guy acted as though he didn't care about anything that did not personally affect his little realm. Without breaking stride, his next comment skirted right to the issue that had brought him to the front yard in the first place.

"People are always using this circle drive to turn around as though it was part of a public throughway," he said. "I get a little tired of chasing them away."

"Well, we just stopped by to thank God for helping us make it through the first year," I said. "We won't be here long."

He seemed to soften a little and then turned and walked back across the schoolyard toward his house. I felt sad for the man's behavior and a little annoyed by his challenging demeanor and unapologetic interruption. In the grand scheme of things, it really didn't matter. He knew who we were, and that was enough.

We stood on the shoulder of the road at approximately the spot where our limp bodies had finally skidded to a stop and looked first at each other and then at the sky. It was a warm, sunny day much like the day when we had taken our last motorcycle ride, which had ended at that very spot one year earlier.

We hugged each other and then let go of the balloons, snapping photos of them as they drifted up and out of sight.

Chapter 34

Wedding in a Garden

—w—

Although Carole and I had found some common ground, our relationship remained apathetic. We had become two strangers living under the same roof. There was nobody else either of us wanted in our lives. We simply gritted our teeth and waited as though something magical would happen to snap us both out of our marital peevishness.

Earlier in the year, Jason and Rhonda had announced their plans to marry on Saturday, August 1, 2008. That was an encouraging bit of news.

"Wow," I said to Carole, "we'll be attending our son's wedding on our thirty-eighth wedding anniversary and my dad's ninety-second birthday. All three events will be on the same day!"

Maybe this is it, I thought to myself. *Maybe my son is coming back home to be with his family and he picked that date to help reconnect with his mother and me!*

I secretly envisioned a milestone event complete with reconciliation, reunion, and celebration. My thoughts ran wild as I eagerly sought ways to help with the arrangements. I was anxious to be reunited with our son and, hopefully, symbolically reestablish a relationship with Carole.

Well, if nothing else, those were pleasantly hopeful thoughts.

The kids were planning an outdoor ceremony at a beautiful park on the outskirts of Frankenmuth, Michigan. Carole and I took a drive one afternoon and located the spot. It was truly an enchanting setting.

Carole and I were allowed peripheral involvement in the planning stages of the wedding until I managed to trip over unannounced protocols and royally mess things up. To this day I don't know what the fuss was about. All grandparents had been invited, but Rhonda's grandmother was the only one of the five grandparents who was still able to travel without assistance. Carole's parents lived near her sister in Florida, and my parents lived near my sister outside of Traverse City, Michigan.

All four of Jason's grandparents wanted to attend the wedding, but someone was going to have to help get them there. The only reasonable option was to ask for our sisters' help with transportation.

"How in the world are we going to tactfully ask our sisters to bring the grandparents to the wedding without allowing them to attend?" I asked Carole. "What are they supposed to do during the ceremony? Wait by the car on the other side of the hedge until it's over?"

"I don't know," she said. "Just invite them to the wedding."

Of course asking our sisters to bring our mothers and fathers to the wedding meant they would bring their husbands with them. I decided that if our sisters and their husbands were going to be at our son's wedding, so were my two brothers and Carole's other sister.

So as the father of the groom, I took it upon myself to let our siblings know that they were all welcome to join us during our son's ceremony, as were their spouses and my younger brother's two sons. The list of guests grew modestly, but the whole arrangement fell radically outside the margins of the official plan.

I was oblivious.

Must be a guy thing, I thought to myself.

Those twelve extra guests accompanying the four grandparents seemed to represent a serious violation of some cryptogram I had missed. I started taking flack for inviting more people than the arranged seating would accommodate, so Carole and I made a trip to Lowe's and picked up twenty more white plastic chairs that perfectly matched the thirty or forty white chairs Rhonda's father had already purchased for the ceremony.

Once again I had interfered with my son's life. I was deeply sorry for having overstepped my bounds, although I had never been made aware of where those boundaries had been set.

After that social blunder, subtle warnings in the form of offhand remarks and uninviting body language served sufficient notice that I was to quit interfering. I got the distinct impression that my wife and I had been granted permission to attend the wedding as long as we didn't invite anyone else, stayed out of the way, and kept our opinions to ourselves. I was not about to uninvite anyone, especially Jason's grandparents, so I remained silent and stepped aside while my soon-to-be daughter-in-law stewed and the wall between my son and me thickened.

I was torn between feeling bad for having spoiled Rhonda's perfect wedding plans and resentment for having been made to feel as though everyone was frowning at me for trying to help. I felt out of place and experienced twinges of self-consciousness for having shown up at all for my own son's wedding ceremony.

Amid a mix of cloudy skies, torrential downpours, fast-moving thunderstorms, and rays of sunshine, Jason finally put the ring on Rhonda's hand. Carole and I quietly stood on the sidelines, watching the ceremony for the duration of our thirty-eighth anniversary. Dad's ninety-second birthday hardly received a mention.

When it was all over, Jason and Rhonda returned to Arizona happily married. Carole and I went home to our empty house wondering what we had done wrong. All hope of our reclaiming any sort of bond with our son had disintegrated, and the funk reclaimed my mood.

Meanwhile the relationship between Carole and me reverted to tepid and testy with brief moments of compatibility occasionally sprinkled in. We just couldn't seem to get a handle on contentment.

CHAPTER 35
MYSTERY SOLVED

—◁◁◁—

That summer, while Carole and I were at the Caro fair, a terrific electrical storm plowed through the area. A frighteningly close lightning strike blew out the fairground's main transformer, and everyone ran for shelter while the sparks flew and the clouds opened up, flooding the streets, parking lots, and carnival midway. The Caro Fire Department was called to the scene, and the fair was closed for the rest of the day. We hung around inside one of the exhibition barns, waiting for the rain to stop before heading back to our car, which was parked in what had become a muddy mire.

By the time we finally drove through the gate and away from the fairgrounds, the fire department had secured the area and returned to the station. That was the department our rescuer was assigned to, and it seemed like the perfect opportunity to look him up.

"I wonder if Dennis would be at the fire station," I said to Carole. "I'd really like to meet this guy and thank him for what he did for us."

"Well, let's drive by and see," she said. "Maybe we'll catch him."

The fire trucks were all parked on the ramp in front of the open doors, and firemen were crawling all over them, cleaning equipment and packing things away. I walked over to one of the firemen and asked if Dennis was around.

"Yeah," he said, pointing to an office inside the building. "I think he's back there somewhere hanging up his turnout gear. I'll go get him for you."

A few moments later, Dennis emerged from the building, walking toward us with a grateful grin on his face. As soon as he spotted us, he knew who we were. He had us at a disadvantage.

He introduced himself and said, "You sure look a lot better than you did the last time I saw you!"

Carole hugged him and I shook his hand, thanking him for saving our lives. Typical of most emergency volunteers we know, he just shrugged his shoulders and looked at his feet, a little embarrassed by the recognition.

"Well," I said, "you can be as humble as you like, but the truth is, we owe our lives to you."

He just smiled again.

"They caught that guy, didn't they?" he asked.

"You mean the guy we ran into?" I asked

"Yeah. Didn't the police finally catch up with him?"

"Yes, they did," I said, "but I doubt the guy will receive any sort of punishment for what he did. There were no witnesses, and he has given the police four different versions of what happened. None of his stories match the evidence. The official police report says that we hit him from behind while he was waiting to make a left turn. If that were true, the back of his car would be caved in. The only marks on the back of his car were a dent and a bloodstain on the left tip of the bumper.

"Damage to his car clearly proves that we piled into his left rear wheel. My skid marks up to the point of impact indicate that I was on the right-hand side of the centerline in our lane of traffic. His vehicle had to have been sideways in the road when we slammed into it. If he was making a left turn, he sure wasn't doing it from a legal left-hand turn position in the road! All of the evidence confirms that his car was still over the fog line to the right at the time of impact. We may never know exactly what happened."

"You know," Dennis said, "I remember hearing the description of the car that had been impounded, about three days after the accident, and I swear that's the vehicle I saw on the shoulder of the road next to the southbound lane of traffic when I got there. There was a guy standing next to the car looking back at us, but I thought it was just a gawker—somebody who had stopped to take a look. I didn't pay any attention to him because you guys were in bad shape. I was just focused on keeping you alive."

"You may have just solved the mystery," I said. "Spotting him at that part of the intersection after the crash may be the one missing piece of evidence that will help resolve exactly what happened and who was at fault."

An eyewitness placing that car on the shoulder of the highway next to the southbound lane meant the driver had to have pulled a U-turn directly into our path from the shoulder of the northbound lane of traffic. That would explain why we had hit him in the side of his car while we were riding in the center of the northbound lane. I shared that revelation with Dennis, and he agreed that the scenario made sense.

"Would you be willing to talk to our attorney?"

"Happy to," he said. "I'm just as interested in seeing the right thing done as you are."

"The guy they caught claims he got permission to leave the scene from the ambulance guy who was working on us," I said. "Was anyone there besides you?"

"Nope," he said. "I was the first one at the scene. I'm not an ambulance guy, but if he's referring to me, there's no way I would have given anyone permission to leave, especially if I suspected he had been involved. For that matter, no emergency personnel would have given him permission to go anywhere. That is a direct violation of procedure."

We exchanged phone numbers and addresses and hugged again. We thanked him once more and then left for home.

The next morning I got on the phone and shared my encounter with our attorney.

"Is he willing to take a deposition?" our attorney asked.

"Yes," I said. "In fact, he said he would be happy to."

I gave Dennis's contact information to our attorney, who arranged to come to Caro two days later to meet Dennis and put his story on record.

Dennis's eyewitness account, along with the photographs our son Jason had taken of the scene and the other vehicle were enough evidence for our attorney to place the blame clearly on the guy who had been driving the car we ran into. The homeowner's testimony in the police report placed the driver west of the intersection, changing the flat tire with the bent rim before hightailing it out of there.

The official conclusion was that the driver of that car had entered our lane of traffic from the shoulder of the road while making a U-turn at the intersection, exactly the way I had figured. After the collision, he got out of his car, saw us lying in the highway, jumped back into his car, performed another U-turn, and fled the scene down the gravel side road.

Telling the police that he had been given permission to leave was just one of the many lies the driver told the deputies after he had been taken into custody three days later.

Dennis's revealing story was a bittersweet discovery that answered the blame issue, but I found no comfort in knowing that the accident had not been my fault. A motorcycle rider can be 100 percent blameless, but he still loses to the idiot driving the car. No matter how you cut the cake, the fact remained that we were the ones who had been left to die in the road, and the injuries we had sustained would be a constant reminder for the rest of our lives.

On August 21, 2008, I went to the courthouse to witness the man's sentencing. During a conversation with the prosecuting attorney that morning, I learned that he had used the official police report as his sole source of information. That report contained nothing but the lies the driver had given the police. No further investigation had been conducted. Until I showed the prosecutor the photographs that my son Jason had taken of the scene, the motorcycle, and the guy's car, the prosecutor had been under the impression that I was at fault.

The prosecutor softened his position but did nothing to amend the charges that had been filed.

The sentencing was scheduled to take place at three o'clock in the afternoon. Everyone but the defendant was present. His court-appointed attorney nervously wondered if his client would show up. Finally, at four o'clock, the would-be fugitive entered the courtroom. He was alone, having driven himself to his own sentencing.

The judge, showing great restraint for the defendant's obvious contempt, patiently started the proceedings.

The defendant had been charged with the following:

Count 1: Failure to stop following an accident, serious injury (hit-and-run, a felony offense)
Count 2: Failure to report the accident (misdemeanor)
Count 3: Habitual offender, second offense

The habitual offender charge took me by surprise. *Does that mean this guy has actually done this before?* I wondered to myself. *Why on earth is he still being allowed to drive?*

His court-appointed attorney managed to negotiate a plea bargain that dismissed counts two and three by entering a plea of guilty for count one: the felony.

When I was allowed to approach the bench, I asked the judge not to send him to jail.

"Your Honor," I said, "anyone capable of driving off and leaving two human beings on the highway to die needs psychiatric help. Jail isn't going to help this guy. Please consider some form of justice that will provide this man with some counseling, or he is going to remain a menace to society."

Then I turned to the defendant and addressed him with my prepared speech.

"I have been protecting you," I said, "and I will continue protecting you. Many of my friends have been looking for you so they can hand you their own form of justice for putting a biker down on the road and then driving off. I have not and will not provide your identity because I don't want your blood on my hands. Besides, that is not the form of justice I endorse.

"However, young man," I continued, "if I ever see you so much as sitting behind the wheel of another vehicle I will personally rip your head off and leave you there to bleed to death."

Before his attorney had an opportunity to object, I spun around and faced the judge.

"Thank you, Your Honor," I said, and I then returned to my seat.

As near as I was able to decipher, citations had been issued for counts one and two, neither of which put points on his driving record. By the time the gavel fell, that guy's sentence had been reduced to ninety days in the county jail with work-release privileges and credit for time already served.

I'm pretty certain his punishment would have been more severe if he had been charged with beating up on his dog.

Justice? Really? Okay, O. J.

CHAPTER 36

PRESCRIPTIONS AND PAYMENTS

—m—

The rest of that summer passed slowly as we worked our way through therapies and into the colors of autumn. Although a year had gone by since Carole's discharge from the Lighthouse, we were still connected as outpatients.

Michelle, Carole's counselor at the Lighthouse, was married to a guy who rode a motorcycle. She had confided in Carole about wanting to ride with her husband on the back of his bike but said that because of an automobile accident that she had been in, she was afraid. During a Friday morning session in October, Carole shared a bit of her caution-to-the-wind philosophy and told Michelle that she should just get on the back of that motorcycle and take a ride.

"You'll love it," she said. "Go have fun with your husband."

"Maybe I will," Michelle told Carole. "It really does sound like fun."

When Carole and I showed up for our appointments on the following Monday, we were greeted by the news that Michelle and her husband had been in a serious motorcycle accident over the weekend. Carole was devastated by the news. She immediately blamed herself for having encouraged her counselor to climb on the back of her husband's motorcycle, and she noticeably crawled further into isolation from the world around her.

Since Michelle had been sidelined by the accident, my counselor, Dan, temporarily took over part of Michelle's list of clients and inherited Carole as one of his patients. It was an appropriate transition because Dan already knew my side of the story so he could easily interpret Carole in greater depth.

Dan immediately picked up on Carole's self-persecution and tried to defuse the demolition, but Carole would not stop blaming herself for everything bad that had happened, including Michelle's accident. Carole dutifully continued her sessions with Dan at the Lighthouse for psychological counseling and crisis intervention from the added trauma generated by Michelle's accident. She hated talking about those things that haunted her, even though she was well aware that ignoring the issues was obviously not the cure.

Dan knew that my wife was in deep denial on several levels. He saw through Carole's quiet attempts to deceive him into thinking that she was happy and healed, but there was little he could do to bring her back without her cooperation.

Her medications were critical to her neurological healing, and the psychiatrist was specific about Carole diligently taking her prescriptions on schedule without fail, so we made certain to keep the pillbox stocked. But the no-fault insurance company was so far in arrears with medical payments that by the time December 2008 rolled around, the pharmacy refused to fill any more of Carole's prescriptions unless we paid for them with cash on delivery. We were also advised that we would probably be receiving collection notices for past-due amounts. I came unglued.

We didn't have the money to cover the cost of prescriptions and then wait for reimbursement. It was unconscionable to have been put in a position where we would have to float the insurance company's responsibilities. My stomach churned, and the tension built in the back of my neck from the injustices we had been expected to endure. We were barely getting by as it was because of the way the insurance adjusters had been handling our other reimbursable expenses and benefits. Cutting us off from the funding needed to purchase medications we had been prescribed was cruel and deviously abusive.

I felt another spring in my emotional suspension system snap. I had done my level best to be the cooperative nice guy, but I was sick and tired of being told to sit still and wait while those responsible for our welfare ignored us.

The next day, Carole met with Dan at the Lighthouse and shared our dilemma. Dan went ballistic. Without batting an eye, he grabbed the telephone, dialed our case manager's cell phone number, and got her voice mail. Dan did not mince words. The message he left our case manager was brief and very professional, and it contained a clearly defined ultimatum.

And that aggressive behavior came from the man who has been counseling me for anger issues! I thought to myself. His attack made me smile. *Maybe this encounter will help him understand why I am always so out of sorts and angry.*

On the morning following Dan's telephone tongue-lashing to the case manager's voice mail, we returned to the pharmacy and handed the pharmacist our private medical insurance information. I told him to transfer all previous bills owed by the no-fault insurance company over to our medical insurance carrier. I knew there would be deductibles and co-pays to cover, but those amounts would be much more manageable than the cost of filling prescriptions with the money we had available. Then I requested a detailed summary of all of our transactions with that pharmacy so that I could forward the information to our attorney and let him fight it out with the insurance adjusters, medical providers, collection agencies, and whomever else had their fingers in the pie. I was all through with being treated as though my wife and I were the ones who had done something wrong.

The no-fault insurance company's nonpayment to the pharmacy turned out to be the tip of the iceberg. One month following the prescription incident the adjusters pulled our files and suspended all further activity without warning or explanation. Our lost wages compensation was placed on hold, and reimbursements for our out-of-pocket medical expenses remained in limbo.

About the time I was becoming aware that the insurance company had unplugged us, I learned that the Lighthouse, having provided continuing care for both my wife and me for more than a year, had not received payment and was being advised to file a lawsuit to collect amounts due. The accountant for the Lighthouse, quietly continuing to defer the debt while I scrambled to satisfy the no-fault insurer's financial responsibility, demonstrated more faith in my ability to resolve the issue than I had in myself. I had promised Connie on the first day that we met, shortly before Carole was released from Hurley, that I would sell everything I owned, if necessary, to pay for the medical care the Lighthouse provided. Through our relationship with the administrative staff at the Lighthouse, it gradually sank in that their concern was not so much about being paid—although payment is necessary for survival—as much as they were concerned about caring for and curing their patients.

Our attorney had been made aware of the past-due account. Aggravated by the constant waiting game we had been forced to play, I called his office and left instructions for him to do whatever was necessary to get our medical providers paid and eliminate the delinquencies—and to find out why we had been cut off. Then I wrote a check against our home equity for over thirteen thousand dollars to satisfy the pecuniary obligation. All the while I continued praying for something to break loose before I had to start selling off our personal assets to pay our bills and avoid defaulting on our mortgage. We were left twisting in the wind. Our attorney was perplexed.

The strain had become unbearable, turning all of my dreams for a peaceful, secure retirement to dust. The ordeal had also diluted my sanity. The human consciousness can only absorb so much before it begins to shut down. After a certain point, the body goes numb and simply absorbs all additional shocks without flinching.

I had watched friends and fellow soldiers coming back from the war zone during Vietnam with expressions on their faces we commonly referred to as the thousand-yard stare. The look in those eyes was an outward reflection of a traumatized mind. I had finally arrived at that place. There was nothing anyone could do to me that would have increased the intensity of the discouragement I already felt. At that moment in time, leveling the sights on those responsible for our agony, and squeezing the trigger with no remorse, would have been easy.

CHAPTER 37

INTERROGATION ROOM

—w—

A few days after writing that check to cover the insurance company's debt to the Lighthouse, we drove to our attorney's office in Royal Oak for predeposition briefings. The following day, we returned to his office and sat through depositions conducted by legal representatives for the no-fault insurer.

The interrogations conducted by those insurance lawyers were intended to trip us up and get us to say something that would let their employer off the hook for what they owed in medical bills and reimbursable expenses. I responded to their ridiculous line of questioning with curt responses and blank stares. Although they did not appear to be the least bit intimidated, there is no doubt that my expressionless answers caused them to phrase their questions carefully.

I had been warned that certain words or phrases could be twisted to mean whatever might be convenient for them. We were cautioned beforehand not to use words like "speculation" or phrases like "I believe" in any of our responses. We were told that those types of words and phrases could have multiple meanings, giving rise to false implications. "Just the facts, ma'am," as Joe Friday would say.

The whole deposition process was a grand display of redundancy. It made me want to stand up and scream, "What part of 'wrecked' are you people having a hard time understanding?"

Over a year and a half had passed since the accident, and those people acted as though they were still trying to figure out whether or not there had been an accident.

A month later we were ordered to drive to Birmingham for an appointment with an independent medical examiner hired by the insurance company. That guy was a genuine quack! Not only was he unprepared, but he was also unequipped. I was in no mood to be jerked around anymore, so when he asked for the name of our attending physician, I recoiled.

"Which one?" I asked him bluntly. "We have each been seen by at least a dozen physicians that we are aware of. Look at your records and you'll find everything you need to know."

There was a brief pause as the guy leafed through the small stack of files lying on the table in front of him.

"You do have our records, don't you?"

"Well, no," he said. "They haven't been forwarded to our office yet."

This guy has no idea what we have been through, I thought to myself, *and I don't think he cares. How can he even pretend to conduct an examination without knowing what he's looking for?*

"If there is any information you need that has not already been provided through the company that hired you," I said to him, "you are welcome to call our attorney in Royal Oak. He has copies of all of our medical records."

That clown was a fraud hired by the no-fault insurance company to formalize exactly what the insurance adjusters wanted him to say. There was nothing about that independent medical examination that resembled a medical examination, and he knew it. What's more, he knew that I knew.

"Uncooperative" was what he put in his report. "Patient displays anger issues."

Well, duh!

By the time we left that medical examiner's office, I knew we were being bamboozled. I called our attorney's office the first chance I had and told the associate handling our case that they needed to bring this thing to an end. I had become nervously reckless with my attitude, but I was tired of playing games. Our attorney knew I was right. He shared my frustration. Twice in

March, depositions were scheduled and then cancelled at the last minute. No explanations were offered.

Near the end of April we were ordered to appear for another independent medical examination in Novi, Michigan—another two-hour drive to satisfy the bureaucracy. I told our attorney's associate that I would not waste my time again.

"You can't just ignore this stuff," he said. "We just have to play their game a little while longer."

"Why?" I said. "This is not a game. That clown who left us for dead has failed to cooperate at every turn. According to what you've told me, he hasn't shown up for a single deposition and nothing has happened to him!"

"I know; it's not right, but he's got nothing to lose. Just work with me. We'll get this over with as soon as we can."

I told him that unless I could be assured the doctor in Novi would have a complete set of our records far enough in advance to sufficiently acquaint himself with our medical history, I refused to cooperate.

"If I get there and find out this guy is as unprepared as the last quack we had to see, I'm walking out."

He assured me the examiner in Novi would be properly briefed before our arrival.

I woke up in another foul, defensive mood on the day of the medical exams. Carole and I climbed into the car and reluctantly headed for Novi. After some seriously wrong turns provided by our GPS, I was ready to thumb my nose at the whole process and go home.

"The insurance company can send their examiner to our house if they really want to obtain our blood pressure," I said to Carole.

"Let's just keep looking for the place," she said. "It's got to be around here somewhere."

With all of the medical facilities we had been through and all of the medical doctors who had examined us, there should have been more than enough corroborating history to establish the fact that my wife and I had been seriously injured. That goose chase was nothing but harassment!

When we finally located the medical complex that housed the examiner's office near Novi, I realized why we had not been able to locate it with our GPS. It was a brand-new building with an address that had not yet been logged into the map database. My mood softened, and a more forgiving spirit took over.

We parked the car, entered the building, and walked up to the receptionist's window. The lady on the other side of the glass asked what she could do for us, and I told her that we had been instructed to report for an independent medical examination and gave her our names.

It may have been my misinterpretation of her response, but it appeared to me as though she was stalling for some reason. My forgiving spirit immediately disappeared. Without hesitation I dispensed my foul attitude in liberal, sarcastic doses. The lady behind the counter began to protest with a little of her own attitude, but I refused to let her finish. I suggested that she could either get us in to see the doctor or be prepared to explain to our attorney why we were being stonewalled.

Carole and I were immediately ushered into separate examining rooms, ordered to strip down to our underwear, and told to dress in the paper gowns that had been provided. The room I was in was chilly, and paper was not the proper attire to retain body heat. When a nurse came in to take my blood pressure, she asked me how I was feeling, and I told her that I was freezing to death. She asked me a series of seemingly redundant questions, scribbled in her notebook, and left the room. I sat there on that cold plastic chair all alone in a drafty space, feeling vulnerably exposed. Finally, after it felt as though hypothermia had begun to set in, the doctor entered.

Unlike the clown we had been forced to visit in Birmingham, this doctor was a well-groomed young man who seemed to be kind and understanding. I immediately got the impression that he had read our files and was embarrassed for having been put in a position to make us prove ourselves to anyone.

"This will only take a few minutes to fill out the forms and get you on your way," he said. "You and your wife have obviously been through some serious trauma. We'll get the reports finalized and filed right away. You should have no more trouble."

The doctor shook my hand and left the room. I got myself dressed and went back to the lobby, looking for my wife. A short while later we were on our way back home.

The next morning, an associate from our attorney's office called and asked how the examination in Novi had gone. I told him the whole story, including the part about nearly turning around and going back home. I also shared with him that I would not honor any further requests to be examined by anyone representing the insurance company. Apparently unsure exactly how to respond to my commentary, he remained silent.

CHAPTER 38

BATTLEGROUNDS

—◦◦◦—

It was early April 2009. We needed a break before we were broke and broken. I figured that if we were going to go down the tubes, we might as well do it in a blaze of glory.

Our oldest son, Jeremy, and I had been talking about him, me, and Carole visiting Civil War battlefields along the East Coast in chronological order, starting at Harper's Ferry and ending at Gettysburg. He lived close enough to Manassas and Fredericksburg to use his home as our overnight quarters for the majority of our adventure, so we decided to launch the tour regardless of the cost and make an attempt at creating some positive memories before our cash was gone altogether.

Jeremy was excited to hear that we were coming. While he was on the Internet, lining up our adventure, he tracked down Billy Lee Cox, an old friend of mine from the air force. Bill and I had hooked up and played bluegrass music together while we were stationed in Taiwan. While there we entered a talent contest and won a trip to Japan, where we were invited to perform as guests of honor at the 1971 Japanese National Bluegrass Festival in downtown Tokyo.

With a little more research Jeremy discovered that Bill and his bluegrass band Remington Ryde were scheduled to perform on Saturday night at a little place called Beck and Benedict's Hardware in the town of Waynesboro, Pennsylvania, located about twenty miles west of Gettysburg.

We circled dates on the calendar and planned our trip, looking forward to a tour through Civil War history and a reunion with my old air force pal. When the day came, we packed our stuff and headed for Virginia, hooking up with Jeremy at Harper's Ferry. Day two of our trip was spent learning about John Brown's uprising. The third day out we took off for Manassas and discovered how Jackson earned the nickname Stonewall.

Carole and I were at peace. Spending time with our oldest son proved a refreshing change of pace, but the quiet interlude did not last long. The fourth day started with a disaster.

Carole said she had to go to the car to get something. A minute after she stepped out the door, I decided to carry some things out to the car while Carole had it unlocked, and I was totally unprepared for what I stumbled into. Hunched down behind the open door on the passenger side was my wife with a cigarette hanging from her lips. This woman who had sworn she was no longer smoking was still sneaking around filling her lungs with poison and lying about it. My anger escalated. I berated her for lying to me, and at that moment, an invisible eight-hundred-pound gorilla climbed on board for the rest of our trip. We continued our tour of the battlefields, but for me our visit had been ruined.

We finally made it to the end of our weeklong history expedition and met up with Billy Lee. It was a great reunion, but I found myself wishing I could have made the trip alone. When we returned to Michigan, I actively avoided Carole. My trust had been wrung out too many times to care any longer. I was simply tired of being hurt and angry. The only way I could find peace was to stay away.

—ɯ—

A day or two after Carole and I returned home from our tour of the Civil War battlefields and had settled back into our own separate bunkers, I received word that our attorney had finally decided to pull out the artillery and go on the offensive. He called the insurance adjuster's bluff and filed suit for nonpayment.

I asked about damages and was informed that the only penalty imposed on the insurance company for failure to pay would be finance charges on past-due amounts. The attorney told us that insurance companies were immune from lawsuits for pain and suffering arising from hardship caused by their delinquency.

"So what you're telling me," I said, "is that those people can bully me and I can't do anything about it."

"That about sums it up," he said.

"Well, where does the pain and suffering part of the law come in?" I asked.

"That's a whole separate issue," he said. "We have filed a suit for damages owed, but their failure to pay is not considered grounds for filing a lawsuit for pain and suffering."

No wonder they dragged their feet! I thought to myself.

Filing the lawsuit guaranteed a minimum delay of sixty more days—the allotted time for the insurance company to respond. That meant the only thing certain about the next two months was that we would continue living without an income unless one of us returned to work.

We had no choice but to tighten the belt another notch and try to squeak through.

I thanked God once again for having miraculously kept our home intact. There was literally no logical explanation for our survival, but we had, in fact, survived. On faith alone I continued approaching every new day thankful for another chance to take a stab at the monster that would not release us.

CHAPTER 39

BACK TO WORK

—◊◊◊—

The second anniversary of our accident was just around the corner. Although Carole and I had become noticeably estranged, I felt obliged to do something to commemorate the day. If anything, I had become more driven than ever before to prove that I was right. If our marriage fell apart, it wasn't going to happen because of a lack of effort on my part.

Sorting through e-mails one morning, I came across an advertisement for tickets to see *Chicago* in concert with *Earth, Wind & Fire* at DTE. The performances were to take place in the evening on June 24, 2009, the second anniversary of our accident. It was an omen, a chance to see the concert we had missed two years earlier. The timing was perfect. Without even checking the calendar to see if the date was open, I clicked the Buy button on the screen, and four tickets for pavilion seating were on their way.

Well, I thought to myself, *if I wind up going alone, I'll have plenty of room!*

That night I called our daughter, Nicole, to see if she and Rodney wanted to go with us. Somewhere in the back of my mind, I had already come to the conclusion that Carole and I would not be able to go to the concert, or anywhere else for that matter, without someone to act as a buffer. It never crossed my mind that whoever joined us would also have to put up with that invisible eight-hundred-pound gorilla.

Carole was distant, and I pretended that I didn't care. Our daughter and her husband tolerated us. The truth was that in spite of our recovery, my life was empty and the person who could fill it was sitting right next to me.

Instead, my mind was on stage with those musicians that night. I dreamed of returning to the music scene and experiencing the incredible rush that comes from wowing a crowd with a stellar performance.

It was an amazing show in more ways than music and choreography. When the lead singer for *Earth, Wind & Fire* stood at the front of the stage to thank the packed hillside for the warm reception, he first raised his hand toward the sky and thanked God for the opportunity to perform.

I was struck nearly to tears by his gesture. It was as though he had pointed his hand at me and shattered that glass bubble I had built for protection.

My heart softened, and for the first time in months, I saw the beauty of unconditional love in my wife's eyes. I knew at that moment that even if our marriage ended, there would never be another woman in my life.

One month later Carole returned to her job at the courthouse, accompanied by an occupational counselor assigned to shadow Carole's work activity. The counselor spent four days observing the working conditions and analyzing Carole's ability to perform her assigned tasks. Not surprisingly, my wife slid right back into her work routine without skipping a beat. Carole had proven herself competent and capable and resumed her responsibilities as court administrator. No further oversight was required.

Carole's transition back to work was anticlimactic. There was no celebration or ceremony commemorating the end of a death-defying drama that had consumed two years of her life. The judge and the bailiff continued their daily routines while she sat at her desk and resumed her duties.

There was one change in the lineup, however, that spoke volumes about Carole's work ethic prior to being flown to the hospital. She had finally been given an assistant to help carry the workload.

During her two years away from the office, three full-time replacements with experience at that job had struggled to keep up the insane pace Carole had maintained all by herself before the accident. After that wake-up call, the judge had finally managed to secure the help Carole should have had twenty years earlier. Carole's job would no longer be the pressure cooker she had dreaded going back to.

Ironically, Carole saw the addition of a sidekick as a sign from her employer that she was no longer capable or competent.

Near the end of July, our attorney called to tell us that the insurance company had finally decided to own up to its legal and financial responsibilities. We received settlement checks in amounts large enough to afford a comfortable retirement nest egg. The waiting had finally come to an end, and we were financially out of the woods.

Part of the reimbursement we had received was for services to which we were entitled but had never been provided. We had been forced to do without help mainly because we could not afford to pay out-of-pocket for the support when it was needed. We had simply been reimbursed. No, it didn't make any sense to me either, but I accepted the money without asking for an explanation. I regarded that money as partial reparation for the insult handed down a year earlier when lost wages compensation had been calculated at less than 20 percent of what it should have been.

In spite of the good news, I had forgotten how to smile, consumed by how much of our life had been stolen from us. Surviving the war with the adjusters and averting financial disaster should have alleviated the pressure, but the deliberations had gone on far too long for me to relax. The endless mental, emotional, and physical stress had turned me into an angry, bitter man. I simply felt no sense of closure. We could have been awarded a settlement worth ten times the amount that we received and I would not have been satisfied. I would have gladly traded every penny of it for the chance to turn the clock back to the day before our accident—back to that time when I thought we were happy.

CHAPTER 40

WEDDING RINGS

—✠—

What I had seen in my wife's eyes that night at the concert stirred something inside. There was a reason I had married that woman and stayed with her through thick and thin. It was not a sense of guilt, pity, or convenience that had kept us together. We truly completed each other.

Those words I had spoken to my wife while she was lying comatose inside Hurley's ICU echoed in my head: "I promise that I will see to your care and well-being, even if I have to spend the rest of my life feeding and bathing you. I will never leave your side."

The day I stood by Carole's hospital bed and made that promise, I obviously had no idea whether she would even survive, let alone recover as a fully functional adult. Neither did I have any idea that the handicaps I would be helping her work through would be more emotional and behavioral than physical.

Flub-a-dubbing through attempt after failed attempt made that vow feel more like a sentence. I had no intention of breaking the promise, but mismatched seclusion certainly was not the way I wanted to spend the rest of my life with this lady. Regardless, the promise I had made fueled my drive to get our marriage back on track.

Carole had mentioned on numerous occasions since the accident that she could not understand why I stayed married to her.

"Because I love you," I would say to her.

She kept telling me that she was boring and that she didn't measure up.

"You still cannot describe what it is you think you should be measuring up to," I would say. "How do you measure up to a standard you cannot identify? And whether or not you are boring is a decision you are not at liberty to make."

That's all it would take to get me back on my soapbox.

"It's none of your business what other people think of you. There are people you can't wait to spend time with, and at the same time, there are those whose company you really don't enjoy. It's that way with everyone.

"Getting along with others has nothing to do with any of us being good or bad at what we do; it's just a matter of personal preference. But in the final analysis, whomever you choose to spend time with is your decision, not theirs—and vice versa. We are who we are and that's just the way it is."

The minilecture always ended with, "So please quit telling me that you're boring or that you don't measure up."

I desperately needed to find a way to shore up Carole's sense of self-esteem. She was beginning to convince me that maybe she had simply chosen to become just another boring individual. Nevertheless, I continued trying different ways to bring her out of her shell with the hope of making some sort of reconciliation between us.

Our thirty-ninth wedding anniversary was fast approaching, and I wracked my brain to come up with something that would make the day special for my wife. Restating our wedding vows? A gift, maybe?

The wedding ring!

Carole had always regarded the vows spoken between a man and a woman as sacred. She had worn her ring faithfully since the day I slipped it on her finger at the altar and over the years had put more effort into maintaining our relationship than she had ever put into her spiritual faith. Marriage was that important to her.

The diamond set that was in Carole's ring was all that I could afford at the age of twenty, and even though she wore it with pride, I had always dreamed of someday adding to it. The time had finally come.

After the accident, the surgeons had to cut the ring off Carole's swollen hand to save her finger from strangulation. Nicole and I had gotten it repaired while Carole was still at Hurley. Carole had been wearing it ever since, but I decided that having it inspected for other damage would be a good excuse to get it back off her finger for an upgrade without her becoming suspicious.

I took Carole's wedding ring to the local jeweler to have an additional diamond-studded band permanently fixed to each side of the original set as a symbol of my commitment and support. The jeweler skillfully transformed my vision for that wedding ring into a work of art.

The next challenge was figuring out how to present the ring to my wife with some sort of a semiformal ceremony short of renting the church and restating our vows.

Our anniversary was on the same day as Dad's birthday. Dad's and my brother Geoff's birthdays were only two days apart. On the off chance we might be able to combine their birthdays and our anniversary into one event, I called my sister, Shirl, who lived next door to our parents, and asked if she had made any special plans to spend the day with Dad.

"Geoff and his family might be driving in for the weekend so Geoff and Dad can celebrate their birthdays together," she said. "Other than that, we're spending the day like it was just another day. You guys want to join us?"

"Sure!" I said, relieved at not having had to invite myself.

I told my sister about Carole's wedding ring.

"Maybe you could give it to her while you're here with the rest of the family," she said.

"That's a great idea," I said. "I'll tell Carole we're heading to your house for Dad's birthday, and while we're there, I can give her the ring."

Carole thought going to my sister's house for Dad and Geoff's birthday celebration sounded like a good idea. I do not recall whether the concept of fun ever entered the conversation, but that didn't really matter. I was on a mission to make a statement in the presence of witnesses that would convince my wife once and for all that I was committed to our marriage.

When the moment came on the day of our joint celebration, my sister quietly directed everyone's attention toward my wife and me. My wife sat motionless as I told her that there was nobody else I would rather have spent the past thirty-nine years with. Then I opened the box and presented the ring.

Although it felt as though she understood and accepted my gesture as a positive sign, her reaction seemed less than enthusiastic. I was slightly disappointed.

Carole knew the disparity between love and hate. She also understood the difference between happy and sad. But what I had failed to understand was that her ability to feel any of those emotions had gone missing. For her, understanding passion and feeling her passion had become two entirely separate matters. It was as though the linkage between her disposition and the outside world had been disconnected.

Whether or not her condition would be permanent was anybody's guess. Brain injuries are invisible, the effects are unpredictable, and the changes they effect are undeniable.

In an attempt to learn about and understand what my wife was experiencing and why, I did some research and unearthed hugely vague psychiatric descriptions relating to her condition that would undoubtedly require years of schooling to decipher. The only thing I gained from my soirée into the world of psychoanalytical science was a much clearer understanding of just how little any of us really knows about the consequences of brain trauma. In other words, I found no answers to "why," but only descriptions of "what," and I had already been provided with firsthand experience in that arena.

CHAPTER 41
LAST-DITCH EFFORT

—◆—

Disquieting thoughts raced through my mind like bees around a hive. My inability to understand my wife's self-persecution and indifference toward life in general had me in a quandary. In spite of my efforts to make things right between us, it felt as though our marriage were still slipping through my fingers.

I feared that something inside might finally snap under the strain of a continually dissolving partnership. The intensifying anxiety made me irritable and edgy.

A healthy connection between two people relies on absolute mutual trust. Once that confidence has been violated, it is finished, and from then on each deception is a little bit like a heart attack. Every tall tale bruises another part of the human spirit and erodes a needed sense of security the way a cramped heart muscle threatens to send a man to an early grave.

For whatever reason, Carole was afraid to be straight with me. Her dishonesty had seriously weakened the bond between us. There was absolutely no way I could know when my wife was telling me the truth. Her lack of interest in interacting with others remained a puzzle. Withdrawal and denial had become her prime directives. She had cemented herself in a place where issues ignored were expected to be forgotten.

I could not imagine spending the rest of my life living with someone who acted that way.

More than once the suitcases came out and I found myself packing her things, ready to help her find an apartment. But I had promised to take care of her, and in spite of her willful behavior, I could not bring myself to break that vow. In spite of the dissention between us, I knew that it was my responsibility to provide and protect, but there would no longer be any presumption of shared companionship.

It was finished. There was no getting over the fact that I loved my wife with all of my soul, but like those dreams we once shared, our marriage had forever been changed. The lines were untied, our ships were launched, and our lives sailed off in separate directions. I kept an eye on her from a distance, wishing and wanting without waiting.

Hoping to regain some semblance of a meaningful life, I resumed pursuing personal goals and left the unresolved issues between us under the rug, where they had been swept.

During my search for resolution, I found a support group that met monthly at a rehabilitation facility in Saginaw. The drive was over an hour one way, but I joined the group anyway. The meetings were held in a very friendly atmosphere. Sadly, there seemed to be no direction for the people who attended those sessions. I needed help, not just camaraderie.

I dragged Carole to a couple of those gatherings, but the discussions and recreational activities did nothing for her. She hated talking about the accident, the injuries, and the therapies and had become emotionally numb out of self-defense. After seeing no appreciable results, I quit wasting the gas and never went back.

Carole's friends and coworkers would not leave the topic of our accident alone, continually talking about people they knew who had suffered the way they assumed that she had. In an attempt to get away from the constant reminders, she further isolated herself socially.

It remained a real challenge for anyone to be near me. I was geared to expect the worst, constantly waiting for the other shoe to drop. As far as I was concerned, there was no longer any such thing as good news. Everything seemed to have a downside, and I usually found it, even when there wasn't one. Instinctively I was in survival mode and had to make some raw choices, desperately in need of finding purpose that could help block out the pain.

Not the least bit concerned about overcommitting myself, and determined to make up for lost time, I surveyed my options and pulled out all the stops.

The first thing I did was dust off the music career that had been shelved. It seemed as though I had only been away for three or four years, but when I started looking back, I realized that it had actually been more than twelve years since my last gig. Everyone I spoke with wondered why I had so completely walked away from the music business.

In September 2009 I was invited to an artists' night hosted by a music store in a neighboring community. A songwriter I had met at the Lighthouse was performing with some friends and asked if I would like to come and play the drums for him.

Following that session, I accepted an invitation to join that songwriter's group for a couple of upcoming gigs and a concert. During one of our rehearsals, the band discovered that I had written and recorded a few songs of my own. One song in particular that drew their attention was a slow blues tune depicting life in the aftermath of our accident. The boys in the band liked the song well enough to include it in the set list for our concert. My creation was well received by the audience:

We're in a prison with broken bones and strife.
There's no bars on our prison, just broken bones and God-awful strife.
He may think he beat me,
but he won't walk away with my life.

Before long I was laying down tracks for the band's new CD, with a couple of my own songs in the lineup.

Meanwhile the singer from a local band I had played with for years asked if I would be interested in getting back together for a performance at a Halloween party.

"Sounds like fun," I said. "You think we'll need to do any rehearsing before we play?"

"Naw," he said. "We played together for so long it'll just be like old times."

Around that time I heard about an open jam session going on in a neighboring town, so just for fun I went to check it out. When I walked through the door, Ginger, a friend and fellow musician, announced my name over the public address system. A few people in the room applauded, and others started cheering.

That was embarrassing, I thought.

A drum kit had already been provided, so I accepted Ginger's invitation to return for weekly sessions. I didn't have to carry anything but my sticks. Every night was amateur night.

So it went, picking up a gig here and jamming with some guys there. Before long I found myself involved with three different musical groups, two separate jam sessions every week, and a CD recording project with some guys who rarely performed outside the studio. It was a welcome distraction from the stress of dealing with adjusters, attorneys, and a strained marriage.

In spite of it all, I missed that connection with my wife. Most of my music activity had been taking place without her anywhere near. She had always supported my music career in the past, but now she seemed to have lost interest in being anywhere near it.

In October of that year, I urged Carole to get back into counseling with her psychologist from Hurley, cautioning her that she was not likely to fix her problems without help from someone. We attended the first few sessions together, but it soon became clear to me that the psychologist was merely attempting to change my expectations to match my wife's behavior.

"Are you trying to tell me that I need to accept being lied to by my wife?" I asked the counselor one evening.

I do not remember specifically what the psychologist said in response, but her message was basically that I needed to back off, give my wife space, and bite my tongue.

That was the end of it for me.

What is it with people? I wondered to myself. *Doesn't anyone get it?*

Carole ended her sessions with the psychologist a short while after I quit going. Both of us had had our fill of trying to find someone to help whose only experience had come from a textbook. Nobody but an alcoholic can fully understand another alcoholic's struggle. A drug addict is the only person who can know what it's like to need a fix. I came to the conclusion that there was no way anyone else would ever be able to help us through the issues we were dealing with unless he had been through the same trials we had faced.

We had been forced to find the solution on our own.

Maybe it's time to take another trip somewhere, I thought to myself.

"What do you think about spending Thanksgiving in Arizona this year?" I asked Carole.

"You mean with Jason and Rhonda?"

"Yeah."

"That would be fine," she said.

"If I can figure out how to get in touch with Jason, I'll run the idea by him," I said, "but if I don't get a positive vibe, I'm not even going to bring it up."

When I finally tracked him down, Jason seemed comfortable talking with me, so I tossed the idea into the conversation to get his reaction. It was encouraging when he sounded excited about the chance to spend the holiday with us, so I circled the dates on the calendar and booked a flight to Arizona.

Generally speaking, we had a good time reconciling with Jason while he and Rhonda showed us the sights around Phoenix, Scottsdale, and Sedona. We took a trip to Tortilla Flat and on the way back stopped for a burger at a saloon where cowboys still rode in on their horses and tied them up to the hitching post out back.

That was the first time either of us had ever visited that part of the country. We enjoyed the dry, cactus-strewn scenery, but I could not help wondering why anyone growing up in the lush green state of Michigan would want to permanently relocate to a place where it was a major accomplishment just getting grass to grow. I secretly hoped that someday our son would come to the same conclusion.

Everything was going well during our visit until I spotted another half-empty pack of cigarettes tucked inside Carole's open purse. The wind went out of my sails again. Another unpleasant confrontation ensued, followed by more lies; and just like that, the eight-hundred-pound gorilla was back.

Another piece of the bridge between us disintegrated, along with the few repairs I had been able to make.

The day we boarded the plane in Phoenix to come back to Michigan, I got the distinct impression that Jason and Rhonda were glad to see us go.

Just after Thanksgiving that year, I reopened my repair business three days a week. I really needed to be busy doing something constructive that didn't involve a pair of drumsticks, a piano, or a guitar.

As I had feared, I was faced with starting the business back up from nothing. I still had inventory, equipment, and a building, but my customer base was gone.

After some aggressive advertising, work started trickling through the door again, but months passed before I was able to develop enough revenue to even cover the utility bills. The profitability had gone out of the rebuilding industry with the flood of cheap imported alternators and starters showing up at every discount store in the country. I knew the stuff was selling below cost, but that doesn't matter to a public with a garage-sale mentality.

Although the business was barely staying afloat, I was at least busy working with my hands again. I felt useful and thanked God every day for having allowed me the opportunity to resume doing what I did most comfortably.

December 25 was just around the corner, and Pastor Mike asked if I would be willing to perform for the Christmas Eve service at Grace. It took some doing, but I finally screwed up the courage and put together a couple of arrangements on the guitar.

Performing for a worship service was something I had always dreamed of doing, and only once years earlier had I been given the opportunity. Since that one time, I could never muster the courage to carry through with it again.

I don't know if the people attending the service that Christmas Eve felt anything different for my having been there, but for me the ceremony was a deeply moving experience. My songs were interspersed throughout the service and ranged from a simple guitar piece to *O Holy Night* with full orchestral accompaniment that I had recorded in my studio.

The service ended with Holy Communion as I played the guitar and led the gathering through *Silent Night*. Pastor Mike's brother, Marv, sat down to the piano to add accompaniment while the congregation sang. The children's voices drifting through the cozy, candlelit sanctuary that night made magic. Playing music and listening to the spirit of Christmas fill the air, leading all of those smiling, singing faces through the verses of that timeless melody, carried me to a peaceful place in my soul.

Afterward I thanked God privately for the gift he had sent to me through that healing experience.

—

Near the end of January 2010, I received a call from Brian Bennett, one of my longtime journeyman musician friends. Brian had been a legendary keyboard player in the Saginaw Valley area with connections to Alice Cooper through his experience doing shows with Dick Wagner.

Brian had suffered a paralyzing stroke one week to the day after our accident three years earlier. He was told that he would never walk, talk, or play music again, but he, like any other true-blue musician, was not willing to accept that death sentence.

Although Brian's entire left leg and arm had become nearly unusable, he had regained the ability to walk. More amazing was his ability to cover keyboard parts with his right hand more proficiently than most two-handed musicians were able to. He openly credited his miraculous partial recovery to God's grace.

Brian had called me to find out if I was doing anything on the drums.

"I'm involved in some jam sessions and doing some recording," I said. "Why do you ask?"

"*Crabtree* is getting back together, and we're looking for a drummer and a bass player. I told the band you were the perfect guy to sit behind the kit," he said.

"Brian, you've never heard me play! In all the years we've known each other, we have never worked together, and you have never made it to one of my gigs. What makes you think I'm the guy you're looking for?"

"I called you based on your reputation," he said. "I don't have to hear you play. I know enough people who have. Trust me; you're the guy this band is looking for."

"Okay," I said. "I'll give it a shot."

He was right. *Crabtree* turned out to be one of the best combinations of musicians I had been with in years. I was flattered to have been considered for the position, and it was a comfortable fit.

Full rehearsals started up twice a week in Bay City, sixty miles from home, with additional hours of personal rehearsal time spent on my kit at home. Within a few weeks we were polished enough to go on deck and put most other groups in the area to shame, and the band had not yet come close to reaching its potential.

We were a hit wherever we performed. Although there were some minor personality clashes between the guitar player and me, the potential was as encouraging as anything I had been involved with up to that point.

Just like that, I was back in the business.

As soon as word was on the street that I had come out of retirement, the telephone started ringing. I was flattered by offers to join bands and invitations to attend jam sessions. It was a heady experience, one that I couldn't quite figure out. I knew that I could muddle my way through and apply the appropriate rhythm to just about any style of music, but I had never been a flashy drummer. I quit trying to understand it. I was just thankful that I had a foot and was capable of using it to play the kit with anyone who needed a percussionist.

Sometime in the middle of the winter of 2010, Geoff Gibor, a friend and another fellow musician, called for about the umpteenth time and asked me to come to one of his weekly jam sessions in Caro. Because I was already involved in open mike Friday nights with Ginger in Brown City and rehearsing feverishly with *Crabtree* twice a week in Bay City, I was reluctant to add yet another activity to my list of diversions.

"A couple of guys from a band that opened for REO Speedwagon at the Casino in Mt. Pleasant last weekend are still in town," he said. "They're coming to Monday night's session. We could really use a drummer who knows how to stay in the pocket. I hope you can make it."

I was hooked. I could not turn down an invitation with that caliber of musician showing up, so when Monday night rolled around, I grabbed my sticks and headed for Geoff's jam session in Caro.

That session was a memorable moment in time for me. I could not believe what unfolded before my eyes and ears. When my turn came to play, I sat down behind a drum kit where every pedal and cymbal stand was positioned in the wrong place and screwed to the floor.

This is likely going to be my first and last chance to play with these guys, I thought to myself. *I'll just make the best of it and let the cards fall where they will.*

One of the guitar players took off on Stevie Ray Vaughn's "Pride and Joy." I had played the song with *Crabtree* a few times, so the arrangement was familiar. I just followed his lead.

The music carried me away. *God in Heaven,* I thought. *I think I have finally died and made it to the place He has reserved for musicians!*

When the song was over, the guitar player turned around and looked at me through the glass.

"I can't believe it," he said. "We've been doing these jam sessions for three years, and we finally found a drummer who knows how to play a blues shuffle!"

I felt very self-conscious, but whatever I had done seemed to please the players around me. I almost cried.

Burying myself in music allowed me to live in the present, blocking out the pain and loneliness at home. Given the offer, I would have been happy to climb aboard the tour bus with those guys and get lost out on the highway, playing for food.

On my way home that night, it occurred to me that although I had put music between Carole and me, God had me right where I needed to be. I was still a part of the music community, and the players were happy to have me back, which was a huge boost to my self-confidence. I was finally beginning to heal emotionally. Pieces of my life were beginning to have meaning again. It felt as though someone had done an appraisal of my net worth as a human being and had drawn the conclusion that I was worth having around.

The strange thing was that I no longer cared about retirement. I had given up on being happily married, so planning for the future just did not matter anymore. My sense of responsibility for keeping things moving forward had not disappeared, but my focus had changed. I decided to spend every remaining moment of my time living life to its fullest, free as a bird until my last breath, which did not seem to be all that far away. A little voice in my head kept telling me that the relentless strain and distress of the past three years had taken tenfold that much time away from my stretch here on earth.

CHAPTER 42

WHEELS-UP LANDING

—ɯ—

Although I knew Carole had no desire to go with me to band jobs or jam sessions, I continued to extend the offer, leaving the door to reconciliation open a crack. What struck me was that even though she rarely accepted my invitations, she usually declined through sad eyes.

I got the same reaction from her whenever the phone would ring and another musician or friend was on the other end of the line. She would listen to my side of the conversation and then clam up and withdraw. After hanging up the telephone, I usually found her holed up in the bedroom, buried in a book with the door closed; or hiding in the TV room, staring blankly at the screen.

Something was bothering her, and for the life of me, I could not figure out what it was. Desperate for a solution, all I could do was throw my hands in the air and quietly walk away frustrated. It took a while for me to realize that my wife was jealous. I was moving on with my life and leaving her in the dust. She was uncomfortable following me because she had become too self-conscious to relax around other people. Still, she didn't want to be alone.

It was extremely unsettling knowing that my wife was miserable, and her misery fueled my unhappiness. There I was, standing at a crossroads. In one direction was a life of recluse alongside my wife. In the other direction was a life of solitude in the company of friends. Neither option sounded palatable. I finally sat Carole down one day and told her point-blank how I felt.

"As much as I want to be with you," I said, "there is no way either of us will ever be happy living like this, unplugged from our dreams and avoiding everything that once held our interest."

"I don't know what interests me anymore," she said.

I had already heard that complaint more than a dozen times.

"Well, neither do I," I said. "I've done everything I can think of to make you happy. I have nothing left."

Her response was a blank stare.

"You're free to choose your own direction," I said. "If you think you can survive as a recluse, I won't stop you, but I'm not going to join you."

She knew that if she wanted to be with me, she would have to crawl out of her shell and meet me somewhere in the middle. Her choices were to follow me, follow her own dreams, share our dreams together, or stay out of the way. I had come to the conclusion that until she was willing to help herself, there was nothing further I could do for her.

That was the day that I emotionally divorced my wife, consciously deciding that I did not want to be married to her anymore.

All of the counseling we had received up to that point had done little to nothing to support our marriage. It was always the same advice: Carole had suffered a brain injury, and I needed to adjust. I could not make any more adjustments. I had already lost my identity trying to become the person everyone seemed to think I was supposed to be, and nothing had improved. The last thread holding my emotional suspension intact had finally snapped, and I felt myself falling away.

It was fascinating the way my brain could logically rationalize a separatist's attitude. What a horrible dilemma I faced in being with someone I loved more than life and whose behavior I could not tolerate.

The end brought a curiously peaceful, welcome relief. It was not the hoped-for finale, but at least the turmoil was over. I had simply decided that I would be okay living alone. That was the end of it, plain and simple.

We actively avoided each other, awkwardly living separate lives under one roof, two renters sharing the same kitchen. Curt remarks and cold politeness had replaced every aspect of our marital relationship. What a ridiculous existence!

From somewhere out of the murky gloom, a strange and confusing curiosity about suicide resurfaced in my mind. Because it was such a mystery, I had no way of knowing whether those thoughts were a red flag or simply random musings. In a strange way it was understandable how someone could find himself so closed-in that turning out the lights might seem like the ultimate alternative to all of life's misery.

Could I do it? Would I do it? Nobody truly knows, but I was so desperately tired of scraping the bottom of the barrel emotionally that I had begun seriously asking God to take me home.

—◊—

At the end of the last day in March 2010, Carole walked through the front door, dropped her things on the kitchen table, and made an announcement regarding something that had happened at work she thought might be of interest to me.

"A show cause came across my desk today," she said.

A show cause action is a judge's order summoning an individual to appear in court and provide an explanation, or show reasonable cause, for violating a court order. Part of Carole's job as court administrator included the preparation and processing of those hearings.

"For who?" I asked.

"For the guy who nearly killed us," she said. "The judge who sentenced him wants him to appear before the bench and explain why he hasn't paid his fines and court fees."

"Well now, there's a bit of irony!" I said. "You're hauling the guy who nearly killed you into court for failure to pay his fines."

That guy's negligence seemed to know no limitations.

The order was processed and served April 1, 2010. His debt was finally paid in November of that year, three years and five months after he committed the act that had nearly put my wife and me in the grave.

The proceedings offered no satisfaction that justice had been served.

During the month of June that year, I made the final payment on our mortgage. Although I had missed my original goal of burning the mortgage by fifteen months, we did still own our home. Short of paying the State of Michigan's rent (taxes) every year on the land we had struggled for so long to own, our household was finally debt free. That too was an anticlimactic event: no fanfare, handshake, or even a backyard barbecue. I just sent a check for the final payment to the bank, and a month later I received the copy of our deed to the property and the original mortgage with "Paid in Full" stamped across the front.

There I stood with a piece of paper in my hands that summarized thirty-six years invested paying for a dream home that had been transformed into a reformatory. There was not a room, closet, or corner in that house that had not been contaminated with bad memories.

When August 1 arrived, we spent our fortieth wedding anniversary in separate parts of the state. Instead of trying to do something that resembled an attempt at reconciliation, I went to the family reunion near Gladwin and stayed at my parents' house in Mesick. Nobody was home at Mom and Dad's, so I spent the nights alone, sarcastically wondering what other wonderful experience life had in store for me.

Did I mention I had also become sensationally cynical?

It had always been a puzzle to me how anyone could be married to the same person from high school and make it through the trials of building a home and raising children, only to wind up going separate ways after years of wedded bliss. Through firsthand experience, that mystery had finally been solved. It was a violation of trust that had destroyed our marriage. "Estranged" would have been a very inappropriate description of our relationship. "Wrecked" was more like it.

Dealing with a failed marriage was a key factor in my reconnection with the music business losing its allure. The 110-mile round trip to Bay City twice every week had drained me financially, and band rehearsals had become emotionally stressful, unproductive battles of the wills. The clash between the guitar player and me finally came to a head just after the weekend of our anniversary. I had been in the music business far too long to be treated as though I were a novice, especially by someone who I later discovered had been fired from every musical group he had been involved with. Regardless of how talented and polished he was on his instrument, his vulgarities, filthy habits, and uncongenial attitude had become more than I could bear.

I finally pulled the plug on my involvement with *Crabtree* and told the band members that I would fill in for as long as it took to find my replacement.

That resulted in a hit-and-miss schedule lasting another three months until the guitar player who had given me so much grief was caught pulling a fast one with the band's income one night. After that confrontation, he packed up his gear and left town.

For the final three months of 2010, I had volunteered to perform every Friday night at a musician friend's bar/restaurant in Brown City. His cancer had resurfaced, so a few of us decided to help him through the trials of chemotherapy by keeping him busy playing his piano. That diversion temporarily took my mind off a crumbled marriage and the slow disintegration of *Crabtree* as I escaped from both battle scenes for about six hours every Friday night. Geoff's open jam sessions had become somewhat disappointing. Beginners mostly still learning their instruments gradually replaced the seasoned players who had been showing up. It was a great group of guys overall, but I had lost interest.

Just before Halloween that year, I took another pile of insurance claims to Linda, an attorney and close friend, and asked if she could help us. She accepted the box full of documents and told me that she would call if there were any questions.

Battle fatigue from the long, drawn-out war with insurance adjusters had taken its toll, but the battle was far from over.

Following the settlement negotiated by our accident attorney over a year earlier, medical bills and reimbursable expenses from continued therapies and doctor appointments had continued to pile up. Once again, reimbursable medical expenses were digging deep into our pockets.

I had been submitting monthly claims without any response from the uncooperative no-fault insurance adjusters. Fourteen months passed before I finally admitted to myself that without a lawyer to handle the claims, those insurance adjusters would never get off their "buts."

I had faith in Linda's ability to do whatever could be done, but I had no confidence in the adjusters' inclination to do the right thing. I figured it would be months, maybe years, before we saw a penny—if ever. I just mentally closed that door and redirected my attention toward getting my business back up to speed.

To my surprise, a little over a month after Linda's clerical staff had summarized and resubmitted our claims, we received checks reimbursing us for every penny we had spent. The outcome was an amazing relief, but I still felt no sense of closure.

Christmas 2010 was approaching, and I was dreading the holidays. There was no way we would be spending time with any of our kids. Jeremy had his family in Virginia, Nicole was involved with her husband and two-year-old son, Brody, and Jason was nowhere to be found.

Carole and I may as well have been living in separate countries, tenuously coexisting under the same roof. We had reached another truce, but unless I found some way of keeping myself busy, I was facing a potentially deadly season of lonely depression.

Pastor Michael asked me if I would perform for the Christmas Eve service again at Grace, so I accepted the invitation. Once again the strains of *Silent Night* accompanied by those innocent voices filling the sanctuary softened my soul with a peace I had not experienced for over a year.

Carole's spirit also seemed to have softened that evening, which was a fortunate turn of events.

A couple of days earlier, I had decided to book a hotel room in Frankenmuth and geared up to spend Christmas away from home, either with my wife or alone. In a left-handed way, I was preparing myself for the day when I would spend every one of my nights alone.

Gambling on the possibility that a more conciliatory mood would prevail, I packed Carole's bag without her knowing and formulated a plan to go for a ride through the countryside to look at lighted decorations after the Christmas Eve service had concluded. Carole agreed with the notion that a quiet drive would be a pleasant way to spend the rest of the evening, so instead of taking her home and going off alone, I drove away with her.

Gradually I made my way toward Frankenmuth. Neither of us had seen that city's world-renowned Christmas store's decorations at Christmastime, so that became the target destination. Carole suspected nothing about the plans I had made to spend the night away from home.

Up to that point the evening together had actually turned out rather pleasantly, so I took the next step.

"I really don't feel like going back home tonight," I said. "The house is empty, and it just doesn't feel much like Christmas. It looks like there are a few hotels open. Do you want to see if there are any rooms available?"

"Sure," she said.

With that endorsement, I pulled up in front of the hotel in downtown Frankenmuth where I had made my reservation. Carole still did not have a clue what was going on until I went to the front desk to sign in and pick up the room key. She couldn't believe that I had managed to pack all of her personal belongings, a nightgown, and a full change of clothes without her knowing anything about it.

I had also packed a cooler with some snacks, a bottle of wine, and a few gifts I had purchased earlier in the week. Had the joint venture been aborted, my plan was to leave those things at the house for her to open on Christmas morning.

The hotel was situated on the banks of the Cass River and was located within walking distance to most of the attractions in downtown Frankenmuth. Our room had a Jacuzzi and a view that overlooked a beautiful, elegantly lit park on the other side of the river below. It was a romantic setting that served as a welcome interlude from the feud that had been going on between us.

The next morning, we ventured downstairs and enjoyed a private breakfast buffet. We were two of only four guests who had spent the night at that hotel, so we basically had the entire facility to ourselves. It was ironic waking up in an empty hotel on Christmas morning, considering the whole purpose of the night out was to avoid waking up in an empty house.

After breakfast we sat by the fireplace in the lobby, visiting politely until checkout time. We then loaded our bags and left for home. The overnight retreat had been an encouraging interlude. Our daughter had invited us to spend the afternoon at her house with her in-laws, so Christmas day also promised to be pleasantly filled with comfortable companionship.

On the drive home from Frankenmuth, my cell phone rang. Thinking it might be our son Jeremy calling, I answered the phone. It turned out to be Sheila, our female singer from *Crabtree*. She knew that I had planned to spend the night in Frankenmuth and was anxious to see if I had somehow coaxed Carole into going with me.

That phone call went over like a lead balloon. Sheila was single, and she could keep a crowd entertained with wit, humor, singing, and a little borderline lewdness. It was all part of the act. That's entertainment, and Carole was fully aware of it. Regardless, Carole was insanely jealous of Sheila.

Sheila knew that I was married. That was one of the reasons she wanted me in the band. She needed to work with men who weren't going to be making passes at her. What's more, she really adored my wife. In fact, if Sheila thought I might be tempted to stray into unfaithful territory, she would have personally kicked my teeth in. She had that much respect for Carole. She also knew how hard I had been trying to salvage our marriage.

I handed the phone to Carole so Sheila could wish her a Merry Christmas. They talked briefly, and then Carole handed the cell phone back to me. I finished the conversation, closed the lid on my phone, and looked over at my wife. She was squeezed tight against the passenger-side door, hugging her knees to her chest with tears in her eyes.

Her display of jealousy came across as a statement that she didn't trust me, which sent me over the edge. In a fit of anger, I flung my cell phone over my shoulder and heard it hit something in the back of the car. Then I launched a few terse comments at my wife, put my eyes back on the road, and drove the rest of the way home in silence.

After we finished unpacking, Carole loaded some of her own things back into her car and departed for our daughter's house. I spent the rest of that Christmas Day at home alone. Suffice it to say that neither of us had behaved appropriately. Carole was terminally unhappy, and I had no patience. There was no logical reason for the unpleasantness between us. I may not have hit the bottom of the barrel, but I was certainly kissing the sludge that had settled there. Fortunately I had no place to run, or I may have done just that. I envied my son Jason for having found the courage to leave home without ever looking back. I had already passed that point in my life forty years earlier, but it appeared as though I had come full circle and was about to start all over. My flight through life had been intercepted and diverted to a deserted patch of ground, and all I had to look forward to was a wheels-up landing.

I distinctly remember reflecting back on that Christmas season as the absolute worst holiday experience of my entire life. With the exception of Christmas Eve and the celebration of Christ's birth, that was the year that I learned to literally hate everything else about Christmas.

CHAPTER 43

SOLVING THE PUZZLE

For where your treasure is, there will your heart be also.
Matthew 6:21 (KJV)

—⟋⟍—

Capricious thoughts of leaving home reminded me of the little boy who bundled up everything he owned in a bandana, tied it to a stick, and headed out into the cold, cruel world to make it on his own. I always wondered what the little guy had wrapped up in that bandana. A sandwich? A pair of socks?

If I ran away, what the heck was I going to leave behind that I was truly willing or able to live without? That flight of the imagination reminded me of Steve Martin in the movie *The Jerk*—specifically the scene in which he walks through his house, randomly picking up things of no relative value along the way to the door as he leaves his girlfriend behind.

There is probably some psychological term for that sort of behavior—"avoidance," or maybe "self-pity." The thing is, I did not need a psychologist to tell me that I needed help. I knew I was facing a serious problem. I just could not seem to find anyone capable of helping me. All I wanted to do was flee.

Our son Jeremy sensed my desperation and shared with me something called the Kübler-Ross five stages of grief: denial, anger, bargaining, depression, and acceptance.[7] The five stages were developed to help identify the way people react to the loss of a loved one, but generally speaking, anyone suffering any type of loss will usually experience every one of those emotions to some degree.

For all practical purposes, Carole and I had lost each other. We had also lost our dream, sense of security, and hope.

The impenetrable life Carole and I thought we had established had obviously been built upon a slippery foundation. We thought we were protected, but when we nearly lost our lives through no fault of our own, the reality of human vulnerability hit us both pretty hard. The psychological, emotional, and financial ripple effect created serious, long-lasting disillusion.

Recovering from our injuries had placed us at the center of a man-made game of life and death with players on three sides of us: the adjusters, the lawyers, and the medical billing authorities. In other words, we had put our faith in snake oil peddled by flimflam artists, and when the crisis hit, the vultures collectively capitalized on our misfortune. Realizing just how insignificant we were in the grand scheme of things made us both feel like bugs waiting to be squashed.

Frustration had become our prime emotion, and we had learned to expect the worst. We both entered the five stages of grief multiple times. Rarely did we complete one full cycle before reentering. We had been caught in an endless loop like the guy in the old Kingston Trio song *Charlie on the MTA*.

I bounced back and forth randomly from one stage of grief to another. The one constant was that no matter where I bounced, I always seemed to land on anger, which masks myriad emotions, including pain.

I was as mad as blazes at everyone and everything except God.

The Kübler-Ross model also suggests that anger is just another indication of the intensity of love.

Well, that made sense. I loved my wife more than life itself. I just didn't like her very much for the way she had lied to me. Being lied to hurt, and that made me angry.

On a cold winter morning in February, during a PTSD counseling session at the veterans' hospital, I was asked a very pertinent question: "With everything you've been through," the counselor said, "how could anything have been any different?"

He was referring, of course, to state of mind, personal experiences, and reactions to particular trials in life. His question was not meant as a reference to the way my marriage had fallen to pieces, but nevertheless I made the connection.

He's right, I thought to myself. *How can anything be different if I don't change?*

I had been trying to find happiness by tinkering with my wife's behavior, forcing her into submission. I was the kind of guy I would never have chosen to hang around with. Most things had to be my way or the highway. The impossible paradox was that my wife had to be happy before I could be happy.

While I talked with the VA counselor that morning, scenes from various stages of the past flashed through my mind, shedding light on why life had turned out the way it had. One by one, pieces of the puzzle fell into place.

When everything came to an abrupt halt in the middle of the highway that day in June, a Pandora's box full of minitraumas finally sprang open. Facing each issue one at a time would have been manageable, but the way everything came at me all in one mass of confusion had been overwhelming.

Stepping away helped me to sort things out and put them into perspective. Enlightenment did not make the puzzle any less difficult to assemble, but at least I had finally found a way to compartmentalize and deal with matters one at a time.

The VA counselor was right. All things considered, nothing could have turned out any differently.

Hands down, the one unsettled issue that stood out among the rest was the state of affairs between Carole and me. I knew we both needed to change our ways, and it had become painfully obvious why change was in order. Neither of us was happy.

Unfortunately I had manipulated my relationship with Carole in much the same way I had managed the business. She had become a resource. She cooked, cleaned, went to work every day, and took care of the kids. I took her for granted, and she had become her own survivor.

Carole seemed to enjoy being my security blanket, and she was good at feigning contentment. I believe she learned those particular skills from her mother. All through Carole's formative years, servitude had been the slogan. Her mother's personal philosophy was that nothing worth doing would ever be worth doing for oneself.

Carole's hellfire Baptist upbringing did not turn her away from God, but it definitely cultivated in her a serious distaste for guilt-producing religion. Right or wrong, Carole learned to hide a lot of her social activity from her parents while growing up. Nevertheless, her Christian conscience would not leave her alone. She had always been torn between doing what she had been taught was righteous and what she believed was right. At some point during those developmental years, the art of deception had taken over.

My exacting methodology eventually encouraged Carole to regard me as unapproachable. I had unwittingly extended her childhood environment into our married life. In her mind, facing me with the truth without engaging in conflict was impossible, so she simply avoided the truth. My wife knew how to lie straight to my face without batting an eye.

Lying made her feel guilty. Then, as if to make up for being less than honest, she seemed to be driven to do things, as though she were paying penance, a sort of militant servitude: serving others whether they liked it or not.

I had been attending Grace Bible regularly, occasionally with Carole at my side, and had also joined an informal weekly Bible study group with a handful of folks from that congregation. It was refreshing to learn that they mostly believed, as I did, that Christianity is a personal relationship between the believer and his Savior. There was peace, support, and fellowship among that modest collection of misfits. Everyone there seemed to understand. Each member of that congregation had his own heartbreaking story, and they all accepted me just as I was. And I was a broken human being.

It wasn't long before I realized that those misfits were healthier than most "normal" people who served their mainstream religions.

The people at Grace were misfits in the same way Christ was a misfit among the Pharisees.

Carole also joined me at the Bible study sessions on occasion, but most of the time I was alone. Those evenings spent with that small group of friends provided the peace and confidence I needed to keep pushing forward.

—m—

In May 2011, I was invited to a private session with some of the players I had met at Geoff's jams; I was unaware they had lured me into an audition.

At the end of an hour of just playing songs at random, Geoff put his guitar down and made the pitch to Rick, Natalie, Rob, and me. They were already a unit but lacked a percussionist who could play up to their caliber. Geoff sold the other members on bringing me into the group, and from that point forward we were known as *East 81*.

Once again I found myself with a group of true professionals who were sober, seasoned players. And for the first time after forty-five years of performing around the world, every member of the group I had joined was a practicing Christian.

With a healthy, stable group of friends in music on one side and a solid collection of Christians at church on the other, I was finally able to step back and analyze the wreckage in my personal life without feeling as though I were being hurled off a cliff.

Solutions to the dysfunction between Carole and me remained elusive, but the primary causes were becoming clear. Both of us had been so consumed by what had gone wrong that there was no room left to focus on what had gone right. We had unconsciously reprogrammed ourselves to identify with the wounds rather than with the healing that had taken place. Looking back, it was easy for me to see how the previous five years had been filled with issues that would have required a lifetime for some people to sort through.

Suffice it to say that I had lost the ability to be thankful for what we had. I had also forgotten how to forgive. Probably the most fundamental snag was that any effort to rebuild our marriage relationship had been overshadowed by trust that had been destroyed. Restoring trust is important, but even more basic is learning how to forgive.[8] Forgiveness is the ultimate choice—the cancellation of debt. But talking about forgiving is a whole lot easier than actually doing it.

Forgiveness is difficult because we are programmed as a society to interpret forgiveness as a form of weakness and a sign of approval for the wrong that has been done. Forgiving others doesn't mean we approve of their behavior; it just means that whatever they did does not matter anymore. What's done is done.

Forgiving someone requires the kind of strength found in very few people. It means turning the other cheek, and taking that leap is risky.

Before I could ever risk exposure to another painful episode of being deceived, I had to somehow give up being the person I had been without feeling as though I had given up on myself. That was a tall order.

Forgiving my wife for having so thoroughly betrayed my trust was one of the most difficult things I had ever faced. I had every legitimate reason for throwing her under the bus. Many were the times I nearly made tracks, but the truth is that I was still in love with her.

While doing some soul searching, I came across a couple pieces of sage advice that helped me conquer my own stubbornness enough to make another run at repairing our marriage.

The first was a tip from a friend who told me to look at her as the person that I had married, not as the person that she had become. It took a while for that to sink in.

Turning that thought over in my mind made me realize that I needed to be more like the person my wife had married and put away the person I had become. We had grown apart because we had both changed who we were without ever realizing it.

The next piece of help came from something I read: "I may not be able to trust my wife, but I can trust God in my wife."[9] Translated into my own words, this means, "Don't get hung up on the person's behavior; focus on his or her intent." That was a little easier to understand and appealed to my sense of fair play.

Most people do and say foolish, hurtful things without intending any harm. Carole and I had both committed the blunder with impunity. Carole did not hurt me intentionally; she had just become defensive out of self-preservation.

While trying to figure out exactly how to approach the situation without turning it into a train wreck, I came across the Alcoholics Anonymous "Serenity Prayer." Therein was a solution.

SERENITY PRAYER
God, grant me the SERENITY to accept the things I cannot change,
The STRENGTH to change the things I can,
And the WISDOM to know the difference.

Recalling how it felt when someone tried to change me to meet his or her expectations made it crystal clear that I could not change my wife. I could only pray for help in accepting her the way she was.

The process began with changing myself after wrestling with the notion that change was even necessary. The reality was that nothing could improve in my life until there was a major overhaul from the inside out.

Then came the part that involved learning how to forgive. I struggled with memories of every embarrassing encounter or error in judgment until finally giving up and forgiving myself for being so stupid, self-centered, and full of control. That took a lot of willpower.

The second half of that challenge was to forgive others. It was not long before the ultimate test in forgiveness stared me square in the face.

CHAPTER 44

THE SILVER ROSE

—⟋⟋⟍—

The father and mother of the guy who had left us for dead in the highway had barely escaped with their lives when their house had rapidly been consumed by fire. Two days after they had been left homeless, one of the local firefighters stopped by my shop to deliver the news.

"Well," he said with a devious smirk on his face, "it looks like everything that goes around really does come around."

"What do you mean?" I asked him.

"The guy who left you for dead in the highway—his parents just lost their house to a fire two nights ago."

"Are they all right?" I asked.

"Yeah," he said, "but they lost everything except the clothes on their backs."

He seemed proud to be the bearer of such tragic news.

Admittedly, my first reaction was a silent, *There, that'll show 'em!*

Immediately I felt a surge of guilt for even having had that thought.

"Man, nobody deserves that," I said.

My friend was startled that I would have any compassion for anyone in that family, but he didn't challenge me. We talked a little about the fire, and then he left.

Is that what people think will make me happy? I thought to myself. *Wow, have I delivered the wrong message!*

I was genuinely sorry for their loss. They weren't the ones who had hurt us. I mulled their tragedy over in my mind for several

301

days, but I couldn't shake that feeling of guilt for what I had initially felt.

A week later I mailed the following letter:

> Dear C—,
>
> I heard about the house fire and saw your home. I have a pretty good idea how you're feeling right about now.
>
> I am sorry for your loss. This has got to be devastating for you and your wife.
>
> You and I are neighbors, C, and we're all children of the same God. If there is anything you need that will help you and your wife get back on your feet, please let me know. I will do whatever is within my power to help.
>
> You are on our prayer list.
>
> Regards,
> David Stieler

About that time I was introduced to the hit-and-run driver's ex-mother-in-law. Little did I know that she had been a member of the congregation at Grace Bible and had been there nearly every Sunday that I had attended services. The secret was out when she stood up in church before the service began and asked for prayers for her grandchildren's other grandparents, explaining that they had just lost their house to a fire.

After the service, I approached her and asked what the connection was between her and the folks who had lost their house.

"Those kids belong to my daughter," she said. "My daughter was once married to the young man who was driving that car that was involved in your accident."

"And you have known all this time that it was my wife and me that he left for dead?" I asked her.

"Yes, but I didn't want to say anything," she said. "I didn't want to make you mad."

I looked her in the eye, told her that I was sorry she had thought that about me, and then gave her a hug.

I did not know until a week later that several people in the congregation had been watching and holding their breath as I approached that lady. They all knew the connection and were likewise afraid of the way I might react. Nearly five years had passed, and none of them had breathed a word to either Carole or me.

That was another moment of truth. When everyone started verbally patting me on the back and expressing relief for the way I had handled the situation I knew instinctively that every one of them had been preprogrammed with entirely the wrong impression.

A week after I had mailed the letter to C—, a man stopped by the shop. I didn't recognize him until he spoke.

"I just stopped by to tell you how much that letter you wrote meant to my wife and me," he said.

"C—?" I asked, more than a little surprised. "Is that you? I didn't recognize you."

"Yes, it's me," he said. "Your letter really touched me."

I shook his hand, and we talked for half an hour before he had to leave to finish some errands. During our conversation I discovered that his health was failing as a result of side effects from his exposure to Agent Orange defoliant during his tour as a US Marine in Vietnam.

Ever since the war in Vietnam had been cancelled for lack of support, Vietnam veterans have been crippled and dying by the thousands as a result of their exposure to Agent Orange defoliant. Unfortunately, none of those casualties of war is entitled to the Purple Heart.

The Order of the Silver Rose is a nonprofit organization determined to recognize those veterans. The group's position is that all Vietnam veterans with an illness related to exposure to Agent Orange deserve the Purple Heart because their illnesses are, in reality, war-related wounds. Those wounds may not have shown up until years after the war had been called off, but their wounds, nevertheless, are a direct result of having served their country in time of war.

Since neither the Department of Defense nor the officials in the US government will acknowledge that fact, the Order of the

Silver Rose has launched an effort to stand in the gap. They are reaching out to all Vietnam veterans suffering from documented Agent Orange-related illness in order to provide them with the Silver Rose in lieu of the Purple Heart they deserve.

Our local VFW post was in the process of adopting the Order of the Silver Rose project. I invited C—to our next VFW meeting and sponsored him as our post's first candidate for the Silver Rose.

Heads turned when I introduced C—to the membership at that meeting. Anyone who had made the connection between C—, his son, and me was amazed that I was even talking to the man, let alone standing in as his advocate.

I had no way of knowing beforehand how sending that letter to C—was going to turn out, but looking back, I see that I definitely felt a sense of completion for having made the effort. For days following that episode, visions of reconciliation with Carole danced around my brain.

The encounter with C—had been another wake-up call from God, but in typical, thickheaded fashion, I had slept through the alarm, and the overriding message from the entire experience had eluded me.

Chapter 45

The Resurrection

Not that I speak in respect of want: for I have learned, in whatsoever state I am, therewith to be content.

Philippians 4:11 (KJV)

———————

The tap on my shoulder came again in the middle of the night when a silent alarm grabbed my attention, bringing me out of a sound slumber. The message I should have picked up through that encounter with C—had finally come through crystal clear: *Dave, you have been treating your wife with less respect than you have paid the family of the guy who almost killed you.*

That eye-opener also helped me to understand that Carole had been avoiding honesty as though it were the kiss of death because I would not quit persecuting her for being deceitful.

Provoked or otherwise, together we had completely crucified our marriage.

Not unlike the encounter with C—, as long as our fragile partnership remained intact, there was always a chance of us resurrecting our relationship. We needed to plow some new ground and start fresh to make it work. It would be an uphill battle for sure.

I prayed that it was not too late.

I had become accustomed to that numbing coldness that started in the pit of my stomach and worked its way up the back of my neck every morning right after opening my eyes. Such a helpless feeling it was, knowing I had painted myself into a corner simply by standing my ground and sticking to principle. Being right was of little comfort to me, knowing that I had lost the biggest battle of all—saving my marriage.

Carole had no excuse or reasonable explanation for lying to me about anything. Convincing her that I could be trusted with her honesty seemed impossible.

The shortcut solution, of course, would have been to abandon principle and cave in, but changing expectations to match unacceptable behavior was definitely not going to happen. We were at a stalemate, Carole and I, and I stood alone in a place where wrong ruled and right had become irrelevant. There was obviously no quick fix.

—m—

On one particular morning in March, nearly five years after the wreck, I awoke with the strange sensation that I had just returned home after a long absence. The dawn greeted me the way it had on that first morning in my own bedroom after spending fourteen months in Southeast Asia.

The fresh sunlight cast an odd hue, creating an indescribable aura. For a moment I actually wondered if I was alive or experiencing the opening chapter of the afterlife. Had I finally made it through the twilight zone?

Sitting up in bed, I looked around the room and took a quick inventory. The surroundings were familiar but felt strangely different. There were no flashes of gut-wrenching reality, and the tension was gone, along with those consuming, temple-throbbing, nightmarish thoughts. It was just a peaceful, thirst-quenching feeling, almost as though the night had been filled with violent lightning, thunder, and drenching rain that had left a freshness in the crisp morning air.

The storm was over, and we had survived. Although the bond between us remained thin, Carole and I were still together. The strain associated with nearly losing everything to the insurance machine would have been enough for most couples to throw in the towel, yet we had not given up. That same tenacity had kept us together as allies against a common enemy.

There had to be some good in that.

In an effort to blank out the bad things we had been through, I began focusing on the blessings we had shared in our relationship, consciously filling my mind with nothing but positive thoughts.

Keeping our ship from coming apart was not our only victory. We had trampled the opposition on several battlefronts, and in spite of the scars and stiff joints, we were finally limping away from the wreckage victorious. We looked forward to our future free of debt. Who, other than each other, were we willing to share that with?

Reflecting on the trials that we had faced over the previous five years, it seemed as though our survival was nothing short of a miracle. Too many components had fallen perfectly into place for any of them to be coincidence. There are those who would refer to our victory as luck, but we both knew that God's hand of protection had kept the enemies at bay. Prayer had no doubt been the strongest weapon in our arsenal.

I shared those visions of a new dawn with Carole during a quiet conversation over coffee that morning. She seemed relieved, as though she had been waiting for me to say those things, nodding in agreement. In that moment I knew that we both wanted peace and security in the presence of each other. It went without saying that there would need to be some serious adjustments if we were to rebuild compatibility.

Focusing on those revelations alone provided strength and hope. We were finally ready to join hands and resume making our way as husband and wife. Hopefully Jason, Nicole, and Jeremy— our three kids—were still willing to join us.

We still owned all of our toys, but they just did not seem all that important anymore. I might have sold the airplane and the Corvette for lack of interest, but Carole wanted to hang on to them. That bit of encouragement told me that I still had a playmate at my side.

At my wife's insistence, I replaced the broken motorcycle with a full-dress Harley Electra Glide Classic, and we resumed riding, enjoying the countryside and the sense of freedom the way we had always dreamed of doing.

My repair business continued recovering. Customer loyalty had not disappeared. Patrons frequently reminded me that quality of workmanship was worth far more than the few bucks saved by purchasing cheap, over-the-counter replacement units. Profitability had gone out of repairing many of the units that had at one time represented the bulk of the workload, but there remained enough custom repair work to pay the bills and maintain a comfortable lifestyle.

It was amazing how revenue always matched expenses with a little to spare. Faith held true. Prayers asking for the opportunity to continue earning my way had been answered.

I did not really need a job to put food on the table; I needed daily, productive activity to heal a broken spirit. Every morning, I thanked God for two things: first for having the work to do, then for the ability to do the work that I had been given. In plain, simple language, my little repair shop made me feel whole again.

Patching up our relationship had become our number-one priority.

Every morning, I made a point of getting up early enough to spend fifteen minutes with Carole before she left for her job at the courthouse so we could focus on starting our day together. At the end of each day, Carole came home from work, changed her clothes, and made a beeline for the shop to say hello.

Although I really did not want to give up music, it made no sense having to choose between performing and spending time with my wife. Convincing Carole to join the crowd at those performances became a personal goal that would likely only be accomplished by making the time she spent with me worth her while. My bringing her up to the front line when making decisions about my music career helped her feel more in tune. She did not need to play an instrument to have a voice in what dominated my time.

Violation of trust had created the deepest wounds. The scars were permanent and remained tender. Regaining trust would require a major leap of faith, but I never quit searching for a sign that it was safe to let my guard down.

Waking up on the recovery side of disaster had radically altered our outlook toward nearly every aspect of life, most notably in the way we integrated our faith in God's watchful eye with life in general. Letting go of the reins did not mean giving up. On the contrary, faith in God gave us the courage to let go. After that, every priority settled into its proper place.

In years gone by, our lives had typically been reduced to a series of daily chores. The purpose behind most of my projects had simply been to get them done. Always on a mission, consumed by project after project, I would lose Carole in the dust after she would jump off the wagon and watch me disappear, frustrated by the intensity of my concentration.

For that to change, Carole and I made a point of standing shoulder-to-shoulder either physically or figuratively before allowing anything to move forward. Whether we slowed down, sped up, or temporarily shelved the task, the decision-making process had to be a joint effort involving both of us before the first nail could be driven or the first spade of sod turned.

Both Carole and I concentrated our individual efforts on slowing down and finding the joy in doing things. We adjusted our philosophical attitudes to face every day in a positive light and do things because we wanted to, not because we had to. We knew there would always be a degree of drudgery in performing chores, but the way we approached them would never be the same.

Together we left the dog-eat-dog world behind. The days of carrying someone else's load along with our own had come to an end. Like healthy tendons knitting back together, Carole and I went to work tearing down the walls that had gone up between us and mending the fences that had once made our house a home.

—w—

So there we were, staring at each other from opposite sides of the room, amazed that in spite of everything we had been through, we were still married and had been handed back our lives with a restart. Our kids were grown and gone, and we suddenly found ourselves unaccompanied for the first time in our married life.

Having been together only two weeks before I shipped out for Southeast Asia, then starting our marriage fourteen months later as a young couple with a baby boy, had left us without a chance to learn how to live as newlyweds. We never thought twice about the three of us setting out together to blaze our own trail, but there were times when we both wondered what it would have been like had we begun our marriage alone.

Our chance to find out had finally arrived. We were standing at the starting gate, not the finish line. We had the toys to play with, and the time had finally arrived to start enjoying them. All we needed to do was go back and experience the beginning that we never had.

CHAPTER 46

LETTING GO

This I say therefore, and testify in the Lord, that ye henceforth walk not as other Gentiles walk, in the vanity of their mind.

Ephesians 4:17 (KJV)

—◊—

Old habits are hard to break and even harder to ignore. A serious inferiority complex had always forced me to put up a front as I tried to appear strong in the eyes of those around me. Learning how not to flinch had become an art form for me. The same was true of Carole.

Both of us had some serious overhauling to do, but that meant making sacrifices. I knew that changing the way people perceived us and accepted us for who we truly were would take a lot of courage. Friends might fall by the wayside, and others would probably find reason to criticize. We faced a fearsome challenge. Regardless, we needed to buck up and be ourselves.

Of course, before we could assert the real us into our circle of friends, we needed to clearly understand ourselves. Figuring out who we were and how we got that way would require some somber soul searching.

Lack of self-confidence had always prompted changes in my behavior the way a chameleon changes colors to match its surroundings. Determined to get along with everyone, I had always bent over backward to please and appease. It was not easy and not always pleasant ignoring annoying habits and disreputable behavior. Nevertheless, I would paste on a smile and suck it up, selling myself for the sake of friendship.

Trying to accommodate was a bad plan. Like a politician canvassing for votes, I apparently came across as wishy-washy and disingenuous.

One by one, as our personality facelift progressed, those individuals whose friendships I cherished distanced themselves. Roger and Leslie slowly drifted away. Rumor had it that Ginger no longer wanted my guitar or me anywhere around while she performed. We stopped receiving invitations to social events. Most of our old haunts seemed to have put away the welcome mat.

I had always believed that true friends would never abandon one another. It was humbling to learn that many of those friends simply expected something I did not have to offer. They were the ones I thought would have been the most brutally honest and straightforward. They were brutal, but the way I had been discarded turned out to be anything but straightforward.

Reconciling those friendships may have been feasible, but it seemed more sensible to let sleeping dogs lie.

Our kids also seemed to have found reasons to keep their distance. Jeremy was moving on with his career in Washington, DC, and had become immersed in launching his third marriage. After Nicole and Rodney witnessed an unpleasant firsthand display of the friction between Carole and me during a joint venture to Mackinaw City, our relationship with them had noticeably chilled. Jason and Rhonda remained distantly removed, and it was obvious that we were at the bottom of their list of people with whom they would spend time. "To thine own self be true." That quote from Shakespeare had become agonizingly accurate.

I was confident that patching up my relationship with Carole would eventually bring the kids back around. They rightfully had no desire to be exposed to conflict. There would be future opportunities for us to demonstrate the peace. The goal would be to prove to them that the war was over.

The same held true for those friends whose companionship had meant so much to us. Unfortunately, without a personal invitation to rejoin them, their presence would slip into the past and become little more than fond memories. Our door would remain open for anyone wishing to reconnect, but many of those who had at one time befriended us would probably not recognize the people we had always been.

—ɯ—

A newfound sense of spiritual awareness came through the church while the family of musicians who had readopted me helped rebuild my self-confidence. I forgave those who had misinterpreted me, and I then forgave myself for the role I had unconsciously played in the game of deception. Throughout the personality makeover, Carole seemed to use my behavior as a template for her own overhaul. "Letting go and letting God" brought a strange sense of peace for both of us. Being thankful for every new day became a point of order. I thanked God daily for loving me in spite of the person I had been and silently thanked those friends who had moved on for the role they each had played in shaping our lives.

Hope and optimism were the elements that had always kept us moving forward, but denial was the smoke screen that prevented us from getting a good look at reality. I had finally slammed headfirst into acceptance, the fifth and final stage of grief, only to rediscover that there is no running from the truth. And the truth was that Carole and I were changed individuals. I had been hoping to return to a normal life with my wife, but survival meant settling for a new normal, and that would require major adjustments for both my wife and me.

Staying busy had become my prime directive, and thankfully, the work that came through my little repair shop was still enjoyable. Do-it-yourself restoration artists and farmers maintaining their equipment brought a variety of challenges and problems to solve. The work itself had become a source of social networking. Keeping the shop doors open was no longer about earning a living; it was more about having a reason to get out of bed in the morning. As I said in the beginning, anyone who believes that happiness is watching a workplace disappear in the rearview mirror has never been forced to sit idle.

As long as the work did not rule the day, I could apply my skills indulging hobbies and live out my years with dignity. Music, aviation, backyard landscaping projects, and wrenching on the old panel truck in the garage—those were things I enjoyed doing in my leisure time. There needed to be no other purpose than to share those things with my wife.

Carole continued struggling to find meaning, but her daily progress was visible. Helping her find peace and enjoyment in leisure activity brought her closer to reestablishing her identity. Her self-fulfillment helped dissipate my loneliness.

Giving up the past brought the heartbreaking reality that our children were on their own. No matter how much we missed having them around, sharing companionship would be their decision, not ours. That is the downside to having children. They grow up and go away.

As the lingering pain from our battle scars and the loneliness caused by separation from family and friends gradually subsided, color began filtering back into the world around me. Once the emotional turmoil of an on-again, off-again relationship with my wife had been put behind us, the fragrance of a fulfilling life filled my senses. Happiness had started popping up in unexpected places.

CHAPTER 47
THE SUNSET

—⁀∿⁀—

The wind was calm and the air was still as we stood on the beach, silently gazing toward the setting sun over the open waters of Lake Huron. Freshwater sport-fishing boats off in the distance trolled the depths across the entrance to Saginaw Bay while waves rhythmically rolled in, gently lapping the shoreline.

Singles and couples strolled along the water's edge, sometimes wading, often stopping to examine an undiscovered treasure that had washed in with the last wave. Kids played in the sand, running in and out of the water, screaming gleefully while their moms and dads opened picnic baskets, swam with their children, tossed Frisbees, or just sat quietly observing and enjoying a short reprieve from the August heat.

In a rebelliously carefree act of audacity, I thumbed my nose at the price of gasoline and pulled the Corvette out of storage for a cruise. Carole threw together a picnic basket full of goodies, and we headed for Oak Beach Park.

It made no sense to postpone life's pleasures one moment longer for the sake of frugality. I felt a little bit like Scrooge on Christmas morning as I dangerously tempted fate and mocked the very discipline that had brought us this far in life. The entire outing seemed deliciously irresponsible, but a little voice in the back of my head kept telling me not to worry, reassuring me that if we ran out of resources we would adjust. Until that happened, we would simply live for the moment.

Ours had been an enjoyable afternoon spent lounging comfortably side by side in our nylon fold-up chairs with our feet in the sand, surrounded by a crowd of vacationing strangers at the tip of Michigan's Thumb. As the fiery ball in the sky inched its way closer to the horizon, bringing another day to an end, the thought crossed my mind that we had spent practically our entire lives together. We silently held hands and stood at the water's edge, taking in the beauty of another Michigan summer sunset.

Where does the light go when the sun disappears over the horizon? I wondered to myself.

When I was a little boy, my dad would tell me to listen for the sizzle as the sun touched the water at the end of the day. There was a short period during my young, impressionable adolescence when I actually wondered where the sun spent the night! I remember wondering how the sun caught fire again every morning when it came back up on the other side of the world.

Carole and I were privately celebrating another wedding anniversary that day at the beach. Not counting the years we dated in high school, we had been joined together, for better or for worse, through sickness and in health, for forty-two years; death had even nearly parted us. It was hard to believe that this living, breathing woman at my side had not been expected to ever walk or talk again—let alone be alive—only five years earlier: a sobering thought. Together we had experienced the ending and beginning of life.

My wife and I were still reeling from the physical and emotional wounds inflicted during the hellish nightmare we had been through while trying to find our way into the next phase of our existence. But we were also reveling in the grace we had been shown through our own form of resurrection. God did not prevent the pain that we had endured, but He certainly made the pain bearable. And we were healing, ever so gradually.

There was nothing pleasant about the tribulation my wife and I had been forced to bear during the previous five years, and there will never be one specific answer for why we were put through the shredder. We were simply two people trying to get through life without making waves, enjoying the afternoon on our motorcycle that Sunday in June. Our style had always been to help those around us and ask nothing in return. In spite of our deeds, we had come face to face with disaster and had every right and reason to be bitter. We did not deserve the punishment that followed our calamity, but it had been meted out just the same.

Silently celebrating life while sitting on the beach alongside my wife, I felt for the first time since the final moments before our motorcycle crash a sense of relaxation and a level of comfort I thought would never return. We had finally found peace by reflecting on the past, looking forward to the future, and reveling in the moment.

The release made my head spin. Nothing could completely describe the tension caused by the fear and disappointment we had endured since that fateful day on the highway, but the experience Carole and I shared was our bond in much the same way that nightmare called Vietnam had bonded me with my band of brothers.

Being together was our comfort zone.

Still, in spite of our victories, our accomplishments, and our achievements, something was missing. It was nice having all of the things we owned, but none of our possessions would have kept either of us alive. We needed to unscramble our priorities and regain the spirit of living. Sitting in the sun was relaxing and comfortable, but for us that sort of inactivity had always served as the reward at the end of our journey. We thrived on doing things, not sitting around dreaming about them. Our craving was for the excitement found in the crossing, not the destination. Our visions always involved going places and enjoying the sights along the way.

We both agreed that our best vacations had been spent aimlessly wandering in the general direction of a destination without any specific deadline for arrival. We still muse over a trip we once took to Florida in the airplane during which we were grounded in London, Kentucky, for four days because of bad weather. Those were the best four days of the entire two-week vacation.

Prior to the day of our wreck, whenever the opportunity presented itself, we always took advantage of the freedom of not having to move according to someone else's schedule. That way of thinking hadn't changed. In spite of a system that discouraged individualism—one that seemed to be infiltrated by people who refused to cooperate—we remained two intensely independent people. We cherished our freedom and both agreed that our sovereignty was best when shared with each other. Our treasure was our mutual admiration, sweetened with the contentment that comes with owning each other's time.

The day we took that ride on the motorcycle through the countryside was one of those days that we had spent a lifetime earning. We weren't doing anything wrong; we were exploring the joys—the adventure—of living. When our heads hit the pavement that afternoon, the spirit of adventure was literally slapped out of us.

Since the day of our accident, the missing ingredient in our life had been that sense of anticipation found in exploring the unknown, visiting places we had only talked about seeing, and doing things we always wanted to do. Sharing an adventure—any adventure—had always been the source of our mutual contentment. The stuff we owned wasn't the root of our happiness. Those things—our toys—were nothing more than evidence of adventures we had shared, the things we had played with during our time together.

We were a team, Carole and I. Side by side we had built a home, raised our children, and filled our own personal clubhouse with the fruits of our labor. Time we spent as one defined our reason for living. Carole had been my girlfriend, my wife, and my soul mate. This lady holding my hand truly was the person I wanted sitting next to me on the front porch swing when all else had been said and done. I knew instinctively that there would never be another. Some people don't find that soulful connection until the second or third mate enters their life, but of this I am certain: Carole is the one God had chosen for me, and I thank Him for all of the pleasures that He allowed us to share.

Retirement was still a thing of the future, so we continued meeting our obligations the way honest, hardworking people were supposed to, with Carole going to work at the courthouse and me opening the shop every morning. However, it wasn't usually until the end of the workday that our life had any meaning, because that was when we came together.

We had finally gone full circle in our search for peace and serenity. How typically human, travelling to the other side of the world and back only to discover that what we were looking for had been staring us right in the face. Retirement did not have to be the end of a career. Retirement for us was going to be what retirement is: choosing to do what we want to do, when we want to do it, and for as long as we choose. We simply needed to redefine the terms of engagement.

The task now was to rekindle that spirit of togetherness and get on with the rest of our lives. Where the adventure was destined to take us from that point forward was anybody's guess, but that is, after all, the real definition of adventure.

I knew instinctively that the door to our past had been slammed shut; going back was not an option. And although the finale was still somewhere in the future it had become clear that *life will have already ended a number of times before death finally catches us.*

The setting sun signaled the end of a life we had desperately clung to. It also marked the beginning of the rest of our lives together. A still, small voice in the back of my mind continued gently whispering that our five-year-long, hair-raising experience would ultimately be looked back upon as a defining moment—the opening chapter of our greatest adventure yet.

Uncertain as we were about our future, I clearly sensed that we would be safe and at peace as long as we followed God's guidance, steering around the potholes through the rest of our life's journey, while staying clear of the idiots on the highways. We would climb back into the saddle and continue charting our course, confidently plunging full-stride into the escapades that awaited us.

Because in spite of what some people may say, nobody wants to be unhappy.

—⁓—

NOTES

1   Romans 8:28 (KJV).
2   The Insurance Code of 1956, MCLA §500.3107a, MCLA 500.3107(1)(a)(b) (passed 1991).
3   The Insurance Code of 1956, MCLA §500.3105 (passed 1972).
4   The Insurance Code of 1956, MCLA §500.3101(2)(e) (passed 2008).
5   Motorcycles and the Michigan Catastrophic Claims Association (MCCA), Fis. Pub. 0227 (Feb. 27, 2012).
6   American Psychiatric Association, *Diagnostic and Statistical Manual of Mental Disorders* (DSM-IV-TR), 4th ed. §309.81: "Posttraumatic Stress Disorder" (Washington, DC: American Psychiatric Association, 2000).
7   Elisabeth Kübler-Ross, *On Death and Dying* (New York: Touchstone, 1969).
8   Cindy Beall, *Healing Your Marriage When Trust Is Broken* (Eugene, OR: Harvest House Publishers, 2011).
9   Ibid.